Corruption
and the Global Economy

KIMBERLY ANN ELLIOTT
Editor

Corruption
and the Global Economy

INSTITUTE FOR INTERNATIONAL ECONOMICS
Washington, DC
June 1997

Kimberly Ann Elliott, *Research Fellow,* is coauthor of *Reciprocity and Retaliation in U.S. Trade Policy* (1994), *Measuring the Costs of Protection in the United States and Japan* (1994), *Economic Sanctions Reconsidered* (second edition 1990), *Auction Quotas and United States Trade Policy* (1987), and *Trade Protection in the United States: 31 Case Studies* (1986).

INSTITUTE FOR INTERNATIONAL
ECONOMICS
11 Dupont Circle, NW
Washington, DC 20036-1207
(202) 328-9000   FAX: (202) 328-5432
http://www.iie.com

C. Fred Bergsten, *Director*
Christine F. Lowry, *Director of Publications*

Cover Design by Michelle M. Fleitz
Typesetting by Sandra F. Watts
Printing by Kirby Lithographic Inc.

Printed in the United States of America
99 98   5 4 3

Library of Congress Cataloging-in-Publication Data

Corruption and the global economy /
Kimberly Ann Elliott, editor.
        p. cm.
    Includes bibliographical references.

    1. Political corruption—Economic aspects. I. Elliott, Kimberly Ann, 1960-
II. Institute for International Economics (U.S.)
JF1081.C673   1996
364.1'3—DC20   96-35400
                                            CIP
ISBN 0-88132-233-4

Contents

II Opportunities and Options for Reform

III Summary and Conclusions

Appendices

Preface

As economic interdependence grows, especially for the United States, more and more issues have taken on an international dimension and have come to be linked with traditional trade concerns. Examples within the realm of economics itself include competition and investment policy. Examples that reach into the social domain include labor standards and the environment. The Institute has completed projects on each of these topics. Along with ongoing work on the overall impact of globalization, the aim of this research agenda is to better understand the substance of these issues and whether or how they should be related to the more traditional foci of international economic policy.

Corruption is a recent addition to this agenda. Corruption is by no means a new issue, but it has only recently emerged as a global issue. With the end of the Cold War, the pace and breadth of democratization and international economic integration have accelerated and expanded. Yet, in some parts of the world, corruption threatens to slow or even reverse these trends.

Ill-gotten gains give dictators like Marcos and Mobutu an incentive to cling to power until the last possible moment, driving their countries ever deeper into political and economic instability. Corruption in many countries of the former Soviet bloc distorts and slows market-opening and pro-democracy reforms. Whenever it is pervasive, corruption can deter investment, impede economic development, and undermine political legitimacy. Even when the consequences appear to have been contained for long periods of time, as in Indonesia and South Korea, relatively widespread corruption can eventually spin out of control. And when corruption becomes linked with liberalizing reforms, those reforms may lose support and eventually unravel.

Corruption also distorts international trade and investment flows, and it facilitates the activities of international organized crime, including drug trafficking and money laundering. The spread of transnational crime, in turn, can impede moves to further open borders to trade. The recent dispute over liberalization of trucking services between the United States and Mexico arose in part from concerns that decreased regulation could facilitate drug trafficking.

As the global implications of corruption have grown, so has the impetus for international action to combat it. Just as this book was going to press, the 29 advanced economies that make up the Organization for Economic Cooperation and Development agreed to negotiate a convention criminalizing bribery of foreign public officials by the end of this year and implement it by the end of 1998. (Though most countries have laws against bribery of their own officials, the United States had been the only nation to prohibit bribery outside its borders.) The Organization of American States has negotiated the Inter-American Convention against Corruption, which calls on signatories to criminalize transnational bribery and cooperate with one another in enforcing laws against corruption and recovering illicit riches. And the United Nations General Assembly passed a resolution last year calling on members to take steps against all forms of corruption.

The World Bank and International Monetary Fund have also vocally denounced corruption as an impediment to economic development. Both institutions, along with other multilateral and bilateral development agencies, now focus explicitly and carefully on the role of "governance" in development. The World Bank has tightened its procurement regulations to ensure that its funds are not siphoned off or diverted.

Additional steps are needed, however, to maintain the momentum and to expand the international attack on corruption:

- The OECD must demonstrate that it can convert words into deeds. Negotiation of an international treaty against transnational bribery on the tight deadlines they have established will be difficult, and continuing high-level attention and pressure by key governments will be necessary to keep it on track.

- Where it has the cooperation of the borrowing country, the World Bank should put more resources into areas often neglected due to corruption, such as education and health, as well as into support for capacity-building and institutional reforms that more directly combat corruption. But in countries where corruption impedes project implementation and undermines economic development, and there are no signs of meaningful reforms, the Bank must be quicker than in the past to withhold funds.

- With respect to government procurement, where much "grand" corruption occurs, the World Bank should exercise leadership by continuing to strengthen their procurement guidelines. The multilateral development banks should conform their procurement regulations to the World Bank standard, and bilateral aid organizations should adopt or strengthen their own anticorruption safeguards. The members of the World Trade Organization should abandon the go-slow approach they have taken on the issue and move quickly to negotiate an agreement on transparency in government procurement.

- To provide the essential political leadership for this entire effort, the G-7 should give corruption the highest priority at its Denver summit in June 1997 and thereafter. The commitment of the world's top leaders is key to overcoming the deeply entrenched forces of corruption and eradicating its pervasive impact on economies and societies around the world.

This volume is based on a conference held by the Institute for International Economics in April 1996, and we are deeply grateful for the active participation of so many people from around the world in the project. We especially appreciate the close collaboration of top officials of Transparency International, which has done so much to call attention to the corruption problem, especially Nancy Zucker Boswell, Fritz Heimann, and Susan Rose-Ackerman.

The Institute for International Economics is a private nonprofit institution for the study and discussion of international economic policy. Its purpose is to analyze important issues in that area and to develop and communicate practical new approaches for dealing with them. The Institute is completely nonpartisan.

The Institute is funded largely by philanthropic foundations. Major institutional grants are now being received from The German Marshall Fund of the United States, which created the Institute with a generous commitment of funds in 1981, and from The Ford Foundation, The Andrew W. Mellon Foundation, and The Starr Foundation. A number of other foundations and private corporations also contribute to the highly diversified financial resources of the Institute. The Ford Foundation, the General Electric Fund, and Merck and Company, Inc. provided partial support for this project. About 16 percent of the Institute's resources in our latest fiscal year were provided by contributors outside the United States, including about 7 percent from Japan.

The Board of Directors bears overall responsibility for the Institute and gives general guidance and approval to its research program—including identification of topics that are likely to become important to international economic policymakers over the medium run (generally, one to three years), and which thus should be addressed by the Institute. The Director, working closely with the staff and outside Advisory

Committee, is responsible for the development of particular projects and makes the final decision to publish an individual study.

The Institute hopes that its studies and other activities will contribute to building a stronger foundation for international economic policy around the world. We invite readers of these publications to let us know how they think we can best accomplish this objective.

C. Fred Bergsten
Director
June 1997

Acknowledgments

I would first of all like to thank all the authors and discussants for their excellent contributions to the volume and for their participation in the conference that launched it. In particular, Susan Rose-Ackerman and Fritz Heimann, along with Managing Director of the US chapter of Transparency International Nancy Zucker Boswell, were extremely generous with both their time and their knowledge in helping us to identify important issues and potential authors. I would also like to thank Fritz and Susan, as well as fellow authors Patrick Glynn, Michael Johnston, Paolo Mauro, and Moisés Naím, for reading my chapter—in some cases more than once—and providing often detailed and always insightful comments. Michael Gadbaw, Frederik Galtung, and James Hines also read my chapter in its entirety and their comments helped me to further sharpen and refine the analysis.

I am grateful to my colleagues at the Institute, who offered their insights during two internal staff discussions on the topic. The suggestions and insights of Geoffrey Carliner, Ellen Frost, Morris Goldstein, Gary Hufbauer, Carol Lancaster, and David Richardson never failed to improve the presentation and substance of my chapter. C. Fred Bergsten's contributions to both the planning and implementation of the conference, as well as his advice and comments on my chapter, are immeasurable.

Thanks also go to those at the Institute who keep things on track and make sure that our research actually gets to our readers. Valerie Norville, as always, did an excellent job editing most of the papers, and David Krzywda was more than patient with my never-ending revisions in the final editing of my chapter. Brigitte Coulton, Helen Kim, and Michelle Pointer expertly shepherded the manuscript through production, with Christine Lowry, unflappable in the face of last minute changes, overseeing the process. Tracy Temanson assisted me with my library research and provided expert bibliographical assistance for the volume. Angela Barnes helped organize the conference and Clavel Hunter did just about everything else related to logistics.

Finally, thanks to Peter who never lets me get away with lazy thinking or faulty analysis and is always there no matter what.

Introduction

KIMBERLY ANN ELLIOTT

Judge John T. Noonan's massive treatise *Bribes* traces the evolution of corruption and responses to it since before biblical times. More than a decade after Noonan wrote his study, the hardiness of the corruption perennial and its ability to take hold in virtually any environment seem not to have diminished. The press reminds us almost daily that corrupt behavior remains ubiquitous. It occurs in democracies and military dictatorships and at all levels of development and in all types of economic systems, from open capitalist economies such as that of the United States to centrally planned economies such as the former Soviet Union's. In the 1990s, however, economic liberalization, democratic reforms, and increasing global integration are combining to expose corruption and raise awareness of its costs. These trends, in turn, have sparked an anticorruption backlash that is spreading around the world.

The number and variety of countries suffering corruption scandals in recent years underscore the fact that corruption differs widely in its forms, pervasiveness, and consequences. In poor countries, corruption may lower economic growth, impede economic development, and undermine political legitimacy, consequences that in turn exacerbate poverty and political instability. In developed countries, the economic effects may be less severe; however, even in rich countries diverted resources will not be available for improving living standards. Corruption also tends to exacerbate income inequalities by increasing the power of those willing and able to pay bribes to the detriment of those who cannot, and this issue is of increasing concern in many developed and developing countries today. Finally, corruption can undermine political legitimacy in industrialized democracies as well as in developing ones by alienating the citizenry from

1

its political leadership and making effective government more difficult. Corruption may have the most deleterious effects in countries in transition, such as Russia, where, left unchecked, it could undermine support for democracy and a market economy.

Yet the record also reveals that corruption plagues countries whose economies have performed relatively well, such as South Korea, Japan, Mexico (until recently), and Italy. And in some of these examples, corruption as political patronage appears to have been more a factor of short-term political stabilization than destabilization. But corruption that once appeared to contribute to stability may over time do just the opposite, as evidenced by the recent turmoil in South Korea, Japan, and Italy and the increasing dissatisfaction in Mexico. More to the point, corruption may stabilize a political situation that is repressive and unjust, in which all but a wealthy elite lack the resources to protect themselves from exploitation. The evidence suggests that pervasive and uncontrolled corruption is usually economically debilitating.

The seeming universality of corruption at one time led many observers to conclude that it was a fact of life about which little could be done. But the conventional wisdom is increasingly being called into question. In 1996 a variety of groups and organizations took steps to combat corruption:

- At the end of March 1996, the Organization of American States (OAS) approved the Inter-American Convention against Corruption, which by the end of the year had been signed by 23 member states.

- Also in March, the executive board of the International Chamber of Commerce adopted a report that proposes strict rules of conduct for corporate self-regulation and makes complementary recommendations for action by governments and international organizations.

- In June 1996, the World Bank announced revisions to its guidelines intended to guard against corruption in procurement for projects it funds. And during annual joint meetings later that year, World Bank President James Wolfensohn and International Monetary Fund (IMF) Managing Director Michel Camdessus publicly condemned corruption and pledged to give greater priority to fighting it in their programs.

- In December, the United Nations General Assembly approved a declaration calling on member states to "take effective and concrete action to combat all forms of corruption, bribery and related illicit practices in international commercial transactions . . . ."

- Also in December, the World Trade Organization (WTO) agreed at its first ministerial meeting in Singapore to undertake a study of transparency and due process in the award of government procurement contracts as a first step toward reducing corruption in these markets.

- In May 1997, the Organization for Economic Cooperation and Development (OECD) adopted a recommendation committing member states to negotiate by the end of 1997 a convention criminalizing transnational bribery and calling on them to promptly implement the earlier recommendation calling for an end to tax deductibility of bribes.

An additional sign of the growing opposition to corruption is the rapid growth of Transparency International (TI), a Berlin-based nongovernmental organization (NGO) established in 1993 to combat international corruption. In less than four years TI has developed a network of over 60 national chapters throughout the world.

A striking feature of many of the incipient anticorruption efforts around the world is the role played by the developing countries and economies in transition that have recognized the threat corruption poses for fledgling political and economic reforms. Many of these countries are also concerned, however, that the corruption issue not be used to deny them access to international markets or capital. For that reason, some developing countries opposed inclusion of an agreement on transparency in government procurement in the WTO and expressed concern about the degree to which World Bank and IMF lending should be conditioned on anticorruption reforms. There has also been resistance to criminalization of transnational bribery in OECD countries because some firms are loath to eschew what they regard as a useful tool in international commercial competition. The initiatives listed above are only useful first steps: the road to full and faithful implementation will remain long and arduous.

The complexity and political sensitivity of the corruption issue poses many challenges to those who would analyze the problem as well as those who would seek an effective policy response. The first objective of this volume, developed in part I, is to identify the most virulent types of corruption and the types of economic and political structures most vulnerable to corruption. Under what circumstances does corruption spin out of control? Are certain institutional mechanisms more effective in keeping corruption under control? To design effective antibribery policies, it is important to understand who gains and who loses from corruption and thus who has an incentive to expose and prevent it. The second major objective, developed in part II, is to describe and analyze the growing number of policy initiatives being pursued to combat corruption, including how they relate to the causes and consequences of corruption as identified in part I.

Plan of the Book

Chapter 1, by Patrick Glynn, Stephen J. Kobrin, and Moisés Naím, describes the economic, political, and technological changes that have contributed to the evolution of corruption as a global phenomenon. The authors note that the increased attention to corruption as a global policy issue is a result of both real and perceived increases in the phenomenon: the magnitude or severity of corruption has probably increased in some parts of the world; but in other countries, what previously was overlooked or ignored has been exposed and declared unacceptable by newly empowered media and voters. This chapter also provides brief summaries of the global policy initiatives that have evolved and that are discussed in more detail in part II.

The remaining chapters in part I explore patterns in the corruption phenomenon. In her examination of the incentives for engaging in corrupt activities, Susan Rose-Ackerman focuses on the allocation of government benefits, costs, and jobs (which become valuable when corrupt opportunities exist). She also discusses the factors that influence the size and incidence of bribes, including the benefits available, the discretion officials exercise, the risks involved, and the relative bargaining power of the two parties to the bribe transactions. Rose-Ackerman explores the economic costs of corruption, including potential inefficiencies in government contracting and services (red tape and delay), and the use of bribe proceeds (capital flight), as well as increased social inequity and weakened political legitimacy. She also discusses possible ways to reduce the worst effects of corruption, by increasing the risks and costs of discovery and by reducing the incentives and opportunities for engaging in corruption.

In chapter 3, Michael Johnston focuses on the potential political sources and effects of several kinds of corruption and suggests political and institutional reforms to contain them. He looks at social and political imbalances that may develop in societies—the balance of political and economic opportunities, and the accessibility of political leadership in relation to its decision-making autonomy. Johnston identifies four types of corruption: interest-group bidding as occurs in the United States and other liberal democracies; elite hegemony as in China; fragmented patronage as found in Russia today; and patronage machines as in Mexico. Johnston does not suggest that democracies are immune from corruption, but he does argue that democracy has "long-term anticorruption strengths."

In the final chapter of part I, Paolo Mauro uses data from two sources that assess country risk in relation to potential investors and other businessmen in his study of cross-country effects of corruption on investment, growth, and the composition of government expenditure. He concludes that corruption deters investment, thereby lowering growth, and also that corruption affects the allocation of government expenditure, and may in fact lower the share of public spending for education. Reduced spending on public education lowers a country's growth potential by reducing human capital formation and tends to exacerbate income inequality.

Part II is largely devoted to policy initiatives currently being explored by various international institutions, national governments, and NGOs. Mark Pieth, chairman of the OECD Working Group on Bribery in International Transactions, traces the evolution of efforts in the OECD to end tax deductions for bribery of foreign officials and to impose corresponding criminal sanctions. He also discusses the regional initiatives in the Western Hemisphere and European Union to enhance the detection and punishment of corruption.

Augustine Ruzindana was Inspector General of Government in Uganda when he authored his chapter. He describes the far-reaching political, economic, and administrative reforms undertaken in his country over the past decade as well as the explicit anticorruption initiatives that are a key component of broader efforts to spur development. Ruzindana also emphasizes the importance of leadership and the role of a strong civil society in controlling corruption. Fritz Heimann, the chairman of the US chapter of Transparency International, discusses private sector initiatives, particularly those of the International Chamber of Commerce, and lays out key elements for corporate compliance programs that would prevent bribery by employees and agents. Heimann also discusses the undesirability of unilateral US initiatives.

Finally, appendix A contains the remarks of US Assistant Secretary of State for Economic and Business Affairs Alan Larson, who presents the US government perspective on international corruption and the various antibribery initiatives in which it has provided leadership, including through the OECD, OAS, and WTO. In addition, the IMF and World Bank have increasingly stressed the role of governance in development and condemned corruption at the annual joint meetings held in Washington in late 1996. The WTO and OAS initiatives and the changes in emphasis at the World Bank and IMF are mentioned in other chapters in part II, particularly chapter 10, which also updates developments since the conference was held and recaps issues raised earlier in part I and in research elsewhere.

As suggested by the papers in part II, the final overview chapter recommends a multipronged approach to combating corruption. To have a lasting effect, corruption must be attacked from both the supply side and the demand side. Corporate codes of conduct and OECD sanctions against bribers would address the first, while public-sector reforms and institution building in countries where government officials are prone to accept or extort bribes could have an impact on the demand. The systemic nature and pervasive effects of corruption throughout much of the world will not allow for silver-bullet solutions. National governments, international financial institutions, the OECD, multinational enterprises, NGOs, and citizens all must take responsibility.

The Globalization of Corruption

PATRICK GLYNN, STEPHEN J. KOBRIN, AND MOISÉS NAÍM

Over the past four years, corruption has been transformed from a predominantly national or regional preoccupation to an issue of global revolutionary force. In less than a half-decade, the worldwide backlash against corruption has swept like a firestorm across the global political landscape. Governments have fallen. Longtime ruling parties have been hounded from office. Presidents, prime ministers, parliamentarians, and once mighty corporate chieftains have been grilled by prosecutors and herded onto the docket. Italy, France, Japan, South Korea, India, Mexico, Colombia, Brazil, South Africa: no region, and hardly any country, has been immune.

It is a revolution that even Karl Marx could scarcely have predicted—a simultaneous, though largely peaceful, public revolt on five continents against one of the world's oldest part-time professions: proffering and accepting bribes.

Campaigns against corruption are, of course, hardly new. But this decade is the first to witness the emergence of corruption as a truly global political issue eliciting a global political response. Since 1992 a half-dozen or more international organizations—governmental and nongovernmental—have energetically taken up the question. The United

The authors are members of the World Economic Forum's Davos Group, which brings together business executives, law enforcement officers, and other experts to address corruption issues. Patrick Glynn is an adviser to that group. Stephen J. Kobrin is William H. Wurster Professor of Multinational Management at the Wharton School, University of Pennsylvania. Moisés Naím is editor-in-chief of Foreign Policy.

Nations, the Organization of American States (OAS), the International Chamber of Commerce, the recently formed Transparency International, the World Economic Forum, Interpol, and—in what may be the most promising initiative of all, the Organization for Economic Cooperation and Development (OECD)—are all making efforts to tackle the problem.

No one imagines that we are about to vanquish corruption, which is deeply entrenched across the globe and shows dangerous signs of spreading. In many countries, new leaders have ridden to office on anticorruption platforms, only to be exposed in turn as thoroughly corrupt themselves. Nonetheless, there is reason to believe we may be at a historical turning point in humanity's long wrestle with corruption. A new global standard appears to be taking shape in human consciousness, with potentially major ramifications for our institutions as well as our political and business lives. The 1990s, we would predict, are unlikely to pass without the achievement of significant legal and institutional anticorruption reforms.

What has been the source of this sudden "corruption eruption" (Naím 1995)? Why is this issue increasingly seen as a global rather than a local or national problem by so many? What international reform efforts are now under way? Are they likely to succeed, and if so why and how? We will attempt here to offer provisional answers to these questions.

Why Corruption Erupted

The corruption eruption has several causes. There have been both real and perceived increases in corrupt activity in various countries. In some regions, systemic political change has weakened or destroyed social, political, and legal institutions, opening the way to new abuses. Elsewhere, political and economic liberalization has simply exposed corruption that was once hidden. But almost everywhere, we observe a marked decrease in the willingness of the public to tolerate corrupt practices by their political leaders and economic elites.

A Legitimation Crisis

In the largest sense, today's anticorruption revolution can be viewed as a continuation of the ongoing legitimation crisis that has become the leitmotif of global politics during the final quarter of the century. From the most advanced democracies to the most repressive states, the balance of power between leaders and publics has been shifting and continues to shift in favor of open, democratic governance. The primary driving forces behind this change are growing affluence and education and the emergence of the Information Age. The increasing worldwide availability and consumption of information, the burgeoning influence of the media, and technological changes that give knowledge and information primacy in economic life have all contributed to an information-rich environment in which leaders, willy-nilly, are forced to give a fuller public accounting of themselves than ever before.

Secrecy and Orwellian manipulation of the truth—those cornerstones of authoritarian and totalitarian rule—have become increasingly difficult to maintain in the ever more transparent postindustrial environment. Empowered by information, people almost everywhere are expressing their revulsion at the traditional sub rosa activities of entrenched and corrupt elites, taking their dissatisfaction to the streets and, where possible, the polls.

The Watergate scandal in mid-1970s America—in which a newly empowered media exposed and brought down a strong president—the peaceful democratic revolutions that toppled dictators across Latin America in the 1980s, Mikhail Gorbachev's fateful decision to revitalize the sclerotic Soviet economy and political culture with a major infusion of openness or *glasnost*, and the subsequent peaceful popular uprisings in Eastern Europe that precipitated the fall of the Berlin Wall and the collapse of the Soviet Union have all been manifestations of this global democratizing trend. The present-day global backlash against corruption is, in a sense, only the latest chapter in this contemporary saga.

The end of the Cold War has clearly accelerated the process. This has been particularly obvious in Italy—the birthplace of the 1990s anticorruption revolt—where fear of communism had long underwritten public tolerance of notoriously high levels of corruption. Beginning in 1992, a coterie of Milanese magistrates discovered that with the demise of the Soviet Union and the elimination of the communist threat it was possible to bring down many of the erstwhile political untouchables on corruption charges. In South Korea as well, the end of the Cold War opened the floodgates of public anger at the antidemocratic and corrupt practices of the politicians and the large conglomerates, or *chaebol*. As *Business Week*'s John Rossant has written, "In every country on the former front of the cold war—South Korea, Taiwan, Mexico, Italy, and even Japan—holding the line against communism was more important than instituting real free markets and political competition. Now, shocks are beginning to rock the Establishments of the industrialized nations" ("Dirty Money," *Business Week*, 18 December 1995).

Our Enemy Left Us

The end of the Cold War and the emergence of a truly integrated international economy have also contributed to the widespread perception of corruption as a problem with inherently global ramifications. With the world no longer divided into two great camps, our sense of global interdependence has increased. There is growing awareness that security and stability depend not simply on air forces, armies, and national arsenals but also on a host of interacting economic and political factors. The security of one nation can be radically affected by purely domestic developments in a seemingly distant state. There is an indissoluble link, for example, between official corruption in Latin America and drug-inspired crime on American city streets. Disputes over alleged corruption can even drive a wedge between allies—as in the recent scandal over American economic espionage in France ("CIA Confirms Blunders During Economic Spying in France," *New York Times*, 13 March 1996).

Potential links between corruption and political instability are particularly obvious in the case of Eastern Europe and the former Soviet Union. In the short run, removal of authoritarian controls, decentralization, privatization, and opening of these economies to international participation have vastly expanded possibilities for corruption; in some places, such as Russia, it is rampant.

Corruption in these emerging markets is doubly pernicious. First, it compromises the efficacy and efficiency of economic activity, making the transition to free market democracy more difficult. Second, and equally important, corruption distorts public perceptions of how—and how well— a proper market economy works. Under such circumstances it becomes all too easy for economically beleaguered publics to confuse democratization with the corruption and criminalization of the economy—creating fertile soil for an authoritarian backlash and engendering potentially hostile international behavior by these states in turn. If it contributes to derailing democratic reform and provoking an authoritarian backlash, corruption in Russia could ultimately engender a major security threat for America and the West.

Nor, as we have seen, are the political ill effects of corruption restricted to emerging markets. One of the unexpected consequences of the end of the Cold War has been widespread malaise and an intensified crisis of legitimacy in advanced industrial societies—aggravated by the public perception of entrenched official misconduct. To quote French political scientist Dominique Moisï, "Our enemy left us before we were ready" (remarks at the Wharton School's International Forum, Bruges, Belgium, June 1994). As a result, governments in many OECD countries are experiencing difficulties or are even floundering. Italy, Japan, Great Britain, and the United States come easily to mind.

The end of the Cold War has affected the developing countries as well. The longevity of regimes such as those of Marcos in the Philippines, the Duvaliers in Haiti, Stroessner in Paraguay, and those of the many African tyrants who oppressed their citizens and looted their central banks was a concrete geopolitical expression of superpower rivalries. Foreign aid and military assistance continued to flow to these countries even though it was widely known that much of the time the titular destination was no more than a stopover en route to the private Swiss bank accounts of the ruling families and their cronies. Nowadays—when aid budgets everywhere have been slashed, when the communist threat is a fading memory, and when public opinion in donor countries is better informed of abuses that take place anywhere on the globe—corrupt regimes can no longer rely on loyalty to the cause as an automatic guarantee of support.

Rent Seeking versus Vote Seeking

Side by side with these shifts in the international climate have come domestic pressures for reform arising from the growth of democracy itself. In 1996 the human rights organization Freedom House classified 117 states as free and democratic—fully 61 percent of the world's countries, up from just 42 percent 10 years before (Karatnycky 1996). Growing democratization has meant the emergence of more active national media and stronger legislatures with the power to hold leaders accountable.

To be sure, there is no simple correlation between levels of democracy and levels of corruption (see Johnston, chapter 3). Democracy bestows no automatic immunization against public malfeasance, as the countless recent scandals in industrial and developing democratic countries show. Nonetheless, it is probably fair to argue that democratic regimes, over the long run, engender more powerful antibodies against corruption than systems in which political liberties are stifled. A regime that has frequent elections, political competition, active and well-organized opposition forces, an independent legislature and judiciary, free media, and liberty of expression is bound to generate more limits on the scope and frequency of corruption than one that does not have them. The recent succession of cleanups in the belt of South American countries that went democratic in the 1980s bears witness to this basic trend.

Still, in countries undergoing a transition from authoritarian rule to democracy and a market economy, the consequences of corruption can be complex—as the aforementioned problems in many postcommunist states evidence. Initially, democracy may mean only that corruption is decentralized; bribes that were once paid at the federal level are now paid to state and local authorities.

Moreover, the sudden deregulation of entire new arenas of economic activity that were once under the exclusive control of the state can vastly expand room for misconduct, opening the door to fraud and all sorts of abuses by firms trying to take advantage of the opportunities created by capitalism. Government officials in charge of privatizing publicly owned assets can become instant tycoons by selling them at low prices for a bribe or even by acquiring them through their families and friends. Indeed, the opportunities for rent-seeking and rent-taking behavior by public officials during such a transition can be manifold.

Rates for newly privatized utilities—phones, electricity, and the like—can be sold very lucratively. These opportunities peak in the early stages of the transition to a market economy, when monopolistic companies are often privatized without an effective regulatory framework in place or the banking system is liberalized without adequate supervision by monetary authorities. During this period, the coexistence of free-price and free-market sectors, with sectors in which central planning still reigns, creates major distortions and many opportunities for graft and abuse.

In the long run, however, a more competitive, less regulated economy is bound to offer less scope for corruption than a centrally planned one, if only by reducing opportunities for official rent seeking and by shifting the balance of power between the private and public sectors, usually with the effect of increased official accountability (see Klitgaard 1988 for discussion of this issue).

Globalization of the Problem

If political interdependence is particularly marked today, economic interdependence is even more so. Indeed, the globalization of the economy is adding new urgency to the corruption problem. Three related and dramatic changes are at work.

Holes in the Dike

First, broadening and deepening of global economic integration increases the probability that the effects of corruption will spill over and resonate throughout the world economy. When the corrupt Bank of Credit and Commerce International went belly-up in 1991, for example, the entire social security fund of Gabon was wiped out (Passas 1994). The increasing permeability of national borders limits the reach of national territorial jurisdiction and makes it impossible to wall off national economies or policies, to separate the domestic from the international.

Second, the emergence of an electronically networked international financial system markedly enhances opportunities for corruption, the difficulty of controlling it, and the potential damage it can inflict. Paradoxically—when we consider the present-day ability of intelligence and other agencies to monitor such electronic traffic—it also may offer new opportunities for its exposure and control.

Third, there has been a dramatic increase in the number of cooperative strategic alliances, both within countries and across borders. In many strategic sectors, the emerging global economy resembles a complex worldwide network of interfirm agreements. The relational nature of alliances makes control much more difficult for both managers and public policymakers. Furthermore, alliances or networks depend on mutual trust to a much greater extent than the traditional, hierarchical firm. Such trust can be compromised directly by corruption. Globalization affects both the problem and its solution: the new global realities facilitate corruption, as well as serve in other ways to expose and inhibit it. In the following sections we explore both sides of this coin.

Atoms and Bits

By the early 1990s, some 37,000 transnational corporations with worldwide sales of about $5.5 trillion controlled roughly one-third of the entire world's productive assets. Interfirm trade between subunits of these corporations now accounts for between 30 and 40 percent of all world trade. Today the value of sales of transnational subsidiaries is far greater than that of world exports (UNCTAD 1994, 131).

At the same time, in Nicholas Negroponte's words (1995), trade in "atoms" is being replaced by trade in "bits." Today the most valuable product in international commerce is information transmitted electronically. It has become increasingly difficult to separate manufacturing from services and goods from information; in fact, in 1995, *Fortune* decided to combine its industrial and service 500s into a single listing.

Many countries that tolerate corrupt practices—to the extent, for example, of allowing corporate tax deductions for overseas bribes—do so under the assumption that the illicit activity in question will take place somewhere else. However, in an integrated international economy, there is no somewhere else. The walls around national markets are crumbling; the separation between international and domestic economics and politics is vanishing rapidly. The very concept of national products, national firms, and even national markets is losing meaning.

Both corruption and standards of conduct are globally contagious today. With an increasing portion of the world economy in the hands of global firms, it is unreasonable to expect that corporate practices, culture, and ethics will not interpenetrate all markets. If it works abroad, why not try it at home?

As a growing number of experts are beginning to recognize, widespread corruption threatens the very basis of an open, multilateral world economy. Multilateralism depends on trust and a belief that others will play by the rules. The tendency to cheat, to free-ride, is a constant threat to the international economic system. Tolerance of corruption tilts the playing field—against firms (and countries) that will not or cannot engage in bribes and other corrupt practices. Corruption distorts competition and may reduce gains from free flows of trade and investment. That is equally true of countries that tolerate corruption domestically and those that tolerate—or even tacitly encourage—corrupt activities by their firms abroad.

Millions by Mouse Click

In no sector of the world economy have bits replaced atoms to the extent that they have in international finance. Today the international financial system comprises hundreds of thousands of computer screens linked by satellites in instantaneous communication with one another; they are in closer contact than the stalls in a village market. The volume flowing through this network is almost incomprehensible—well over $1 trillion a day in foreign exchange transactions alone. In the vast majority of instances, the only physical act needed to transfer funds is a tap on a keyboard or the click of a mouse. Money circulates around the globe literally at the speed of light. Once funds enter the system they can be disbursed in an instant to any number of far-flung locations. As *Time* magazine has put it, law-enforcement officials today are forced to search for dirty funds afloat on the oceans of legitimate payments—a daunting task at best ("A Torrent of Dirty Dollars," *Time*, 18 December 1989).

The globalization and digitization of international finance mean that it is technically easier than ever before to dispose of the fruits of corruption, regardless of the size of the payment. Consequently, corruption and criminal activity such as the drug trade increasingly pose a direct threat to the integrity of the international financial system itself. It is more and more difficult today to draw a clear line between legal and illegal funds, to separate bribes and drug money from less criminal but still dubious corporate and individual transactions designed, for example, to minimize a tax burden. Such an integrated and digitized international financial system only partly under the control of national authorities by nature increases the occasions of sin—and its potential consequences.

Developments just over the horizon threaten to exacerbate the problem. Any number of firms are now working hard to develop electronic cash, E-money, which can be used in the growing number of commercial transactions on the Internet. E-money, in whatever form, will combine the attributes of cash—universal acceptance and a lack of a clear audit trail—with the ease of electronic transfer (Post 1995). From a regulatory standpoint, the one advantage of cash is that it is cumbersome to transport in large quantities and possible to spot as it enters the system. E-money will be instantly transportable at the touch of a computer key and very difficult to track and regulate. It could conceivably make buying a government official just one more transaction on the Net.

A Two-Way Street

Yet if the new global realities in some ways facilitate corruption, in other ways they inhibit it. The globalization of electronic communications makes it easier to transfer money across borders and to launder funds of dubious origin. But it has also given rise to the most unrestrained media in history. Government officials are finding it is far from easy to limit the spread of damning information in the age of CNN, the Internet, the fax-modem, and easily affordable desktop publishing. The global explosion of communication and information not only makes secrecy harder to maintain than ever before, it also forces governments to be more responsive to an influential global audience (investors, journalists, politicians, multilateral bodies, and international public opinion in general) that adds to the constraints under which they have to operate. The risks for government officials, and perhaps even more for corporate executives, of seeing their names blackened by corruption charges on a global scale are higher than ever. Presumably, such heightened risks can have a deterrent effect.

Such forces are limiting the freedom that government officials once had to pursue their private interests at the expense of the public weal. Perhaps as important, they are also lowering the tolerance governments have for harboring corrupt individuals or practices.

Over the past decade, for example, the Swiss government, spurred by pressure from other nations, has made major progress in loosening its once-strict bank secrecy laws. Once alleged to harbor millions in ill-gotten funds, Swiss banks are no longer the banks of choice for money launderers (Andelman 1994). In Cuba, the Castro regime decided it could no longer afford to protect Robert Vesco, the fugitive US financier who had lived on the island for decades. The Samper administration in Colombia also determined it could not afford the sanctions that the United States was going to impose if it did not clamp down on the drug kingpins of the Cali cartel—until the Colombian president was himself accused of soliciting millions in campaign contributions from drug criminals.

A Global Breakthrough?

The final engine of change in the current global environment is the emergence of several concrete, coordinated international efforts at anti-corruption reform. Over the past half-decade, a remarkable number of governmental and nongovernmental international bodies have acted or called for action on corruption.

New International Initiatives

Earliest efforts were aimed not so much at corruption per se as at the related problem of drug money. In 1988, nearly 100 governments approved the UN Convention Against Trafficking in Illicit Narcotics and Dangerous Drugs, committing themselves to criminalizing money laundering and lifting the secrecy barriers to its detection. At the Paris economic summit the following year, the industrial nations formed the Financial Action Task Force, an ad hoc organization of 26 states, to carry out the mission. Since then, the task force has endorsed 40 recommended countermeasures, and member countries have agreed to allow technical teams from other member governments to monitor their efforts. The European Union, a regional member of the task force, has developed its own anti-money-laundering standards based on the task force recommendations (US Department of State 1992).

With the advent of the corruption eruption in the 1990s, the international anticorruption agenda greatly broadened and accelerated. In November 1994, the United Nations sponsored a high-profile conference in Naples on cross-border and organized crime. One hundred thirty-eight nations signed the Naples Declaration, pledging stepped-up domestic action and international cooperation to fight organized crime ("138 Countries Seek to Combat Global Crime," *Los Angeles Times*, 24 November 1994). (That conference host Italian Prime Minister Silvio Berlusconi was himself declared at the time to be under investigation by magistrates on corruption charges underlines the need for a certain skepticism concerning such international declarations.)

In 1995, the World Economic Forum—the largest international organization of chief executives—also called for cooperative action by government and business to fight corruption. They established the Davos Group, an informal association of high-level international business executives, law-enforcement officials, and experts—including Interpol Secretary General Raymond Kendall and Siemens AG Chairman Hermann Franz—to study the problem ("Corruption Goes Global, and So Has to Be the Riposte," *International Herald Tribune*, 29 March 1995).

The most significant and promising effort is an attempt to come to grips with a long-standing, central, and until recently seemingly intractable problem—bribery in international business transactions. With the exception of the United States—which criminalized the practice nearly 20 years ago—multinational firms in industrial countries routinely proffer bribes to officials in developing nations as a means of landing business deals. Many developed states not only legally permit such bribery but also permit firms to deduct such bribes as a legitimate business expense (OECD 1995b). This is not only a widespread and pernicious instance of corruption but also a practice by which the industrial nations, in effect, encourage and contribute to corruption in the developing world. In 1993, a group of former World Bank executives established an organization called Transparency International, loosely modeled on the concept of Amnesty International and dedicated to fighting corruption and promoting increased transparency in business and financial transactions worldwide (Cameron 1996). Remarkably active and effective in the few years since its establishment, Transparency International has given high visibility to the overseas bribery problem.

The most important reform, however, came in 1994 when at US prodding the OECD Council approved an official recommendation calling upon member states to "take effective measures to deter, prevent, and combat the bribery of foreign public officials in connection with international business transactions" (Yannaca-Small 1995). The first such formal political commitment by the industrial countries, the OECD initiative, if successfully carried out, could effect a revolutionary change in international business practices. (A small but interesting development came in 1996 when the Paris-based International Chamber of Commerce, partly spurred by the OECD recommendation, promulgated the first amendments in nearly 20 years to its rules and standards for international business, calling for efforts to combat bribery ["Business, Police Chiefs Urge Anti-Corruption Drive," Reuters, 9 February 1996; International Chamber of Commerce 1996]).

Because it seems a turning point in the anticorruption battle, it is worth examining the events that led to adoption of the OECD recommendation and assessing its prospects for success (see also Pieth, chapter 6).

The Lonely Boy Scout

The deepest historical roots of the OECD recommendation go back more than two decades to the American Watergate scandal of the early 1970s, when congressional hearings exposed a series of corrupt practices by American multinationals, including illegal payments to the Nixon campaign (laundered through foreign banks) and direct bribes by American companies to foreign public officials. In the most infamous such bribery case, exposure of Lockheed Corporation's $25 million in illicit payments to Japanese officials (to secure sale of its Tristar L-1011 aircraft) resulted in the resignation and criminal conviction of Japanese Prime Minister Kakuei Tanaka. Spurred by the reform spirit of the post-Watergate era, in 1977 the US Congress passed the Foreign Corrupt Practices Act (FCPA). As amended in 1988, the act has two primary provisions: the first criminalizes certain payments to government officials abroad, and the second requires accurate accounting of all transactions and establishment of a system of internal controls with periodic auditing (Pitman and Sanford 1994).

The antibribery provisions of the act are detailed and extensive: they prohibit American individuals or corporations from paying, offering to pay, or promising to pay foreign government officials to influence any official act, induce officials to act or fail to act in violation of their lawful duty, or induce officials to use their influence with the government to obtain business. The FCPA (as amended in 1988) makes American managers liable for prosecution, fines, and possible imprisonment if it can be proved they are aware of an illegal act or show conscious disregard or deliberate ignorance of a likely violation.

The FCPA provides for three exceptions. The most important is for facilitating or expediting payments to lower-level officials (often called grease payments) to secure the performance of routine government actions. Exceptions are also made if the payment is legal under the written laws and regulations of the host country or if the payment is a bona fide expenditure, for example, for travel and lodging relating to a product demonstration or contractual performance. The latter provision obviously opens something of a loophole: one US official, for example, was quoted as expressing surprise at Disneyland's growing importance as an international "training site." (See Klubes and Iraola 1995 and Jadwin and Shilling 1994 for a complete review of the provisions of the FCPA and its amendments.)

Still, whatever its imperfections, the FCPA has placed unique restrictions on the foreign operations of American firms. No other industrial country has promulgated or enforced remotely comparable regulations. Not surprisingly, over the past two decades—particularly as overseas business has accounted for an increasing share of American corporate revenues—the FCPA has remained a sore point and issue of controversy with many in the American business community. The complaint has regularly resurfaced that America's effort to play the lonely boy scout placed US companies at a serious disadvantage compared with foreign competitors (Kimelman 1994).

Has the FCPA hurt American business abroad? On balance, evidence suggests that American firms have paid a price for legally enforced virtue —though the extent of losses remains unclear. A 1996 Commerce Department report estimated (with the assistance of US intelligence agencies) that American firms lost $11 billion worth of business over the previous two years to competitors who paid bribes (Trade Promotion Coordinating Committee 1996, 113; see also chapter 10 for further analysis of this estimate). Unfortunately, the underlying analysis remains classified.

Systematic studies in the open literature, meanwhile, are few and far between. A 1981 General Accounting Office study of 250 firms indicated that fewer than 1 percent reported serious losses as a result of FCPA. Almost one-third reported a negative effect of the FCPA on their international business, however, and more than 60 percent felt it affected the ability of American firms to compete abroad (Pitman and Sanford 1994; Sheffet 1995). Two other studies conducted in the late 1980s found negative, if somewhat weak effects, of the FCPA on exports. Beck, Maher, and Tschoegl (1991) found that the FCPA negatively affected US exports to non-Latin American, bribery-prone countries. Using a mail survey of 336 exporters, Prasad (1993) found that 30 percent reported that the FCPA had little or no effect on their business, while 14 percent noted a very large decrease in their business. About half of the respondents felt that their export business was down "somewhat" or "moderately" as a result of the act.

Although a number of American executives have complained about the FCPA, there have also been business voices on the other side of the issue. For example, former Texaco CEO James W. Kinnear has argued that the FCPA actually benefits US companies by preemptively insulating firms from the costs and ethical complexities involved in bribing (Kinnear 1995). Jack Welch, CEO of General Electric, is also on record as saying US companies can "win without bribes." Welch argues that a firm must be the low-cost supplier, "but in almost all cases, if you have the quality, price and technology, you can win—nobody can sleazeball you" (Tichy and Sherman 1993, 133). General Electric has produced what US officials regard, according to a State Department official interviewed by one of the authors, as a model-company ethics code, designed to insulate the firm completely from FCPA violations.

Although compliance has not been perfect, the burden of evidence suggests that most US firms do comply with the FCPA—though recently reported federal investigations of IBM and Boeing under the FCPA suggest that the strains of international competition may be showing. IBM recently fired the top executives of its Argentine subsidiary after Argentine officials alleged it paid $6 million in bribes. Boeing's Canadian subsidiary, meanwhile, is said to have paid a bribe of $1 million to a Bahamian official in a deal to sell airplanes in that country ("Alleged Payoffs Risk Big Penalties for IBM," *Washington Post*, 7 March 1996; "IBM Fires Three Argentine Executives Amid Investigation of Bank Contract," *Wall Street Journal* [electronic edition], 15 September 1995). Both investigations are ongoing.

Whatever their various views of the FCPA, executives of American multinationals have been all but unanimous in their wish for a level playing field, repeatedly urging the US government to take actions to internationalize FCPA prohibitions or to persuade other nations to adopt similar laws.

Congress reflected the desideratum of the American corporate community when it amended the FCPA in 1988. The relevant language, attached to the Omnibus Trade and Competitiveness Act, chiefly aimed at clarifying ambiguities in the original 1977 law. But the amendments also include a "sense of Congress" expression urging the executive branch to negotiate prohibitions on bribery within the OECD—the actual legislative genesis of the talks leading to the 1994 recommendation (Sheffet 1995). Yet, while dutifully complying with the congressional mandate and taking up the issue in OECD councils, the then-presiding Bush administration put little energy into the antibribery talks.

Private Debates, Public Diplomacy

Two factors were critical in producing the strongly worded OECD recommendation on international bribery in 1994: a new, high-level US government decision to press for serious OECD action on bribery and a climate of public anticorruption feeling in Europe that made it increasingly difficult for European governments to oppose the US initiative publicly.

A major shift in American policy on the bribery question came after the trade-minded Clinton administration assumed office in 1993. Departing from their predecessors' back-burner approach, Secretary of State Warren Christopher and Assistant Secretary of State for Economic and Business Affairs Daniel K. Tarullo decided to make the OECD bribery negotiation a State Department priority. According to a State Department official, who described the US role in the OECD negotiations in an interview with one of the authors on condition of anonymity, the two were experienced corporate lawyers by training, with a knowledge of FCPA issues. Both reflected the long-dominant wish in the American business community for a level playing field. (State Department officials also argue that the American motivation is not exclusively economic self-interest: they point to the adverse effects of corruption on economic and democratic development in the developing world.)

Predictably, Germany, France, and Britain at first strongly opposed the US effort behind the scenes—though the British have since become more supportive of the American position. In OECD councils in 1993, the Europeans raised several objections to the US approach. They argued that primary responsibility for policing bribery lay with the (mostly developing) nations whose officials routinely accepted bribes, not with the Western companies that might proffer them. They characterized the FCPA as an illegitimate exercise in extraterritoriality, seeking to extend US law beyond US borders. They also accused the United States of seeking to enforce a uniform international criminal code throughout the OECD, in violation of other members' sovereignty. In addition, Germany argued against mixing taxation with morality—a reflection of its peculiar taxation philosophy (box 1).

US officials countered that the FCPA was a legitimate domestic law that relied on Congress's explicit power under the Constitution's interstate commerce clause: companies became criminally liable under the law by virtue of using either the US mails or the American telephone system (both regulated as interstate commerce) to arrange a bribe—one reason that FCPA cases can be difficult to prosecute and prove. They argued that what the United States sought was not a uniform criminal code but a uniform result: OECD members would be free to legislate against bribery in a manner that conformed with their separate constitutions and legal cultures; all America desired was that such bribery be proscribed.

Yet the key to US success in the negotiations lay with the arguments made not at the conference table but in the headlines. Throughout the negotiations, the American administration made frequent and calculated use of public diplomacy to press its case, according to one US official involved. With scores of French politicians under investigation and with corruption exploding as a high-profile issue in Germany and across Europe and Asia, American officials took their case to the international media, which proved remarkably receptive. (Stories on corruption in the international media have burgeoned. A Nexis search shows the number of articles mentioning the word "corruption" in the *Economist* and the *Financial Times*—which averaged 229 per year over 1982-87 and 502 per year over 1988-92—rose to 1,076 in 1993, 1,099 in 1994, and 1,246 in 1995.)

Whenever the issue went public, the Americans could count on holding the high ground. "The embarrassment factor [in these negotiations] is very high," the official pointed out. Meanwhile, behind the scenes State Department officials collaborated with Transparency International, which helped make a parallel public case for OECD reforms.

Nonetheless, outside observers were generally surprised by the strength of the final language of the recommendation approved by OECD ministers at their May 1994 ministerial. The storm of scandal engulfing Europe at the time was doubtless the critical factor. In the climate of the corruption eruption, European foreign ministers and governments could simply not afford to go on record as favoring bribery in any form.

Even more surprising, however, has been the pace of activity since the recommendation's adoption. The first follow-on task mandated by the OECD after May 1994 was a review of domestic legislation relating to the issue of tax deductibility of bribes. The OECD's Working Group on Bribery, under the chairmanship of Swiss official Mark Pieth, duly embarked on the legislative review. A breakthrough came in 1995, when the British unearthed a long-forgotten 1906 Prevention of Corruption Act, which prohibited such bribery in terms closely paralleling the 1977 American statute. The discovery of this antiquated law, albeit long ignored and unenforced, refuted the European argument that the FCPA had been a unique and unprecedented American exercise in extraterritoriality. It also catalyzed a shift in the British stance on the issue toward the American position.

Coincidentally, the tax deductibility issue arose at a regular meeting of the OECD's Committee on Fiscal Affairs—an expert group comprising mostly economists and tax specialists. For some reason, according to an American official, the OECD tax experts "bonded" on the issue of tax deductibility of bribes—arriving at a powerful consensus on its economic disutility. The fact that OECD tax experts were now on record as opposing tax deductibility of bribes gave new impetus to Pieth's efforts. Allied with the Fiscal Affairs Committee, Pieth's OECD Bribery Working Group during 1995 developed tough new recommendations on tax deductibility that were adopted at the OECD's annual ministerial in May 1996 (OECD 1995b and 1996; "Meeting of Council at Ministerial Level," OECD press release, 21-22 May 1996).

Box 1 From Watergate to Opelgate: Germany's struggle with corruption

Since Congress's passage of the Foreign Corrupt Practices Act in 1977, European and Asian states have been by and large content to regard the US law as yet another peculiar expression of America's Puritanism and penchant for international moralizing. Industrial countries continued to permit their firms to bribe abroad and deduct such bribes on tax returns; not only were European and other governments happy to reap the competitive windfall from America's lonely boy scout posture, but anecdotal evidence suggests that some European embassies also even facilitated such bribery in foreign capitals.

The 1990s have brought an important transformation in the political landscape, however, and such attitudes appear to be changing. The case of Germany illustrates the trend. Germany is one of a number of nations that not only permit overseas bribery but also allow companies to deduct such bribes from their tax returns. In fact, until last year domestic bribery in the private sector was deductible under German tax law—so long as the recipient of the illicit transaction was named. (The provision applied to bribery of businesspeople; bribing public officials remains a serious crime.) Furthermore, criminal sanctions for such bribery have been quite lenient and cooperation between tax and criminal authorities minimal.

Germany has embraced a philosophy of taxation profoundly different from that of the United States. Germans have traditionally prided themselves on a worldly, pragmatic, even cynical attitude toward the financial fallout from morally stigmatized activities. German officials have insisted, with perhaps an almost admirable fiscal realism, that issues of morality and taxation should be kept entirely discrete. For example, German prostitutes operating legally in many cities dutifully pay taxes on their income, in the same fashion as shop clerks or postal workers, and are required to do so by law (see, for example, "Interview mit Klaus Offerhaus [Präsident des Bundesfinanzhofs]," *Süddeutsche Zeitung*, 28 August 1995).

The reluctance to use the tax code to enforce morality has gone hand in hand, however, with a certain national moral self-confidence. Germans have tended to view their society as inherently well-ordered. Traditionally, Germans have taken pride in the self-image of their country as one of Europe's and the world's least corrupt states.

Yet over the past two years this national moral self-confidence has eroded. While corruption in Germany has by no means approached the

As an example of international action against corruption, the OECD initiative has two major virtues. First, it relies on a broad political agreement among states to alter their domestic laws instead of attempting the daunting task of achieving unanimity on language for an international convention or treaty or establishing a new international regulatory agency. Second, paralleling US actions in the drug war, it takes a supply-side rather than a demand-side approach to the problem. In the long run, to prevent companies in well-ordered industrial countries from proffering bribes is clearly a far more manageable task than achieving

Box 1 (*Continued*)

ministers-for-sale levels seen in France and especially Italy, a spate of scandals has dealt powerful blows to the German national self-image, and corruption has emerged as an explosive issue for German politicians. The most widely publicized corruption case involved GM subsidiary Adam Opel, in which 65 executives were investigated for taking bribes in an elaborate kickback scheme with suppliers. Also, a former chairman of the prestigious firm Mannesmann was forced to resign from its board over charges of conflict of interest—an almost unheard-of development in the German business community ("Europe's New Morality," *Business Week*, 18 December 1995). In 1995, a senior prosecutor alleged that the German construction industry paid 10 billion marks to corrupt officials each year (*European Business Report* 1995).

In February 1995, the president of the Federal Criminal Office described domestic corruption as an epidemic (*European Business Report*, 17 February 1995). Adding to the pervasive sense of ethical collapse was the jailing of the father of German tennis hero Steffi Graf on tax-evasion charges ("Germans Fear Corruption Is Eating at Heart of the Nation," *Times of London*, 26 August 1995).

Also in 1995, Berlin-based Transparency International issued its first country-by-country ratings of corruption. To the widespread dismay of Germans, their country was shown to be regarded as more corrupt than Britain or Switzerland, although less dishonest than the United States, France, and Japan. The issue has become one of the leading concerns of the German public. A 1995 poll by *Die Woche* found that three-quarters of Germans believe political and economic life to be seriously threatened by corruption. In eastern Germany, the figure ran as high as 84 percent (*Times of London*, 26 August 1995).

Partly as a consequence, the country's opposition Social Democratic Party was able for the first time to gain partial passage in 1995 of an antibribery bill it has introduced annually for several years. The German Bundestag voted to make tax deduction of domestic bribery illegal, even though Helmut Kohl's ruling Christian Democratic Union successfully beat back an effort to extend the prohibition to overseas bribery by German firms.

In effect, in the 1990s a host of nations in Europe and Asia—Germany, Italy, France, Korea, Japan—have been experiencing an upheaval in many ways comparable to America's Watergate experience 20 years ago. The politics of scandal is no longer a peculiarly American preoccupation but a global political phenomenon.

---

the necessary legal and political reforms in the scores of developing countries where such bribes are routinely accepted (though the United States simultaneously pushed for parallel reforms in Latin America through negotiations that resulted in approval of an Inter-American Convention Against Corruption, signed by OAS states in March 1996). Indeed, the OECD initiative has been one of the most important and unsung achievements of Clinton administration foreign and trade policy—one that could, over time, change the face of international commerce and vastly curtail opportunities for corruption in the developing world.

Yet, despite the progress already made, the most important and contentious issue still lies ahead: concrete recommendations on the actual criminalization of bribery in international business transactions. Governments must agree to pass laws to make such bribery illegal. The target date for final OECD recommendations on criminalization is the organization's annual ministerial meeting in May 1997.

Moreover, even if the OECD ministers manage to agree on final recommendations, it will remain for individual governments and legislatures to pass and, equally important, enforce the laws necessary to make bribing foreign officials a crime. While the combination of a strong OECD stance and the continued public saliency of the corruption issue is likely to wear down resistance to such action over time, there is little question that achieving the needed legal reforms in Europe—and perhaps even more so in Asia—will mean a prolonged and hard fight.

Thus far, the Clinton administration appears committed to the battle. Following reports of the IBM and Boeing overseas bribery investigations, US Trade Representative Kantor blasted America's OECD partners in March 1996 for continuing to permit overseas bribery and threatened to use trade sanctions to combat it (though he reportedly lacked cabinet approval for the proposal and the Clinton administration has since been silent on the threat ["Kantor's Battle against Bribery," *Journal of Commerce*, 18 March 1996]). Kantor also announced he would press for reforms of government procurement standards at the inaugural ministerial meeting of the World Trade Organization in December 1996 ("Kantor Declares War on Bribes," *Financial Times*, 7 March 1996; see Elliott, chapter 10, on the outcome of the WTO meeting).

Conclusion: Seychelles by the Offshore

Still, although the global task of rooting out corruption remains enormous and a world freed even of rampant overseas bribery is undoubtedly still some years away, change is clearly in the air. Take the recent case of the tiny island republic of Seychelles.

In late 1995, the government of the Seychelles islands enacted an innocent-sounding law called the Economic Development Act. One of its provisions offers foreigners that invest more than $10 million immunity from prosecution on all criminal offenses. The language of the statute even ensures that the law can be changed only through a national referendum and a constitutional amendment. It is, in short, an open, official, cynical invitation to money launderers and drug kingpins: come to the Seychelles with your dirty cash.

In a different era, the world would almost certainly have greeted such a development in a tiny island nation with indifference and inaction. Not so today. Almost immediately, the European Commission, the OECD, the Commonwealth Secretariat, the US State Department, the French and British foreign ministries, Interpol, and the Financial Action Task Force all denounced the law, calling for its revision and threatening sanctions.

Furthermore, it was announced that all financial transactions originating from that country or routed through it would be subjected to special monitoring and tracking by regulatory and law enforcement agencies around the world ("Seychelles Condemned over Money Launderers' Charter," *Financial Times*, 3 February, 1996; "Investment à la Seychelloise," *Economist*, 17 February 1996). While the law has not yet been revoked, the international reaction has almost certainly already scared away some of the investors whom the Seychelles government was hoping to lure. It seems doubtful, over the long run, that the law will survive such an international assault.

The Seychelles case provides a vivid illustration of three main themes of this chapter. First, globalization has drastically altered the nature of corruption. Second, while recent changes have opened new avenues for corruption, they have also created new conditions that provide unprecedented opportunities for containing or even reducing it. Third, because corruption is now an inherently global problem, governments acting alone can accomplish little. Systematic collaboration and coordination among the authorities of different countries has become an indispensable precondition for success in the anticorruption battle.

These new efforts at cooperation may seem to be small steps toward tackling a gargantuan problem. They are, however, giant steps compared with what seemed possible even a few years ago—which helps explain why there is a growing sense in many quarters that the fight against corruption need not be a lost battle. Political will is combining with new tools and new institutional arrangements to create a sound basis for cautious optimism.

It is worth remembering that many major, present-day international institutions also began with what at the time seemed rather limited technical agreements. Today's European Union, for example, grew out of an arrangement originally designed to coordinate coal and steel policies. Much of the institutional apparatus that now exists to ensure a modicum of stability in the world's financial markets originated in modest and narrow accords to share information. As Ethan Kapstein (1996) has written, two banking failures in the United States and Germany in 1974 had massive fallout in the world money markets, prompting the central bankers of the Group of Ten industrialized countries to establish the Standing Committee on Banking Regulations and Supervisory Practices, also known as the Basle Accord. The Basle Accord originated as an effort to ensure a minimal level of supervision of international banks. Later, as a result of the 1982 Mexican debt crisis, the members agreed on international guidelines for minimum capital requirements of international banks.

Combatting corruption is certainly a bigger task than regulating financial markets. But the Basle agreement is instructive, both as an example of effective international action and as a model for the form that such action is often likely to take in the present-day environment: some combination of international harmonization of legislation with greater home-country responsibility for multinational firms' actions abroad.

In his classic text, *Bribes*, written more than a decade ago, John Noonan (1984) ventured the bold prediction that "as slavery was once a way of life and now . . . has become obsolete and incomprehensible, so the practice of bribery in the central form of the exchange of payment for official actions will [one day] become obsolete." Even today, Noonan's ambitious prophecy looks premature, not to say utopian. But when a future historian writes the long and ugly story of human corruption, there is reason to suppose that the 1990s could be to corruption what the 1850s were to slavery: a decade of irreversible change.

References

Andelman, David A. 1994. "The Drug Money Maze." *Foreign Affairs* 73, no. 4 (July-August): 94-108.

Beck, Paul J., Michael W. Maher, and Adrian E. Tschoegl. 1991. "The Impact of the Foreign Corrupt Practices Act on U.S. Exports." *Managerial and Decision Economics* 12, no. 4 (August): 295-303.

Cameron, S. 1996. "Dreaming of a World without Corruption." *Macleans* (8 April): 36-37.

Ettorre, Barbara. 1994. "Why Overseas Bribery Won't Last." *Management Review* 83, no. 6 (June): 20-25.

International Chamber of Commerce. 1996. "Extortion and Bribery in International Business Transactions (Revisions to the 1977 Report and Rules of Conduct to Combat Extortion and Bribery)." Paris.

Jadwin, Pamela J., and Monica Shilling. 1994. "Foreign Corrupt Practices Act." *American Criminal Law Review* 31, no. 3: 677-86.

Kapstein, Ethan B. 1996. "Shockproof: The End of the Financial Crisis." *Foreign Affairs* 74, no. 1 (January-February): 2-8.

Karatnycky, Adrian. 1996. "Democracy and Despotism: Bipolarism Renewed? (The Comparative Survey of Freedom: 1996)." *Freedom Review* 27, no. 1 (January-February): 5.

Kimelman, John. 1994. "The Lonely Boy Scout." *Financial World* 163, no. 17 (16 August): 50-51.

Kinnear, James W. 1995. "The Ethics of International Business: Foreign Policy and Economic Sanctions." *Vital Speeches* 61, no. 18 (1 July): 561-65.

Klitgaard, Robert. 1988. *Controlling Corruption*. Berkeley: University of California Press.

Klubes, Benjamin B., and Roberto Iraola. 1995. "The Foreign Corrupt Practices Act: A Compliance Primer for American Business in an Era of Trade Globalization." *Corporate Counsel's Quarterly* 11, no. 4: 56-69.

Naím, Moisés. 1995. "The Corruption Eruption." *Brown Journal of World Affairs* 2, no. 2 (Summer): 245-61.

Negroponte, Nicholas. 1995. *Being Digital*. New York: Knopf.

Noonan, John T. Jr. 1984. *Bribes*. New York: Macmillan.

Organization of American States (OAS). 1996. "Inter-American Convention against Corruption." Washington.

Organization for Economic Cooperation and Development (OECD). 1995a. "Combatting Bribery of Foreign Public Officials in International Transactions: The Role of Taxation (Note by the Secretariat)." Directorate for Financial, Fiscal and Enterprise Affairs. Committee on Fiscal Affairs. Working Party No. 8 on Tax Avoidance and Evasion of the Committee on Fiscal Affairs. Paris.

Organization for Economic Cooperation and Development (OECD). 1995b. "Draft Recommendation of the Council of the OECD on the Tax Deductibility of Bribes to Foreign Government Officials: Report by the Committee on Fiscal Affairs." Paris.

Organization for Economic Cooperation and Development (OECD). 1996. "Bribes to Foreign Officials: Tax Deductibility to End: Intergovernmental Agreement." OECD Letter 5/5 (1996).

Passas, Nikos. 1994. "I Cheat Therefore I Exist? The BCCI Scandal in Context." In W. Michael Hoffman et al., *Emerging Global Business Ethics*. Westport, CT: Quorum Books.

Pitman, Glenn A., and James P. Sanford. 1994. "The Foreign Corrupt Practices Act Revisited: Attempting to Regulate Ethical Bribes in Global Business." *International Journal of Purchasing and Materials Management* 30, no. 3 (Summer): 15-20.

Post, David. 1995. "E-Cash: Can't Live with It, Can't Live without It." *The American Lawyer* 17, no. 2 (March): 116.

Prasad, Jyoti N. 1993. *Impact of the Foreign Corrupt Practices Act of 1977 on U.S. Exports*. New York: Garland Publishing.

Sheffet, Mary Jane. 1995. "The Foreign Corrupt Practices Act and the Omnibus Trade and Competitiveness Act of 1988: Did They Change Corporate Behavior?" *Journal of Public Policy and Marketing* 14, no. 2 (Fall): 290.

Tichy, Noel M., and Stratford Sherman. 1993. *Control Your Destiny or Someone Else Will*. New York: Harper Business.

Trade Promotion Coordinating Committee. 1996. *Toward the Next American Century: A U.S. Strategic Response to Foreign Competitive Practices*. The Fourth Annual National Export Strategy Report to the US Congress. Washington, October.

UN Conference on Trade and Development (UNCTAD). 1994. *World Investment Report: 1994*. Geneva: United Nations.

US Department of State. 1992. "Fact Sheet: Combatting Drug Money-Laundering." *U.S. Department of State Dispatch* 3, no. 9 (2 March): 163.

Yannaca-Small, Catherine. 1995. "Battling International Bribery." *OECD Observer*, no. 192 (February-March): 16-17.

THE SOURCES AND EFFECTS
OF CORRUPTION

2

The Political Economy of Corruption

SUSAN ROSE-ACKERMAN

Corruption occurs at the interface of the public and private sectors. When-ever a public official has discretionary power over distribution to the private sector of a benefit or cost, incentives for bribery are created. Thus corruption depends upon the magnitude of the benefits and costs under the control of public officials. Private individuals and firms are willing to pay to obtain these benefits and avoid the costs. Every state must decide when to legalize such payments and when to label them illegal corruption. The proper link between money and politics is a deep one and will be resolved differently by different countries. Nevertheless, economic analysis can isolate incentives for payoffs to government agents, evaluate their consequences, and suggest reform.

Countries vary widely in the pervasiveness and level of corruption, and within individual countries some industries, government depart-ments, and lower-level governments are very corrupt while others are not. In large, diverse countries such as the United States, India, and China, there is no way to measure the level of corruption. Reliable data on the magnitude of corruption across countries does not exist and probably cannot exist in principle.

Nevertheless, when businesspeople are queried, they indicate that the problem varies widely across countries.[1] Within individual countries,

Susan Rose-Ackerman is Henry R. Luce Professor of Law and Political Science, Yale University.

1. A well-publicized recent example of this type of effort are the corruption perception rankings produced by Transparency International and the University of Goettingen in 1995 and 1996. These rankings evaluated 41 countries in 1995 and 54 countries in 1996 based on an aggregation of other survey work (from various years). The 1996 index is reproduced and explained in *TI Newsletter* (September 1996, 5-8; see also chapters 4 and 10 by Mauro and Elliott, respectively).

surveys demonstrate that some public agencies—for example, customs and tax collection and police departments—are more of a problem than others.[2]

The significance of corruption in international business dealings is also difficult to judge. But, to give a sense of scale, if just 5 percent of the $90 billion of foreign direct investment in the developing world in 1995 were paid as bribes, the total would be $4.5 billion annually. If a similar value of merchandise imports were diverted into payoffs, the combined total would be almost $80 billion (World Bank 1996, appendix 6).

Corruption can significantly affect the efficiency, fairness, and legitimacy of state activities. Extreme cases, although atypical, illustrate the risk of tolerating moderate amounts of corruption. An in-depth study of an irrigation district in India indicated that 20 to 50 percent of the funds the government provided were wasted in corruption and malfeasance (Wade 1982, 1984). Similar work in Pakistan by experts on irrigation indicated that illegal water outlets were purchased from the state, imposing severe costs on downstream farmers (Murray-Rust, Hammond, and Vander Velde 1994; Vander Velde 1990; Vander Velde and Svendsen 1994). A study of corruption in Thailand documented numerous examples of bureaucratic corruption in infrastructure projects, construction, and other areas. Leakage was from 20 to 40 percent of project costs from 1960 to 1990 (Phongpaicht and Piriyarangsan 1994, 25-34). In Brazil under President Fernando Collor de Mello the rake-off on public contracts allegedly increased from 10 to 15 percent to 30 to 50 percent (Fleischer 1995; Manzetti and Blake 1996).

Privatization in Eastern Europe, Russia, and the developing world yields many examples of sales to privileged insiders at below-market prices (Celarier 1996). In Korea, bribery of building inspectors allegedly led to substandard construction of a department store that subsequently collapsed, killing several people (Park 1995). In Indonesia, corruption in the customs service became so ingrown that the head of state signed a contract with a private Swiss firm to take over the duties of the state agency (GATT 1991, 1995). In Guinea, continuous demands for bribes are reportedly a feature of any business deal. Construction contractors locked into a particular site are particularly vulnerable. From Italy to Ghana to Venezuela, allegations of corruption have toppled sitting rulers or led to the arrest of past incumbents (Ayittey 1992; Colazingari and Rose-Ackerman 1995; LeVine 1975; Manzetti and Blake 1996).

As these examples illustrate, corruption is common in both the developing and the industrial worlds. But should it be an object of concern? Some countries alleged to be very corrupt have experienced high levels

---

2. See, for example, the various World Bank surveys reported in de Melo, Ofer, and Sandler (1995); Novitzky, Novitzky, and Stone (1995); Stone (1995); Webster and Charap (1993); and Yabrak and Webster (1995).

of economic growth. In Indonesia, Thailand, and Korea, corruption and growth have gone together. Perhaps poor and transitional countries should not be concerned about widespread corruption in designing economic reform policies. Perhaps corrupt countries with high growth rates should simply accept diversion of funds as normal. There are two fundamental arguments against such tolerance.

First, systemically corrupt countries that have nevertheless experienced satisfactory economic growth risk sinking into a downward spiral. Corruption can feed on itself to produce higher illegal payoffs until growth is undermined. Tolerating corruption that smooths over the rough spots in the system and siphons off 5 or 10 percent of the value of public projects may generate pressures to increase the take to 15 or 20 percent. The very growth that permitted corruption in the past can produce a shift from productive activities to an unproductive struggle for the spoils, harming future growth and investment. Without self-conscious policy reform, corruption is not something a country will just "grow out of."

Second, economic growth is not the only goal worth pursuing. Corruption also tends to distort the allocation of economic benefits, favoring the haves over the have-nots and leading to a less equitable income distribution. In extreme cases, corruption can undermine political stability (see chapter 3). Even when corruption is a way around excessively restrictive government polices, it is a second-best choice. Especially for emerging and transitional economies, a respectable growth record should not be used to justify the continuing existence of inefficient and unfair state and private-sector relations.

Sometimes there is no distinction between public and private purses, and government officials simply "appropriate" state assets. My interest, however, is in the more complex cases in which a private individual or organization bribes a state official to obtain a benefit. Payment may be for the private benefit of the official or his family, or it may be an illegal campaign contribution. Agent-principal relationships are at the heart of such corrupt transactions, with illegal payoffs one way for public agents to allocate the gains and losses of government activity (Rose-Ackerman 1978).

I ignore purely kleptocratic or "vampire" states in which there is no distinction between the public and the private spheres and where the ruler and his associates simply take as much of the country's wealth as they wish (Andreski 1968). Instead, I concentrate on countries that have legal rules outlawing bribery and other forms of self-dealing by bureaucrats, cabinet ministers, legislators, and judges. Most countries today fall into this category.

In seeking realistic reform it is important to realize that, like all illegal activity, the efficient level of bribery is not zero. Bribery is costly to control. Reforms must consider the marginal costs as well as the marginal benefits of anticorruption strategies.

Furthermore, combatting corruption is not an end in itself. The struggle against malfeasance is part of the broader goal of creating a more effective government. Reformers are not just concerned with corruption per se but with its distortionary effect on development and society. Widespread corruption is a sign that something has gone wrong in the relationship between the state and society.

The incidence and level of bribery and other forms of malfeasance depend not just on potential gains from corruption but also on the riskiness of corrupt deals and on the relative bargaining power of potential bribers and bribees. The structural features I stress here can go only part of the way toward explaining the level of corruption. Many officials remain honest in the face of considerable temptations, and many ordinary people and businesses refuse to pay bribes even when illegal payments promise large, short-term gains.

Let us consider several key questions that arise throughout the industrial and the developing world:

- What opportunities for private economic gains exist at the interface between the public and the private sectors?

- What determines the size and incidence of bribe payments?

- What are the political, economic, and distributive consequences of corruption?

- What strategies can be used to reduce corruption?

What Are the Economic Opportunities for Corruption?

The demand for corrupt services—that is, the supply of bribes—depends on the size and structure of the state. Bribes are paid for two reasons: to obtain government benefits and to avoid costs. An effective anticorruption strategy should both reduce the benefits and costs under the control of public agents and limit their discretion to allocate gains and impose harms (Klitgaard 1988; Rose-Ackerman 1978). What are some of the possibilities?

Paying to Get a Government Benefit

The government buys and sells goods and services, distributes subsidies, organizes privatization of state firms, and provides concessions. Officials frequently have a monopoly of valuable information. These activities all create incentives for corruption.

When the government is a buyer or a contractor, there are several reasons to pay off officials. First, a firm may pay to be included in the list of qualified bidders. Second, it may pay to have officials structure bidding specifications so that the corrupt firm is the only qualified supplier. Third, a firm may pay to be selected as the winning contractor. Finally, once a firm has been selected, it may pay to get inflated prices or to skimp on quality.

Governments frequently sell goods or services at below-market prices. Often dual prices exist—a low state price and a higher free market price. Firms will then pay off officials for access to below-market state supplies. In China, for example, many raw materials are sold at both state subsidized prices and on the free market. Payoffs are common (Gong 1993; Hao and Johnston 1995; Johnston and Hao 1995).

When the supply of credit and the rate of interest are controlled by the state, bribes may be paid for access to credit. Interviews with business-people in Eastern Europe and Russia indicate that payoffs are frequently needed to obtain credit (de Melo, Ofer, and Sandler 1995; Webster 1993; Webster and Charap 1993). In Lebanon a similar survey revealed that loans were not available without the payment of bribes (Yabrak and Webster 1995).

Similarly, multiple exchange rates often do not reflect underlying economic fundamentals, thus producing incentives to pay bribes to get scarce foreign exchange at good rates. A World Bank economic memorandum on Paraguay, for example, notes that in the 1980s that country's multiple exchange rate system led to corruption (World Bank 1994). Allocation of scarce import and export licenses is also a frequent source of payoffs and patronage, with bribes linked to the value of the monopoly benefits conferred (Herbst and Olukoshi 1994, 465).

Corruption can also occur when the level of subsidies and benefits for the worthy is too low to satisfy all who qualify, or when officials must use judgment in deciding who is qualified for an entitlement. A service may be scarce so that people will pay to be named recipients or the service may be an entitlement to all who qualify so people pay to be included among the worthy group. In the administration of public housing programs in the United States, for example, the number of qualified households always far outstrips the number of places in subsidized units. In India, some states provide a means-tested pension to the poorest people. The number who qualify exceeds the funds available. Nongovernmental organizations that work with the poor report that applicants must pay to qualify and then must pay postal workers to deliver the benefit checks. Payoffs may be made to alter test results required for university admissions or to induce doctors to declare people disabled so they can qualify for subsidy payments.

Privatizing state-owned enterprises can improve the performance of the economy and in the process reduce corruption. Turning over state assets to private owners can, however, itself create incentives for corruption. Sale of a large parastatal or public firm is similar to tendering for a large public infrastructure project. Thus the incentives for malfeasance are similar. A firm may pay to be included in the list of qualified bidders or to restrict their number. It may pay to obtain a low assessment of the public property to be leased or sold off or to be favored in the selection process. Some corrupt transactions may undermine the efficiency rationale that lies behind economic justifications for privatization. Thus if firms pay to preserve the monopoly power of the enterprise after it enters private hands, the result may simply be a transfer of profits from the state to the new owners. Employees of the newly privatized firm may then face demands from suppliers and customers seeking to share in monopoly benefits.

Before the process was reformed, privatizations in Argentina allegedly favored those with inside information and connections (Manzetti and Blake 1996). Privatizations in Thailand have supposedly involved kickbacks and commission fees (Phongpaicht and Piriyarangsan 1994, 10). Some privatizations in the former eastern bloc have apparently involved similar corrupt transfers (Celarier 1996).

Finally, for all types of government programs, officials are likely to have information that is valuable to outsiders. Thus private individuals and firms may pay to obtain such information or to obtain it sooner than their competitors. Such information as bidding specifications for contracts, the actual condition of soon-to-be-privatized firms, or the location of future capital projects is likely to be worth paying for.

Paying to Avoid Costs

Governments impose regulations, levy taxes, and enforce criminal laws. Officials can delay and harass those they deal with. They can impose costs selectively in a way that affects the competitive position of firms in an industry.

Under public regulatory programs, firms may pay to get a favorable interpretation of the rules or to get a discretionary judgment in their favor. They may pay to avoid or lighten the regulatory load or to clarify regulatory requirements when laws are unclear. Incentives for corruption may be especially high for newly privatized state enterprises dealing with fledgling regulatory agencies with no well-developed track record. Thus those who advise developing and transitional economies on setting up regulatory agencies for public utilities emphasize transparent and open processes (Tenenbaum 1996).

In a federal government, inconsistent rules can make payoffs hard to avoid. A World Bank study of private enterprises in Brazil recounted the (perhaps apocryphal) tale of one entrepreneur who reported that he was visited by state and federal inspectors simultaneously. The goal of the joint visit was to be sure that the firm would be observed violating at least one of the two governments' inconsistent rules on the placement of fire extinguishers (Stone, Levy, and Paredes 1992, 29).

Taxes are always burdensome, so businesses and individuals may collude with tax collectors to lower the sums collected. The savings are divided between the taxpayer and the official. In some parts of Eastern Europe and the former Soviet Union, where nominal tax rates are very high, businesspeople report high payoffs (de Melo, Ofer, and Sandler 1995; Novitzky, Novitzky, and Stone 1995; Webster and Charap 1993). In Italy many allegations of corruption involved payoffs to tax inspectors. Customs officials are particularly likely to engage in corruption since they control something that firms value—access to the outside world. Payoffs are used to reduce tariffs and export fees and to obtain import and export licenses. Customs reform in Indonesia and Mexico resulted from widespread evidence of corruption ("Airport Customs Harnesses 3 Billion Mexican Pesos Per Year," *El Economista*, 13 February 1992; GATT 1991). Here is an area in which the prescriptions of the market-oriented economist and the anticorruption reformer go together. Free-trade policies both improve efficiency under most conditions and reduce the economic rents available to corrupt officials. Tolerating corruption as a way around restrictive trade policies leads to widespread inequities and inefficiencies. Studies show that as tariff rates rise, tariffs collected fall as a share of nominal tariffs and the variance of rates actually paid increases (Pritchett and Sethi 1994). These results are consistent with the view that corruption incentives rise with tax and tariff rates.

Illegal businesses are especially vulnerable to extortion. Law enforcement authorities from the police to prosecutors and judges can demand payments to overlook violations or limit penalties. If evidence of criminal behavior is clear, such businesses will be unable to credibly threaten to report corrupt demands.

But, of course, illegal businesses are hardly innocent victims. They may actively try to corrupt the police. They seek not only immunity from prosecution for themselves but also assurance of monopoly power in the illegal market. In the United States, for example, gamblers and drug dealers have paid officials to raid their competitors or to restrict entry (Rose-Ackerman 1978, 163). At the local level in Thailand, some public authorities shelter criminal enterprises both from competition and from the law (Phongpaicht and Piriyarangsan 1994, 51-97). Instead of inducing state officials to harass their competitors, some illegal businesspeople may engage in outright intimidation of potential rivals, often paying off the police not to intervene in their private attempts to dominate the market (Handelman 1995).

Since time is money, firms and individuals everywhere will pay to avoid delay. For example, if the government or a parastatal does not pay its bills on time, contractors or customers may bribe government officials to get speedy payment. In Argentina a scheme in which insurance companies paid to get claims settled by a state-run reinsurance company degenerated into outright fraud against the state organized by corrupt state officials and middlemen (Moreno Ocampo 1995). In many countries, informal payoffs are required to obtain expedited services such as a telephone, a passport, or a driver's license. Sometimes the service is available only to the corrupt and not to the patient but honest citizen. In St. Petersburg in 1992, the going rate for a telephone installation was $200 (Webster and Charap 1993). An Indian newspaper recently published a list of the "fees" for a range of routine public services ("Bribe Index," *Sunday Times of India*, 17 December 1995).

Paying for Official Positions

When corruption is pervasive, positions in the state bureaucracy become valuable assets, and there will be derived demand for jobs in the state sector. In some developing countries there is a lively market for positions in the bureaucracy that generate large bribes (Wade 1982, 1984). Positions in a corrupt police department are likely to be especially valuable (Phongpaicht and Piriyarangsan 1994, 99-129). Jobs in departments with few such opportunities, such as the foreign service, may attract few qualified applicants. But if government pay scales exceed those in the private sector, people may pay for such jobs even if few bribes are possible. Because public schools in India pay teachers more than private schools, some people purchase these jobs with their wives' dowries or loans from relatives.

What Determines Bribe Size and Incidence?

The level of corruption is a function of the honesty and integrity of both public officials and private individuals. Holding such factors constant, however, the size and incidence of bribes are determined by the overall level of benefits available, the discretionary power of officials, the riskiness of corrupt deals, and the relative bargaining power of briber and bribee.[3]

Benefits and Official Discretion

I have already explained how the nature of government programs creates corruption incentives in all societies. It is important to recognize,

---

3. For a fuller discussion of these issues, see Klitgaard (1988) and Rose-Ackerman (1978). Klitgaard (75) reduces this list to a simple heuristic in which corruption equals monopoly plus discretion minus accountability.

however, that the level of benefits is not necessarily exogenous. Corrupt public officials can frequently use their discretion to increase the supply of benefits up for negotiation. There are several ways this can be done. Officials may be able to extract some of a contractor's profits by introducing payment delays or inventing *ex post* regulatory hurdles. They can threaten to enforce criminal and regulatory laws more vigorously than is the norm. They can behave in arbitrary and unclear ways to create a demand for clarity. They can propose white-elephant projects, which are an inefficient way to encourage economic development or use scarce budget resources.[4] Officials may also be able to structure privatization projects or natural resource concessions so that they include a high level of monopoly profits for whomever obtains the newly privatized firm or the concession.

In general, we can distinguish between two kinds of corrupt market structures. Some corrupt systems are roughly competitive. Routine government services often fall into this category. The market is imperfect because of the costs of secrecy and the exclusion of the scrupulous, but approximately the same bribe price is charged to all for such services as a telephone line, a gas connection, or a passport. When the bribe market is less competitive, however, corrupt officials may bribe-price discriminate. They extract bribes that are proportional to the monopoly profits of bribers. Those with higher gains from obtaining the corrupt benefit pay more for it. Tax collection and customs officials may be able to price discriminate in this way if the taxes owed are related to the firm's profitability. One-of-a kind procurements or privatizations fall into this category and can generate very large dollar payoffs. The level is a function of the overall gains and of the relative bargaining power of the parties.

Since officials can create economic rents and control their distribution, the study of corruption must include an analysis of the organization of public officials. Freelance rent seeking creates externalities among public officials. The level of rents can be thought of as a common pasture that is overgrazed by the officials. In the extreme, such overgrazing could seriously undermine the economy. A monopolistic autocrat could rationalize rent collection with efficiency gains all around. Thus some authors suggest that centralized corruption is less damaging than low-level corruption (Rodrik 1994; Shleifer and Vishney 1993). Corrupt top officials with a long-term perspective will not push their greed so far as to destroy the economy. This argument is correct within the terms of the model under which it was developed. It is simply a straightforward application of a result in industrial organization theory. It is not a general conclusion, however, since it ignores the fact that higher-ups are

---

4. For examples from Nigeria, see Diamond (1993) and Faruqee (1994). See also Ayittey (1992), Ouma (1991), and Werlin (1972) for other African examples.

likely to have greater freedom to create extra rents than lower-level functionaries. The ruler can commit the resources of the entire state to his own corrupt ends. Even a large number of venal low-level officials are unlikely to be able collectively to accomplish so much (Rose-Ackerman 1994). The damage caused by high-level corruption can be especially serious if the ruler is insecure and expects to leave office soon, perhaps as a result of his corruption being revealed. Such a ruler can be in an unstable situation in which his own corruption increases the chance of his overthrow, which in turn encourages him to be even more corrupt, and so forth. Concentrating on reducing low-level corruption ignores these possibilities and is also unlikely to succeed if civil servants are aware of the peculation of their superiors.

Risk and the Division of Gains

The higher the probability that corruption will be detected and punished, the lower the effective benefits available. If the likelihood of detection and punishment is high, either the supply of or the demand for bribes may fall to zero. The analysis can proceed much like any discussion of the economics of crime (Becker and Stigler 1974; Rose-Ackerman 1978, chapter 6). The expected cost of bribery is the probability of being caught times the probability of being convicted times the punishment levied. A risk-neutral briber or public official compares this expected cost with the expected benefit and is corrupt only if the balance is positive. A risk-averse actor must also be compensated for the uncertainty involved in corrupt transactions. In the simplest version of this model, the briber and the official are bribe price takers who do not bargain over the level of the bribe or the service provided in return.

Bribery, however, seldom occurs under competitive market conditions. Instead, a bargaining framework is often appropriate. As the cost of corruption rises, it is not obvious how its remaining gains will be split between briber and bribee. The answer will depend in part on their relative tolerance for risk. It may also depend on whether the probabilities of detection and punishment and the penalties imposed are a function of the level of bribes paid. If they are, payoffs may be quite low but also very common. In contrast, one possible result of stepped-up enforcement is a lower incidence of corruption but an increase in the size of bribes paid in any remaining corrupt deals. This would be most likely if the consequences of being caught are worse for government officials and politicians than for outsiders, a common situation. Thus a larger share of the corrupt gains would need to be given to the official compared with the firm. Officials are either entirely honest or demand large bribes.

The briber's willingness to pay also depends on the alternatives available. First, the potential briber may be able to obtain the same benefits by relocating to another jurisdiction or country. Second, the firm may have the option of following legal procedures at some additional cost. Third, the firm may have access to specialized technology or a type of financing not available elsewhere, or it may have monopoly power in its dealings with the state. Fourth, a private individual may be able to get his or her way by using threats and intimidation instead of payoffs. Fifth, the individual may be able to apply to a different official in the same government to obtain a comparable benefit. This possibility will be credible when many officials can provide a benefit such as a license, a passport, or help in smuggling goods across the border (Rose-Ackerman 1978, chapters 7 and 8). Similarly, in a democratic legislature in which a majority must be bribed, no one legislator has much bargaining power (Rasmusen and Ramseyer 1994).

In short, firms can resist corrupt demands if they have other options. A firm trying to decide where to locate its plant will be in a strong position in relation to corrupt officials if it has several feasible jurisdictions available. In contrast, a firm competing for a privatized company or a mineral concession can be subject to corrupt demands if monopoly profits are expected. In such cases, competition between potential buyers or concessionaires can produce a situation in which most of the economic benefits go to some combination of the state itself and its corrupt officials. Corruption reduces gains to the state through deals in which individual officials take bribes in return for assuring high profits for the successful firms.

The illegality of bribery introduces another cost—the cost of keeping the illegal transaction secret. Corrupt businesses and officials may create an elaborate structure of shell companies with off-shore addresses to hide their peculation. They may engage in other costly efforts to cover their tracks. Furthermore, high transaction costs mean that there is less information available than in a legal market. This may help explain why bribes in many countries are reported as stylized percentages of the value of transactions or as fixed fees—10 percent of the value of a contract, $100 for a license—and that they seem to remain unchanged over time.[5] These pricing conventions may arise from the costs and risks of negotiations. Only for very large, one-of-a-kind deals are specialized negotiations worthwhile. Even those who have been implicated in past corruption may report payoffs if officials start to get too greedy (Alam 1991; Cartier-Bresson 1995).

---

5. In Thailand, for example, both businesspeople and bureaucrats view a 10 percent commission paid by contractors and suppliers to officials as normal. A higher demand would be labeled corrupt. Most ordinary citizens, however, view even a 10 percent payoff as wrong and many understand that such payments increase the cost or lower the quantity and quality of public services (Phongpaicht and Piriyarangsan 1994, 134-35, 155).

What Are Corruption's Consequences?

Corruption can produce inefficiency and unfairness. It can undermine the political legitimacy of the state. Corruption is also evidence that deeper problems exist in the state's dealings with the private sector. The most severe costs are not the bribes themselves but the underlying distortions they reveal—distortions that may have been created by officials to generate payoffs.

Inefficient Government Contracting and Privatizations

When payoffs are commonplace, government contracts, privatized firms, and concessions may not be allocated to the most efficient bidders. One might, however, argue that the most efficient firm can pay the highest bribe. This will not be so, however, if the firm happens to be scrupulous. Corruption favors those with no scruples and those with connections over those who are the most productively efficient. Although there is no necessary relationship between honesty and efficiency, the need to pay bribes is an entry barrier. Only those who already have a close trusting relationship with government officials and politicians may enter the bidding. Officials may refuse to deal with those they do not know for fear of exposure. Furthermore, the high briber may expect to make payoffs, not just to win the contract or the privatization auction but also to obtain inefficient subsidies, monopoly benefits, and regulatory laxness in the future.

Corruption introduces other inefficiencies into government contracting. Projects may be too large and too numerous if bribe revenues increase with the dollar volume of procurement. They may also be more complex than necessary since corrupt payments are easier to hide if projects are one-of-a-kind. An experienced World Bank official mentioned to me that complaints about "inappropriate capital-labor ratios" in evaluation reports were often a way of flagging corrupt deals. Quality may suffer if contractors make payoffs in order to be allowed to skimp on quality.[6]

In privatizations, there is a subtle reason why the most corrupt firm will not necessarily be the most efficient. A corrupt bidder with good access to insiders may persuade officials to bankrupt or badly manage a parastatal so its value is lowered in the subsequent sale. This tactic will make it difficult for outsiders to evaluate the company, and more of the benefits will go to the successful bidder, who is also an insider, than to

---

6. Although there is no systematic evidence on the role of corruption in contracting, considerable evidence suggests that much investment in the developing world has little or no productive impact (Pritchett 1996).

the government. This kind of behavior will be difficult to detect since, *ex post*, the privatization will appear to be a smashing success.

The efficiency costs of corrupt privatizations will be especially high if the winning bidder must actually operate the company for a time. If the winner can sell out to a more efficient competitor, it can cheat the state from some of the gains of privatization, but the privatized firm eventually will be operated efficiently. An inefficient corrupt firm might not sell out, however, if it can continue to use payoffs and connections to gain illicit advantages in the future.

Delays and Red Tape

Officials may raise a firm's costs by introducing delays and unnecessary requirements as a way of inducing payoffs. This can happen either in contracting and auctioning or in administering regulatory and tax laws. In addition, paying bribes is itself costly. A portion of a long-distance trucker's load may rot as it waits at roadblocks established to extract payoffs (Rogers and Iddal 1996). Construction delays caused by rent-seeking officials push into the future the date at which the project begins to bring in returns. An efficient bribe seeker would only threaten delays, not actually impose them. But such threats are not likely to be credible unless they are sometimes carried out. Furthermore, the bribe-generating technology may itself be rather primitive. Trucks must be physically stopped; inspectors must actually show up at the building site.

Private production may be of low quality if bribes are paid to induce officials to overlook dangerous conditions or to permit firms to supply low-quality services. Contractors who maintained irrigation systems in Pakistan and India, for example, were found to skimp on quality. Close observers of the operation of several irrigation districts were convinced that the low quality resulted from payoffs to officials to overlook shoddy work (Wade 1982, 1984; Murray-Rust, Hammond, and Vander Velde 1994).

Regulatory laws that are justified by the inefficiencies of the private market will not be effectively enforced. The safety of the workplace and compliance with environmental regulations can be reduced by payoffs. Firms that benefit from such situations are likely to be opponents of regulatory reforms that they would otherwise favor if the system were honest and the laws well-enforced.

Inefficient Use of Corrupt Payments

Illicit funds may be used for consumption by top bureaucrats, may be invested in legitimate businesses at home or abroad, or may be diverted into illegal businesses. Payoffs are more likely to be diverted into illegal activities or foreign bank accounts than other funds because they are already illegal and must be kept secret. Of course, if bribes are paid out of a multinational's profits, the diversion of bribes abroad may have marginal effect on society. The bribe is just a transfer from the excess profits of the contractor to public officials. This is not a general result, however. Bribes may be paid out of profits that are themselves inflated because of the corrupt nature of the transaction. Then the export of bribes is a form of capital flight that is likely to be costly for a nation's citizens.

The net cost of such transfers, of course, depends on whether other capital investment comes in to take its place. If capital markets were perfect, funds from international investors would replace any inefficiently exported corrupt payments. But, especially in the developing world, where knowledge of local conditions is likely to be valuable, the assumption of perfect capital markets does not seem warranted.

Inequities

Corruption has distributive consequences. As with discussions of tax incidence, the actual distribution of gains and losses will often be difficult to calculate. However, a few observations are possible.

In a corrupt contracting and privatization process, a larger share of the gains accrue to winning bidders and public officials than under an honest system. A share of the country's wealth is distributed to insiders and corrupt bidders, contributing to inequalities in wealth. The state must make up for high contract prices and for disappointing revenue generated by privatizations by raising taxes or cutting spending.

If scarce subsidies to agriculture and to business are corruptly distributed, the poorest producers are most likely to suffer. In India and Pakistan, corruption in irrigation systems means that those at the bottom of the system may obtain much less water than they need even for subsistence farming. Some ditches run dry before the end of the system is reached (Wade 1982, 1984; Vander Velde 1990; Vander Velde and Svendsen 1994). Programs that directly aid the poor will be less effective if payoffs are needed to qualify for the service. If applicants pay for a favorable place in line for admission to public housing, the most needy will suffer.

Countries with abundant mineral wealth face special challenges. For example, much of the oil wealth of Nigeria has been dissipated through corruption and other forms of rent seeking (Herbst and Olukoshi 1994; Diamond 1993; Olowu 1993). In 1984, after 10 years of oil boom, the per capita income of the average Nigerian was no higher than in 1974. During the 1980s, the economy declined at a rate of 0.4 percent annually, and in 1990 Nigeria was the 17th poorest country in the world with a per capita income lower than that of India or Kenya (World Bank data cited in Herbst and Olukoshi 1994, 453).

Damaged Political Legitimacy

Systemic corruption undermines the legitimacy of governments, especially democracies (see chapter 3). Citizens may come to believe that the government is simply for sale to the highest bidder. Corruption undermines claims that government is substituting democratic values for decisions based on ability to pay. It can lead to coups by undemocratic leaders. Military takeovers are frequently justified as a response to the corruption of democratic rulers (Ayittey 1992; Brett 1992; Diamond 1993; Gillespie and Okruhlik 1991; Gould and Mukendi 1989; Herbst and Olukoshi 1994; Phongpaicht and Piriyarangsan 1994; Widner 1994).

In contrast, governments that do not depend upon the consent of the governed can use corruption to maintain power by spreading the benefits about. If most wealthy and powerful individuals are part of a network of corrupt payoffs and favors, the threat of exposure can help current rulers maintain power. Thus corruption need not be destabilizing. A stable corrupt state may provide a hospitable environment for business investment in the medium run. Lacking a well-established rule of law, however, such societies always risk an escalating cycle of payoffs and insider deals. In Somalia, for example, autocracy degenerated into warlordism (Coolidge and Rose-Ackerman 1996). Some wonder if Indonesia, which has maintained a stable corrupt system for years, may be verging toward a more kleptocratic situation as Suharto nears the end of his reign (Campos and Root 1996, 136-37).

Slowed Growth

These consequences suggest that widespread corruption is likely both to retard development and to distribute the benefits of development unequally. When corrupt countries grow, this implies that corruption has not gone so far as to undermine economic fundamentals. Growth may, however, be a cause of corruption since it creates gains to share. Although individual bribe payments can facilitate business transactions, tolerating pervasive corruption is not a recipe for growth. Rather, economic development increases the rents available for distribution. The task for developing economies is to maintain conditions that reward productive entrepreneurship. Otherwise, those seeking wealth may instead become rent seekers, using resources to shift benefits from others to themselves without generating any value added. Countries with mineral wealth such as oil, copper, or diamonds can maintain a standard of living similar to their neighbors and still siphon off a high level of payoffs. If a downturn occurs, entrenched corruption is likely to become less accepted because there is no longer a growing pie.

Recent cross-country research suggests a negative association between growth and high levels of corruption and other measures of ineffective government (Mauro 1995; Keefer and Knack 1995; see also chapter 4). Other work suggests that the smallest businesses find systemic corruption especially costly and that arbitrary and corrupt governments push firms into the informal sector (Rose-Ackerman and Stone 1996; Kaufman and Kaliberda 1996), that development projects are less likely to be successful in countries with high levels of corruption (Kilby 1995), and that illegal payoffs can significantly increase the cost and lower the quality of public works projects.[7]

Solutions

Widespread corruption is a symptom, not the disease itself. Eliminating corruption makes no sense if the result is a rigid, unresponsive, autocratic government. Instead, anticorruption strategies should seek to improve the efficiency and fairness of government and to enhance the efficiency of the private sector. I argued above that the size and incidence of corruption depended upon four factors: the overall level of public benefits available, the discretionary power of officials, the riskiness of corrupt deals, and the relative bargaining power of briber and bribee. Anticorruption strategies can be similarly categorized under headings: those that lower the benefits under the control of officials, those that reduce their discretion, those that increase the costs of bribery, and those that limit the bargaining power of officials. Strategies must be designed not just to reduce corruption but also to reduce the distortions that corruption either makes possible or reveals. In other words, we need to distinguish between cases in which payoffs themselves produce inefficiency and unfairness and those in which payoffs are a response to underlying pathologies in public programs.

I begin with strategies that increase the risk of corrupt payoffs. I go on to discuss structural and substantive reforms designed to limit the "economic rents" in the public sector and to reduce the discretion and bargaining power of officials. I conclude with some ideas about how the international business community and development institutions such as the World Bank might productively help control corruption.

Increasing the Risks and Costs of Corruption

Strategies that reduce the net benefits of paying and receiving bribes provide a background for substantive legal reform. Government policy

---

7. On this last issue the evidence is anecdotal. See, for example, Faruqee (1994) and Diamond (1993) for examples from Nigeria.

can increase the benefits of being honest, increase the probability of detection and punishment, and increase the penalties levied on those who are caught.

Reforming the civil service is an obvious first step. If officials are paid much less than people with similar training elsewhere in the economy, only those willing to accept bribes will be attracted to the public sector.[8] The rest will work in private enterprises or emigrate. Furthermore, if the level of benefits under the discretionary control of some officials is very high, they may need to be paid above the going rate for people with similar skills. This must be done to increase their willingness to resist the high bribes they may be offered. Thus a country will face a choice between a high-corruption equilibrium with a low-wage bill and a low-corruption state with a high-wage bill (Besley and McLaren 1993). In a country with few skilled workers, a high-wage strategy for public servants not only inflates the government budget but also lures skilled workers away from the private sector. Such countries should be especially interested in the strategies discussed below that lower the opportunities for corruption.

When civil service reform is a realistic option, adequate civil service pay is a necessary, but not a sufficient, condition. High pay reduces the marginal value of the extra funds available from taking bribes but does not reduce the value to zero. Paradoxically, high pay may simply increase the bribe an official demands to overcome the risks of losing what is now a quite desirable job. Thus the incidence of bribery falls as fewer officials are solicited or accept payoffs, but the size of the bribes that are paid increases.

Therefore, civil service reform must include features that are tied to the marginal benefits of accepting payoffs. This is a reason for setting civil service wages above the going private-sector wage and for giving public employees generous benefits such as pensions that they will receive only if they retire in good order (Becker and Stigler 1974). Whatever penalties the criminal law imposes on someone convicted of corruption, the costs of losing a government job for malfeasance will be added on. This strategy, however, must be combined with a transparent system of selecting civil servants or else a new form of corruption will arise—people will pay the powerful to be allotted a desirable government job.

Even these reforms may not be sufficient. Although they are tied to behavior that leads to loss of a government job, they are not tied to the marginal benefits of individual corrupt deals. Thus once officials have stepped over the line and begun to take bribes, these policies will

---

8. Some claim that Botswana's status as a relatively clean African country stems from its rulers' commitment to a professional and well-paid civil service (Raphaeli, Roumani, and MacKeller 1984).

encourage them to take ever higher and more frequent payoffs. If they face a high probability of losing their jobs anyway, why not take as much as possible?

Thus a third strategy is needed. Penalties must be tied to the marginal benefits of the payoffs received. To some extent, this is a job for criminal law and for internal monitoring processes. There are two aspects to this—the probabilities of detection and punishment and the level of punishment, given conviction. Both should be designed so that the expected penalty increases as the level of peculation increases. The marginal penalty will increase with the number and level of payoffs if the chance of detection and conviction is a function of these variables. Similarly, it can increase, even with a fixed probability, if the penalty imposed on those found guilty is tied to the overall amount of money they have received (Rose-Ackerman 1978, chapter 6).

In short, behind all proposals for civil service reform is an effective set of internal controls or antibribery laws with vigorous enforcement. The laws must apply both to those who pay and to those who receive bribes. Thus not only should convicted public officials pay a multiple of bribes received but convicted bribers should also sacrifice a multiple of their gains from bribery. Because bribes represent a cost to those who pay them, penalties should be tied to their gains (their excess profits, for example), not to the amount paid. If potentially corrupt firms are repeat players with the government, they can be deterred by debarment procedures that prohibit corrupt firms from contracting with the government for a period of years. To have marginal effect, the debarment penalty should be tied to the seriousness of the corruption uncovered.[9]

Outside institutions can complement systems of internal control. They must themselves be free of corruption in order to exercise effective oversight. Thus an independent and honest judiciary, including lower-level clerks, is obviously a necessary condition for the effective use of legal sanctions (Buscaglia 1995; Malik 1995). Alternatively, or as a supplement, other independent review and investigative systems such as an anticorruption commission, an ombudsman, or other independent administrative tribunals have been proposed by some.[10] External review bodies, such as Hong Kong's Independent Commission against Corruption, can be valuable, but such a body risks arbitrariness if it reports only to the country's ruler, who could bias its work toward political rivals (Klitgaard 1988, chapter 4; Quah 1993).

---

9. For examples of debarment, see "Singapore Blacklists Scandal-Tinged Firms," *Nikkei Weekly*, 19 February 1996, and Thacher (1995), who describes the practices used by the New York City School Construction Authority.

10. See Jeremy Pope (1996, 73-78). This source book, produced by Transparency International, a nongovernmental organization committed to fighting corruption, reviews in more detail many of the reforms proposed here.

Reporting the peculations of others can be dangerous. If corruption is systemic, one risks being disciplined by corrupt superiors and attacked by co-workers. The whistle-blower may even end up being accused of corruption himself. Yet uncovering evidence of corruption is notoriously difficult because both sides to the transaction have an interest in keeping it secret. Thus governments should consider promulgating whistle-blower statutes that protect and reward those in the public and private sectors who report malfeasance (Pope 1996, 59-61). The United States, for example, has a statute that rewards those who report irregularities in government contracts (*US Code* 31, sections 3729-31; Kovacic 1994).

Furthermore, when corruption is systemic, solutions that appear reasonable in other contexts can be counterproductive. Thus some recommend rotating officials so that they are unable to develop the close, trusting relations needed to reduce the risks of accepting payoffs. However, if the entire bureaucratic agency is corrupt, superiors can use their ability to reassign officials as a punishment for those who will not play along with the corrupt system. A study of corruption in an irrigation system in India found that such practices were common (Wade 1982, 1984), and they have been observed in corrupt police forces in the United States and Thailand as well (Phongpaicht and Piriyarangsan 1994, 99-120; Sherman 1974).

Other sources of information about malfeasance are in the private sector. Those concerned with fighting corruption should support a free press and few constraints on creating and operating watchdog groups. They should support freedom of information laws and oppose restrictive libel laws, especially those that give special protections to public officials (Pope 1996, 129-41; Tucker 1994). Elected politicians should not be immune from facing charges of corruption.

Sometimes, when corruption is itself impossible to observe, its effects on the quality of government services may be evident. Thus nongovernmental organizations should be encouraged to carry out and publish public opinion surveys to determine public attitudes toward government services. Sam Paul (1995) has done pioneering work in Asia, and the Economic Development Institute of the World Bank has sponsored several pilot projects that can provide useful models in this area.

Law enforcement and administrative penalties focus on locating corruption after it has occurred. If effective, the perceived risks of becoming corrupt will deter civil servants from accepting or extorting payments. The goal is to use a combination of carrots (desirable pay and benefits) and sticks (legal and administrative penalties) to deter payoffs. In contrast, other mechanisms focus on creating structures within the public sector that make government actions more transparent. Corruption is deterred because it is more difficult to hide.

One example of this is strong financial management systems that audit government accounts and make financial information about the government public. Procurement regulations that keep the process open and fair are also important (Pope 1996, 93-116). Both accounting and procurement rules, however, must not be perceived as silly or overly intrusive. Officials with discretion can accept bribes without their peculation being obvious to the outside world, yet discretion is obviously necessary for governments to function. For example, rules that the low bidder always be accepted can lead to low-quality work or facilitate bid rigging.[11]

Along these same lines, corruption among politicians can be deterred through campaign finance reform and reform of conflict of interest rules. Limitations on legal donations, however, must not be so restrictive that they virtually push candidates off the books. Legal controls must be combined with effective legal methods of financing campaigns either with public money or with contributions from private individuals and organizations.

It is impossible to evaluate the relative merits of these options in the abstract because the costs and benefits will depend upon the context. Most cannot stand alone. For example, increases in civil service pay and benefits would be pointless unless credible monitoring systems are in place to detect wrongdoing. Furthermore, policies to increase the risks and costs of corruption are usually part of reform strategies also designed to reduce the level of potential benefits. When Mexico reformed its customs service, for example, it not only simplified the underlying regulations but also improved civil service pay and auditing and control.

Reducing Incentives for Payoffs

Reforms that simply make corruption risky are not sufficient. Given the difficulty of amassing evidence and carrying out a successful prosecution, law enforcement can provide no more than a set of background conditions within which government programs operate. Similarly, watchdog agencies and private nongovernmental groups have limited ability to observe state activities. A modern state requires strong financial management systems, procurement codes, and civil service reward mechanisms, but these systems may be overwhelmed by the sheer level of benefits and costs dispensed by the state. Thus reform must also reduce the level of benefits under the control of public officials. The strategy must do this, however, without eliminating programs that have strong public justifications and without simply shifting the benefits into the private sector, where they will show up as monopoly profits. There are several strategies to consider.

---

11. See, for example, Klitgaard's (1988, chapter 6) discussion of bid rigging in US Army contracting in Korea.

The most obvious option is simply to eliminate programs that are permeated with corruption. If the state has no authority to restrict exports or license businesses, no one will pay bribes in those areas. If a subsidy program is eliminated, the bribes that accompanied it will disappear as well. If price controls are lifted, market prices will express scarcity values, not bribes. If a parastatal is the locus of corrupt payoffs, the state should move its functions into the private sector.

In general, any reform that increases the economy's competitiveness will help reduce incentives for corruption. Thus policies that lower controls on foreign trade, remove entry barriers for private industry, and privatize state firms in a way that assures competition will all contribute to the fight against corruption (Ades and Di Tella 1995). As Van de Walle (1994, 136) observes, "Economic liberalization is likely to reduce the amount of rent seeking. . . . Devaluation, tariff reduction, and price liberalization all reduce rent seeking."

But any move toward deregulation and privatization must be carried out with care. Deregulating in one area may simply increase corruption elsewhere. For example, a successful effort to reduce corruption in the transport of agricultural products in Niger simply increased corruption in neighboring countries on the same transport route. A project sponsored by the US Agency for International Development was successful in reducing the number of bribe-extraction checkpoints established by police and customs officials along onion transport routes in Niger. Unfortunately, the ultimate outcome was an increase in payoffs and tax levels in Côte d'Ivoire as the onions neared their destination—the food markets of Abidjan (Rogers and Iddal 1996).

The privatization process can itself be corrupted, as can the new regulatory institutions that will be needed in the privatized world. Instead of bribing the parastatal to obtain contracts and favorable treatment, bidders for the company bribe officials in the privatization authority. A firm privatized with its market power intact may not be corrupt, but it will harm the public by charging monopoly prices. This is not to say that privatization and deregulation are not, on balance, desirable in a wide range of cases but only to caution reformers to look carefully at the incentives for rent seeking that remain.

Limiting Official Discretion

Of course, many regulatory and spending programs have strong justifications and ought to be reformed, not eliminated. Corruption in tax collection obviously cannot be solved by failing to collect revenue. In such cases one solution is to clarify and streamline the necessary laws in ways that reduce official discretion. In the reform of the customs service at the Mexico City airport, for example, the number of steps in the customs process was reduced from 16 to 3. The remaining service was streamlined to reduce delays ("Airport Customs Harnesses 3 Billion Mexico Pesos Per Year," *El Economista*, 13 February 1992).

Rules could be made more transparent with publicly provided justifications. Government might favor simple nondiscretionary tax, spending, and regulatory laws as a way of limiting corrupt opportunities. Obviously, the value of such reforms depends on the costs of limiting the flexibility of public officials. Sometimes a certain risk of corruption will need to be tolerated because of the benefits of a case-by-case approach to program administration. Transparency and publicity can help overcome corrupt incentives even in such cases.

Economists have long recommended reforming regulatory laws in such areas as environmental protection by introducing market-based schemes that limit the discretion of regulators. These analysts also recommend user fees for scarce government services. These reforms have the additional advantage of removing corruption incentives by replacing bribes with legal payments. The sale of water and grazing rights, tradable pollution rights, and the sale of import and export licenses can improve the efficiency of government operations while limiting corruption.

The final group of proposals involves administrative reforms that lower incentives for corruption. Corruption is often embedded in the hierarchical structure of the bureaucracy. Low-level officials collect bribes and pass a share on to higher-level officials, perhaps in the form of an up-front payment for the job itself. Conversely, higher-ups may organize and rationalize the corrupt system to avoid wasteful competition between low-level officials. Top officials may then share the gains of their organizational ability with subordinates, perhaps using them to run errands, transfer funds, and do other risky jobs that expose them to arrest. To break such patterns may require a fundamental reorganization.

The first possibility is to introduce competitive pressures within government to lower the bargaining power of individual officials. When bribes are paid for such benefits as licenses and permits, which are not constrained by budgetary limits, overlapping, competitive bureaucratic jurisdictions can reduce corruption. Because clients can apply to any of a number of officials and can go to a second one if the first turns them down, no one official has much monopoly power. Thus no one can extract a very large payoff, and some officials may give up making corrupt demands. For qualified clients, bribes will be no larger than the cost of reapplication. Unqualified clients will still pay bribes, but even they will not pay much as long as they, too, can try another official (Rose-Ackerman 1978, 137-59).

When officials such as police officers can impose costs, another type of overlapping jurisdiction model should be considered. Police officers seeking to control illegal businesses can be given overlapping enforcement areas. That way, gamblers and drug dealers will not pay much to an individual police officer because a second one may come along later and also demand a payoff. The first one is simply unable to supply protection (Rose-Ackerman 1978, 159-63). This system may work better if the law enforcement officers belong to different police forces—local, state, or federal, for example. Then collusion between officers to defeat the system will be less likely. For instance, the FBI is involved in investigating municipal corruption in the United States. Sometimes the overlap has an international dimension. The involvement of US drug enforcement authorities in investigating the drug business in Colombia led a defector to choose the American justice system over the Colombian and to open the door to information on drug cartel payoffs to Colombian politicians ("Informant's Revelations on Cali Cartel Implicate Colombian Officials," *Washington Post*, 28 January 1996).

Second, if it is difficult to observe the corruption itself, one could design programs to observe its effects. For example, the state might use private market prices as benchmarks to judge public contracts (Ruzindana 1995). Clear rules of proper behavior could be established so violations can be noticed even if the bribery itself is not. Where possible, procurement decisions could favor standard off-the-shelf items to provide a benchmark and to lower the cost of submitting a bid.

Third, many corrupt situations have both winners and losers. Thus the state could introduce ways for potential losers to protest or to organize ahead of time. For example, a land reform program in India was apparently relatively honestly carried out, in part because of a credible, speedy appeals process (Oldenburg 1987). Or the state could make it hard for corrupt officials to organize either themselves or bribe payers. Sometimes bribe payers view themselves as extortion victims who would be better off in an honest world. Such bribe payers are potential allies in an anticorruption effort and will cooperate in efforts to eliminate payoffs. Conversely, in other cases bribery makes both payers and receivers better off with respect to a no-bribery world. Thus control incentives must rest with outsiders not in on the corrupt deal (for example, disappointed bidders, taxpayers, or consumers). The existence of losers such as disappointed bidders with a large stake in the outcome can facilitate efforts to limit corruption (Alam 1995).

Involving Multinational Lenders and Firms

Efficient multinational firms face a "prisoner's dilemma" when they deal with corrupt regimes. Each believes it needs to pay bribes in order to do business, but each knows that all of them would be better off if none of them paid. The playing field is tilted toward unscrupulous but less efficient firms that would not fare as well in an honest system. This realization has led to recent international efforts to limit corruption in international business. Such efforts could complement the solutions outlined above, which largely focus on what a country can do when its leaders are committed to reducing the level of malfeasance.

The World Bank and the regional development banks have a good deal of leverage with their borrowers. They have often been reluctant to use it for fear of being accused of lacking cultural sensitivity or of being heavy-handed advocates of democracy and Western values. The end of the Cold War has, however, changed the balance. Widespread corruption and organized crime's influence in countries such as Russia and others in the former east bloc have made the problem difficult to ignore (Handelman 1995; Shelley 1994). The failure of Africa to develop in the face of substantial progress in many parts of Asia and Latin America raises questions about the role of the state in development. The continuing high level of inequality in many Latin American countries raises similar concerns. The coexistence of corruption and growth in several Asian countries highlights the question of the direction of causation when growth and corruption go together.

In short, multilateral lenders are today freed from the need to support corrupt regimes that in the past could threaten to turn to China and the Soviet Union for help. They remain, however, caught in a bind between the goals of poverty reduction and economic growth on the one hand, and the supporting coalition of developed-country exporters and developing-country governments on the other. Corruption of procurement or privatization is sometimes associated with a close relationship between particular international firms and borrower governments. The home countries of these firms will resist multilateral lenders' concerns with corruption. They have developed a comfortable monopoly relationship that they do not want to disrupt. The opening up of Eastern Europe, the former Soviet Union, and China brings this difficulty into relief. Officials in transitional economies are probably no more corrupt than those elsewhere, but they as yet lack supportive counterparts in the international business community. They also lack strong legal, political, and economic institutions. The wealth of these countries is up for grabs, and potential investors worry that the gains will be dissipated in costly corruption and rent seeking.

The World Bank is proving willing to acknowledge the problem in countries in transition in Eastern Europe and Asia and to consider how its projects might provide constructive help in alleviating the worst excesses. Once such projects are contemplated in Russia and Turkmenistan, it is difficult to argue that they are inappropriate for Guinea, Pakistan, or Brazil. In fact, as private capital becomes more important in some traditional areas of Bank lending, the Bank's role in institutional reform should increase.

The World Bank already supports public-sector management and governance projects in a wide range of areas. Some of these projects began as part of the structural adjustment lending carried out by the Bank in the 1980s and, at a somewhat reduced level, up to the present. This is an awkward vehicle for institutional reform efforts, and free-standing projects are now being carried out. Other loans that aim to reform regulatory authorities, taxation agencies, the judiciary, and other public institutions are being considered or carried out. The Bank frequently advises countries on privatization. All these initiatives require a long-term commitment of funds and expertise and a realization that "output" measures will not be easy to formulate precisely. Nevertheless, the World Bank and other development lenders can provide a framework within which development can proceed as a partnership between the public and private sectors.

Furthermore, greater success in improving the institutional environment for development would be likely if both international aid lenders and borrower governments took a more straightforward approach to controlling corruption and other forms of malfeasance. One recent buzz word in lending circles is "ownership." Projects will fail unless the borrower feels that it "owns" or has a stake in the project. Unfortunately, one form of ownership is all too common. Political figures in borrower countries and firms in lender countries express an ownership interest in projects that produce personal benefits for the politicians and profits for the firms. They will oppose projects that spread the benefits more broadly and that assure free competition. Ownership is a questionable value in cases in which a country's rulers do not seem committed to poverty alleviation. The World Bank tries to maneuver between the economic interests of donor and borrower governments and to manage the tensions between the Bank's broad charitable goals and the politics of lending policy. The issue is a complex one, but acknowledging the problems of corruption and self-dealing in both borrower and lender countries and trying to limit their effect on the Bank's efforts to promote growth and reduce poverty are good places to start. The goal should not be to insulate World Bank projects from a borrower country's corrupt climate or from the payoffs that have become routine in some areas of international business. Instead, it should be to seek fundamental changes in attitudes and institutions in situations in which corruption and governmental ineffectiveness go together.

Conclusions

Some argue that bribes help firms and individuals circumvent government requirements—by reducing delays and avoiding burdensome regulations and taxes. Payoffs seem to be nothing more than the grease needed to operate in a difficult environment. Corruption cannot necessarily be limited, however, to situations in which the rules are inefficiently restrictive. If not vigorously attacked, small-scale, facilitating bribes can feed on themselves. The mechanism is as follows: officials might begin by limiting themselves to bribes that facilitate private business without imposing costs on the rest of society. However, if these officials are unscrupulous enough to take payoffs, it seems unlikely that they will limit themselves to such relatively benevolent forms of corruption. Why not take bribes not only to overlook a pointless and burdensome regulation but also to permit violation of environmental and safety standards or to permit underpayment of corporate income taxes? After all, from the private business point of view, both types of payoffs are profitable. Furthermore, if bribes are paid to avoid burdens, it does not take too much cleverness on the part of officials to recognize that their returns may increase if they threaten to impose additional burdens or promise to award specialized benefits to bribe payers.

Incentives to make and ask for payoffs occur whenever government officials have economic power over a private firm or individual. It does not matter whether the power is justified or unjustified. Once a pattern of successful payoffs is institutionalized, corrupt officials have an incentive to raise the size of bribes demanded and to search for alternative ways to extract payments.

Even when illegal payoffs appear to facilitate commerce, governments and private citizens should not respond with tolerance. Instead, they should move vigorously to avoid creating a culture of illegality. Illegal markets are always inefficient and unfair compared with legal ones. Those with strong scruples will not participate, price information will be poor because of the illegality of the trades, and time and energy must be expended to keep the deal secret and to enforce its terms. In some cases, paying bribes may be more efficient than complying with existing rules, but corruption is always a second-best response to government failure.

Corruption can never be entirely eliminated. Under many realistic conditions, it will simply be too expensive to reduce corruption to zero. Furthermore, a single-minded focus on corruption prevention can have a negative effect on personal freedoms and human rights. Such a focus could produce a government that is rigid and unresponsive. Thus, the aim is not to achieve complete rectitude but rather a fundamental increase in the honesty—and the efficiency, fairness, and political legitimacy—of government.

References

Ades, Alberto, and Rafael Di Tella. 1995. *Competition and Corruption.* Institute of Economics and Statistics Discussion Papers 169. Oxford, UK: University of Oxford.

Alam, M. S. 1991. "Some Economic Costs of Corruption in LDCs." *Journal of Development Studies* 27, no. 1 (October): 89-97.

Alam, M. S. 1995. "A Theory of Limits on Corruption and Some Applications." *Kyklos* 48: 419-35.

Andreski, Stanislav. 1968. "Kleptocracy or Corruption as a System of Government in Africa." In Stanislav Andreski, *The African Predicament*. New York: Atherton.

Ayittey, George B. N. 1992. *Africa Betrayed*. New York: St. Martin's Press.

Becker, Gary, and George Stigler. 1974. "Law Enforcement, Malfeasance, and Compensation of Enforcers." *Journal of Legal Studies* 3, no. 1: 1-19.

Besley, Timothy, and John McLaren. 1993. "Taxes and Bribery: The Role of Wage Incentives." *Economic Journal* 103, no. 416 (January): 119-41.

Brett, E. A. 1992. *Providing for the Rural Poor: Institutional Decay and Transformation in Uganda*. Research Report 23. Brighton Sussex, UK: Institute of Development Studies.

Buscaglia, Edgardo Jr. 1995. "Judicial Reform in Latin America: The Obstacles Ahead." *Journal of Latin American Affairs* (Fall/Winter): 8-13.

Campos, Edward, and Hilton Root. 1996. *East Asia's Road to High Growth: An Institutional Perspective*. Washington: Brookings Institution.

Cartier-Bresson, J. 1995. "L'Économie de la Corruption." In D. Della Porta and Y. Mény, *Démocratie et Corruption en Europe*. Paris: La Découverte.

Celarier, Michelle. 1996. "Stealing the Family Silver." *Euromoney* (February): 62-66.

Colazingari, Silvia, and Susan Rose-Ackerman. 1995. "Corruption in a Paternalistic Democracy: Lessons from Italy for Latin America." Draft prepared for a lecture in the Trinity College Italian Programs, Hartford, CT, 25 November.

Coolidge, Jacqueline, and Susan Rose-Ackerman. 1996. "Rent-Seeking and Corruption in African Regimes: Theory and Cases." Manuscript (May).

de Melo, Martha, Gur Ofer, and Olga Sandler. 1995. "Pioneers for Profit: St. Petersburg Entrepreneurs in Services." *World Bank Economic Review* 9, no. 3 (September): 425-50.

Diamond, Larry. 1993. "Nigeria's Perennial Struggle against Corruption: Prospects for the Third Republic." *Corruption and Reform* 7, no. 3: 215-25.

Faruqee, Rashid. 1994. "Nigeria: Ownership Abandoned." In Ishrat Husain and Rashid Faruqee, *Adjustment in Africa: Lessons from Country Case Studies*. Washington: World Bank.

Fleischer, David. 1995. "Attempts at Corruption Control in Brazil: Congressional Investigations and Strengthening Internal Control." Paper delivered at the Latin American Political Science Association, 29 September, Washington.

Gardiner, John. 1970. *The Politics of Corruption in an American City*. New York: Russell Sage Foundation.

General Agreement on Tariffs and Trade (GATT). 1991. *Trade Policy Review: Indonesia*. Geneva.

General Agreement on Tariffs and Trade (GATT). 1995. *Trade Policy Review: Indonesia*. Geneva.

Gillespie, Kate, and Gween Okruhlik. 1991. "The Political Dimensions of Corruption Cleanups." *Comparative Politics* 24, no. 1 (October): 77-97.

Gong, Ting. 1993. "Corruption and Reform in China: An Analysis of Unintended Consequences." *Crime, Law, and Social Change* 19, no. 4 (June): 311-27.

Gould, D. J., and Tshiabukole B. Mukendi. 1989. "Bureaucratic Corruption in Africa: Causes, Consequences, and Remedies." *International Journal of Public Administration* 12, no. 3 (May): 427-57.

Handelman, Stephen. 1995. *Comrade Criminal*. New Haven, CT: Yale University Press.

Hao, Y., and Michael Johnston. 1995. "Reform at the Crossroads: An Analysis of Chinese Corruption." *Asian Perspectives* 19: 117-49.

Herbst, Jeffrey, and Adebayo Olukoshi. 1994. "Nigeria: Economic and Political Reform at Cross Purposes." In Stephen Haggard and Steven B. Webb, *Voting for Reform: Democracy, Political Liberalization and Economic Adjustment*. New York: Oxford University Press for the World Bank.

International Monetary Fund (IMF). 1994. *Balance of Payments Statistics Yearbook,* part 2. Washington.

Johnston, Michael, and Y. Hao. 1995. "China's Surge of Corruption." *Journal of Democracy* 6, no. 4 (October): 80-94.

Kaufman, Daniel, and Aleksander Kaliberda. 1996. *Integrating the Unofficial Economy into the Dynamics of Post-Socialist Economies: A Framework of Analyses and Evidence.* World Bank Policy Research Working Paper No. 1691. Washington: World Bank.

Keefer, Philip, and Stephen Knack. 1995. "Institutions and Economic Performance: Cross-Country Tests Using Alternative Institutional Measures." *Economics and Politics* 7: 207-27.

Kilby, Christopher. 1995. "Risk Management: An Econometric Investigation of Project-Level Factors." Background paper for the *Annual Review of Evaluation Results 1994,* World Bank, Operations Evaluation Department. Poughkeepsie, NY: Vassar College.

Klitgaard, Robert. 1988. *Controlling Corruption.* Berkeley: University of California Press.

Kovacic, William. 1994. "Whistleblower Bounty Lawsuits as Monitoring Devices in Government Contracting." George Mason School of Law, Arlington, Virginia. Photocopy (May).

LeVine, Victor. 1975. *Political Corruption: The Ghana Case.* Stanford: Hoover Institution Press.

Malik, Waleed H. 1995. "Economic Development and Judicial Reform: Some International Experiences." Prepared for the Judges's Workshop, Consejo de la Judicatura, Venezuela, June.

Manzetti, Luigi, and Charles Blake. 1996. "Market Reforms and Corruption in Latin America: New Means for Old Ways." *Review of International Political Economy* 3, no. 4 (Winter): 662-97.

Mauro, Paolo. 1995. "Corruption and Growth." *Quarterly Journal of Economics* 110, issue 3, no. 442 (August): 681-712.

Moreno Ocampo, Luis Gabriel. 1995. "Hyper-Corruption: Concept and Solutions." Presented at the Latin American Studies Association, 29 September, Washington.

Murray-Rust, D. Hammond, and Edward J. Vander Velde. 1994. "Changes in Hydraulic Performance and Comparative Costs of Lining and Desilting of Secondary Canals in Punjab, Pakistan." *Irrigation and Drainage Systems* 8, no. 3: 137-58.

Novitzky, Irina, Victor Novitzky, and Andrew Stone. 1995. "Private Enterprise in Ukraine: Getting Down to Business." World Bank Private Sector Development Division. Photocopy.

Oldenburg, Philip. 1987. "Middlemen in Third World Corruption: Implications for an Indian Case." *World Politics* 39, no. 4: 508-35.

Olowu, Dele. 1993. "Ethical Violations in Nigeria's Public Services: Patterns, Explanations and Remedies." In Sadig Rasheed and Dele Olowu, *Ethics and Accountability in African Public Services.* Nairobi: African Association for Public Administration and Management.

Ouma, Stephen. 1991. "Corruption in Public Policy and Its Impact on Development: The Case of Uganda Since 1979." *Public Administration and Development* 11, no. 5 (September): 473-90.

Park, B. S. 1995. "Political Corruption in Non-Western Democracies: The Case of South Korea Party Politics." Kim Dae-Jung Peace Foundation, Seoul. Photocopy.

Paul, Sam. 1995. "Evaluating Public Services: A Case Study on Bangalore, India." *New Directions for Evaluation,* American Evaluation Association No. 67 (Fall).

Phongpaicht, Pasuk, and Sungsidh Piriyarangsan. 1994. *Corruption and Democracy in Thailand.* Bangkok: Political Economy Centre, Faculty of Economics, Chulalongkorn University.

Pope, Jeremy, ed. 1996. *National Integrity Systems: The TI Source Book.* Berlin: Transparency International.

Pritchett, Lant. 1995. *Divergence, Big Time*. Policy Research Working Paper No. 1522. Washington: World Bank (October).

Pritchett, Lant. 1996. "Mind Your P's and Q's: The Cost of Investment Is Not the Value of Capital." Washington: World Bank, Policy Research Department. Photocopy (6 May).

Pritchett, Lant, and Geeta Sethi. 1994. "Tariff Revenue and Tariff Reform: Some New Facts." *World Bank Economic Review* 8, no. 1 (January): 1-16.

Quah, Jon S. T. 1993. "Controlling Corruption in City-States: A Comparative Study of Hong Kong and Singapore." Paper presented at the conference on the East Asian Miracle: Economic Growth and Public Policy, Stanford University, Palo Alto, 25-26 October.

Raphaeli, N., J. Roumani, and A. MacKeller. 1984. *Public Sector Management in Botswana: Lessons in Pragmatism*. World Bank Staff Working Papers No. 1709. Washington: World Bank.

Rasmusen, Eric, and Mark Ramseyer. 1994. "Cheap Bribes and the Corruption Ban: A Coordination Game among Rational Legislators." *Public Choice* 78, no. 3/4 (March): 305-27.

Rodrik, Dani. 1994. "King Kong Meets Godzilla: The World Bank and the East Asian Miracle." In A. Fishlow, C. Gwin, S. Haggard, D. Rodrik, and R. Wade, *Miracle or Design? Lessons from the East Asian Experience*. ODC Policy Essay No. 11. Washington: Overseas Development Council.

Rogers, Glenn, and Sidi Mohammed Iddal. 1996. "Reduction of Illegal Payments in West Africa: Niger's Experience." Presented at the Workshop on Good Governance and the Regional Economy in Francophone Africa, 5-7 March, Dakar, Senegal.

Rose-Ackerman, Susan. 1978. *Corruption: A Study in Political Economy*. New York: Academic Press.

Rose-Ackerman, Susan. 1994. "Reducing Bribery in the Public Sector." In Duc V. Trang, *Corruption and Democracy: Political Institutions, Processes, and Corruption in Transition States in East-Central Europe and in the Former Soviet Union*. Budapest: Institute for Constitutional and Legislative Policy.

Rose-Ackerman, Susan, and Andrew Stone. 1996. "The Costs of Corruption for Private Business: Evidence from World Bank Surveys." Manuscript (May).

Ruzindana, Augustine. 1995. "Combating Corruption in Uganda." In Petter Langseth, J. Katorobo, E. Brett, and J. Munene, *Uganda: Landmarks in Rebuilding a Nation*. Kampala: Fountain Publishers.

Shelley, Louise. 1994. "Post-Soviet Organized Crime." *Demokratizatsiya* 2: 341-58.

Sherman, Lawrence W. 1974. *Police Corruption: A Sociological Perspective*. New York: Anchor Books.

Shleifer, A., and R. Vishney. 1993. "Corruption." *Quarterly Journal of Economics* 108, issue 3, no. 434 (August): 599-617.

Stone, Andrew. 1995. *The Climate for Private Sector Development in Pakistan: Results of an Enterprise Survey*. Washington: World Bank, PSD Department. Unpublished background paper for Pakistan PSA (April).

Stone, Andrew, Brian Levy, and Ricardo Paredes. 1992. *Public Institutions and Private Transactions: The Legal and Regulatory Environment for Business Transactions in Brazil and Chile*. Policy Research Working Paper 891. Washington: World Bank (April).

Tenenbaum, Bernard. 1996. "Regulation: What the Prime Minister Needs to Know." *Electricity Journal* 9, no. 2 (March): 28-36.

Thacher, Thomas D., II. 1995. *The New York City School Construction Authority's Office of the Inspector General: A Successful New Strategy for Reforming Public Contracting in the Construction Industry*. New York: New York City School Construction Authority. Photocopy (June).

Trang, D. V., ed. 1994. *Corruption and Democracy: Political Institutions, Processes, and Corruption in Transition States in East-Central Europe and in the Former Soviet Union*. Budapest: Institute for Constitutional and Legislative Policy.

Tucker, L. 1994. "Censorship and Corruption: Government Self-Protection through Control of the Media." In Duc V. Trang, *Corruption and Democracy: Political Institutions, Processes, and Corruption in Transition States in East-Central Europe and the Former Soviet Union.* Budapest: Institute for Constitutional and Legislative Policy.

Van de Walle, Nicolas. 1994. "Neopatrimonialism and Democracy in Africa, with an Illustration from Cameroon." In Jennifer A. Widner, *Economic Change and Political Liberalization in Sub-Saharan Africa.* Baltimore: Johns Hopkins University Press.

Vander Velde, Edward J. 1990. "Field Notes." IIMI Pakistan. Photocopy (18 October).

Vander Velde, Edward J., and Mark Svendsen. 1994. "Goals and Objectives of Irrigation in Pakistan—A Prelude to Assessing Irrigation Performance." *Quarterly Journal of International Agriculture* 33, no. 3 (July): 222-42.

Wade, Robert. 1982. "The System of Administrative and Political Corruption: Canal Irrigation in South India." *Journal of Development Studies* 18, no. 3 (April): 287-328.

Wade, Robert. 1984. "Irrigation Reform in Conditions of Populist Anarchy: An Indian Case." *Journal of Development Economics* 14, no. 3 (April): 285-303.

Webster, Leila M. 1993. *The Emergence of Private Sector Manufacturing in Hungary.* World Bank Technical Paper No. 229. Washington: World Bank.

Webster, Leila M., and Joshua Charap. 1993. *The Emergence of Private Sector Manufacturing in St. Petersburg.* World Bank Technical Paper No. 228. Washington: World Bank.

Werlin, H. 1972. "The Roots of Corruption—the Ghanaian Enquiry." *Journal of Modern African Studies* 10, no. 2: 247-66.

Widner, Jennifer A., ed. 1994. *Economic Change and Political Liberalization in Sub-Saharan Africa.* Baltimore: Johns Hopkins University Press.

World Bank. 1994. *Paraguay: Country Economic Memorandum.* World Bank Report No. 11723. Washington: World Bank (29 June).

World Bank. 1996. *World Debt Tables: External Finance to Developing Countries,* vol. 1. Washington: World Bank.

Yabrak, Isil, and Leila Webster. 1995. *Small and Medium Enterprises in Lebanon: A Survey.* Washington: World Bank, Private Sector Development Department and Industry and Energy Division, Middle East and North Africa Country Department II. Final report (28 January).

3

Public Officials, Private Interests, and Sustainable Democracy: When Politics and Corruption Meet

MICHAEL JOHNSTON

Any assessment of the role of corruption in the world's economies must also address its political dimensions. These include corrupt activities themselves, corruption as a political issue, and the overall health of a nation's politics. Corruption raises important political questions about the relationships between state and society and between wealth and power. It affects political processes and outcomes, but its meaning, and the significance of particular cases, are also influenced by the clash of political interests. Corruption tends to accompany rapid political and economic change, but its significance varies from one society to another: it topples some regimes while propping up others. And corruption is, of course, an increasingly important political and trade issue among nations and in international organizations.

At the same time, many other forces affect a country's well-being, and it is risky to use corruption to explain too much. As Colin Leys (1965, 222) argued, "It is natural but wrong to assume that the results of corruption are always both bad and important." Corruption occurs in many forms, with contrasting patterns and political implications (Johnston 1986). Its effects are notoriously difficult to measure: they must be gauged, not against ideal political and economic results, but rather against what would have happened without corruption—a very different, often

Michael Johnston is professor of political science at Colgate University. The author is grateful to Kimberly Elliott, Ting Gong, Robert Leiken, Sahr Kpundeh, Johann Graf Lambsdorff, Anne Pitcher, Susan Rose-Ackerman, and Christopher Sabatini for their very helpful comments on this chapter as it took shape, and to Shannon Curran for her comments and research assistance.

unknowable, standard. Moreover, because corruption is such a useful (and often inflammatory) political issue, it can be difficult to distinguish real corruption from the claims and counterclaims of conflicting forces. Thus, the question of the political implications of corruption has no single answer.

Defining corruption is another complex issue (Johnston 1996). Most analysts define categories of behavior as corrupt, with many relying on laws and other formal rules because of their relative precision and stability to identify corrupt actions (see, for example, Nye 1967, 417; Scott 1972, chapter 1). Critics reply that in many societies the law lacks legitimacy and consistent meaning, that legalisms tell us little about the social significance of behavior, and that public opinion or cultural standards are best for building realistic definitions (Gibbons 1988; Peters and Welch 1978). Still others dispute the behavior-classifying approach itself, regarding the moral health of society at large as the main issue in defining corruption (Dobel 1978; Euben 1978; Moodie 1980; Philp 1987; Thompson 1993). I cannot settle this issue here; indeed, some cases to be discussed below focus more on controversy over the meaning of corruption than on agreed meanings. I will therefore define "corruption" broadly as the abuse of public roles or resources or the use of illegitimate forms of political influence by public or private parties. Later on, however, I will make an explicit issue of the politically contested meanings of terms such as "public," "private," "abuse," and "illegitimate," for often contention over who gets to decide what those terms mean is the most important political dimension of the problem.

Corruption as an Influence on Politics: Who Gets What?

That corruption affects politics and policy is a familiar notion. Most arguments about these effects raise Harold Lasswell's classic question: "who gets what, when, and how" (Lasswell 1936). Klitgaard (1988, chapters 1-2 and especially pp. 36-48) concludes, rightly in my view, that most corruption hurts most people most of the time. But all corruption presumably benefits someone or it would not occur, and sometimes benefits are widely (if unevenly) distributed.

Most forms of corruption short of outright official theft can be thought of as types of political influence (Scott 1972), distorting decision making and diverting the costs and benefits of policy. The initiative may come from either private clients or public officials: the first may offer bribes; the second may delay decisions or contrive shortages until payments are made, or may simply extort them. The climate of corruption can be so pervasive that no explicit demands are needed: "everybody knows" that decisions must be paid for. But whoever takes the initiative, corrupt influence requires valuable resources such as money, authority, expertise, special access, or control over a political following. Few ordinary citizens have such resources or can compete politically with those who do. Thus, most corruption will tend to benefit the haves at the political, as well as material, expense of the have-nots. The latter may obtain petty benefits—shopkeepers might evade official inspections, and citizens might pay to obtain a license, with small bribes or "speed money" —or partake of petty patronage distributed in the course of someone else's quest for power. But these benefits come at a cost: corruption bypasses due process and weakens civil rights, blocking off legitimate channels of political access and accountability while opening up (and concealing) illicit new ones. Patronage or avoidance of official harassment often comes at the cost of lost political choices and inferior public services. Many people pay the costs of corruption again and again.

Actual calculations of who gets what are admittedly complex and unreliable. Much corruption never comes to light: those who know about it usually have a stake in concealing it, and some kinds of corruption can be used to cover up others. Costs and benefits are difficult to compare: most benefits, such as a job or a contract, are tangible, divisible, and immediate and might have come to the recipient anyway (Sacks 1976). By contrast, many costs, such as loss of trust in the political system or the cumulative effects of one-party politics on representation and political choices, are widely shared, intangible, and accrue over the long term. Corruption changes the institutions, economies, and societies within which it occurs. This creates problems for any proposed distinction between "good" and "bad" varieties, for often we cannot say what would have happened without corruption. An economic development agency might have serious corruption problems, but it does not follow that without corruption it would necessarily have produced economic development or have avoided its actual failings.

The Effects of Politics on Corruption: Who Decides?

Politics is a high-stakes game, and its rules have much to do with who wins and loses. Corruption is a hot political issue: despite (or because of?) its moral dimensions, it is used in contentious and politicized ways and can elicit strong public responses. Corruption and scandal are different things (Moodie 1980), and either may occur in the absence of the other. For these reasons, the meaning of corruption, its application to particular cases, and who gets to decide these matters can be hotly contested issues.

In the long run, such contention contributes to the emergence of accepted standards of political behavior (Johnston 1993). In the short term, however, it can politicize the concept and obscure its working boundaries, making it difficult to distinguish actual corruption from partisan scandal. Particularly in undemocratic systems, officially orchestrated scandals may tell us more about the political interests of elites, or about conflicts among them, than about the real extent of official wrongdoing (Simis 1982; Lampert 1985). Critics of the existing order, barred from raising genuine social and political issues, will also find corruption a useful way to criticize government without directly challenging its claim on power. In China, for example, corruption has become a "bandwagon issue" for an extraordinarily broad range of grievances (Sands 1990, 86, 90; Hao and Johnston 1995, 119-21).

Often, reactions to corruption (real or perceived) are at least as important as the problem itself. Relatively minor transgressions, or even just the perception that they have occurred, can elicit major public outcry. Anticorruption coups are common, though corruption is often just a pretext for seizing power and continues unabated under the new regime. Reactions to corruption can mean bad news and good news: serious controversy might occur, but that may also contribute to pluralization of politics. Was the major significance of the Collor de Mello scandal in Brazil the fall of a regime or the fact that strong popular forces emerged to object to elite misconduct? Reforms are another kind of response; many are beneficial, but others, such as antimachine reforms in American cities, confer major political advantages on their advocates or make government less responsive than before (Lowi 1968; Lineberry and Fowler 1967). Still other "reforms" are simply camouflage for continued profiteering.

In democratic societies, reformers must consider not only the nature of corruption problems but also public perceptions and expectations. American campaign finance reforms, enacted during a time of widespread concern about political money and the abuse of power, raised expectations of an era of fair, responsive politics. But the new rules did little to enhance ordinary citizens' feelings of efficacy, and reformers did not educate them about the actual workings of the political process. As a result, public disclosure provisions served mostly to persuade many people that the system was awash in dirty money and that politics had become debased. There is probably much less corruption at all levels of American politics today than a century ago, but opinion polls repeatedly reveal a public sense that the political process is sick in fundamental ways. For example, the recent scandals revolving around President Bill Clinton and Speaker Newt Gingrich—while involving well-documented movements of funds (Clinton) and violations of rules regulating the activities of political committees (Gingrich)—are poorly understood by the public and have not (so far) revealed substantive abuses of public policy. Still, they contribute to the widespread perceptions of a sick political system.

Disclosure for its own sake has not contributed to enlightened political debate; instead, it has encouraged parties and interest groups to engage in competitive scandalmongering as a (poor) substitute for offering real policy choices to the public.

Comparing Political Effects

Can we compare corruption—either levels or causes and effects—from one country to the next? Some analysts have used aggregate economic data and corruption indices from business organizations to develop intriguing international comparisons of the effects of corruption on investment and economic growth or of the relationships between corruption and domestic economic competition (Mauro 1995; Ades and Di Tella 1995). Another approach has been to compare relative levels of corruption across countries by averaging several corruption "rankings" in a "survey of surveys" (Lambsdorff 1995), or by conducting one's own survey based on judgments by international businesspeople (Lambsdorff 1996). Here, validity problems often arise from the need to reconcile qualitatively different kinds of evidence or conceptions of corruption. Reliability questions are posed by the comparatively small differences among rank-ordered cases, which often exceed the level of precision of the original data. Nonetheless, extensive public interest in these scales confirms the importance of continuing research.

Still, overall levels of corruption, its economic effects, and its political implications are all different things. What links various levels and types of corruption on the one hand and political pathologies on the other? Table 1 offers a tentative attempt—based on my own and others' reading of press reports and the scholarly literature on corruption over the years—to distinguish between cases in which corruption has led to systemic political change (such as the breakdown of the political process or fundamental shifts in the bases of political power) and those in which its effects (while still major) have been on the order of changing or preserving regimes and alignments of political competition. I have tried to list all nations that clearly fall into these two categories (although as we shall see, the categories pose many difficulties of classification) but have omitted others that have merely experienced episodes of scandal (even if politically significant), for that includes nearly every country.

These categories do not reveal absolute amounts or the material value of corrupt activity. Corruption in Zaire under President Mobutu Sese Seko, for example, has probably been greater (by either measure) than that of several nations in the left-hand column, but Zaire appears on the right-hand side because its corruption has been more a mechanism of control than a force for systemic change. Similarly, the categories do not

Table 1   Linkages of corruption to systemic change and major political effects by country since the mid-1970s

Systemic change[a]	Major political effects[b]	
East Germany	Argentina	Bangladesh
Liberia	Brazil	Burkina Faso
Mauritania	China	Colombia
Nicaragua	Gabon	Greece
Niger	India	Indonesia
Nigeria	Italy	Ivory Coast
Panama	Japan	Kenya
Philippines	Malaysia	Mali
Former Soviet Union	Mexico	Pakistan
Sierra Leone	Paraguay	Peru
Sudan	South Korea	Spain
Uganda	Tanzania	Thailand
	Venezuela	Zaire
	Zambia	

a. Including complete collapse.
b. Ranging from regime preservation to significant political realignment.

permit comparison of costs to benefits: by no means are all of the regimes brought down by corruption the sorts we might support. In addition, placing a country in one category or the other is at times a judgment call, one that might change as events unfold.

But the most striking aspects of the table are, first, the wide range of countries listed, and second, the breadth of variation within categories. The right-hand category includes countries in which corruption has been used to forestall change (Paraguay, Mexico, Zambia)—perhaps even serving as a substitute for political or economic reform—as well as those in which it has been destabilizing (Colombia). In others (China, Peru), popular or official reactions to corruption have been at least as important as the problem itself. At times, the major effect has been on social structure.[1] In the Sudan, for example, corrupt accumulation of wealth helped create a new "parasitic *comprador* capitalist class" (Kameir and Kursany 1985, 8), and Zambia saw the rise of a business and property-owning class that got its start exploiting public office (Szeftel 1982). Both columns include cases in which political change has imposed new definitions of corruption. Consider the trials of two former presidents in South Korea and of former East German officials. In other cases, such as Liberia's tragedy, corruption has been just one contributing factor in a general collapse. We could devise more categories to capture these variations, but they would quickly become numerous and thinly populated,

---

1. I am grateful to Sahr J. Kpundeh for suggesting the following two examples.

ultimately telling us more about the complexity of the phenomenon and the difficulty of drawing broad generalizations.

There are thus many kinds of corruption problems, and their effects are linked to the nature of the societies in which they occur. If benefits flow to one group and the costs to another, for example, that may exacerbate existing fault lines in society, but a different distribution might ease conflict. Groups excluded from influence on racial, nationalistic, or ideological grounds may well buy their way in through the back door, particularly if they have significant political resources and nonideological agendas. Huntington (1968, 59-71) suggests that corruption may function in those situations as an alternative to violence. Nye (1967) points to the levels at which corruption occurs, the kinds of inducements involved, and the extent of deviation from approved procedures as affecting its consequences. Corruption often flourishes under one-party politics (Doig 1984, chapters 5, 6), whether the system is uncompetitive by circumstance or design. Conversely, fragmented corruption can lead to a collapse in political competition; if there is little to gain and much to lose by being in the opposition, politics may take the form of a disorganized scramble for the spoils.

Corruption influences politics, but politics also influences corruption as people seek or defend positions of advantage. If corruption leads to scandal, the resulting disputes can reshape accepted relationships and boundaries between wealth and power. The challenge is to understand corruption as a kind of process, and form of influence, within political systems, but to do so in ways that still allow comparisons and are not so relativistic as to drain the concept of meaning. In the section that follows, I will suggest that sustainable democracy offers some insights into this problem.

Corruption and Sustainable Democracy

Corruption is not something that happens to a society like a natural disaster. It is the doing of real people and groups as they trade in influence within a particular climate of opportunities, resources, and constraints. Sometimes these actions and choices shake whole governments and regimes, but more often they affect politics in more specific ways— ways that reflect the nature and continuing development of the societies in which they occur. Much depends on relationships between state and society, and on the ways wealth and power are held and used. Are the political elite at the mercy of private interests or so entrenched that they exploit them? Do people use wealth to buy political influence, or do they use political power to enrich themselves? If corruption is a politically contested concept, by which standards and values can we judge its seriousness and any progress toward reform?

Sustainable Democracy

One way to bring these questions together is to consider them in terms of the development and viability of sustainable democracy. In so doing, I do not mean to suggest that corruption is solely the province of undemocratic systems. No democracy is free of corruption, and some authoritarian regimes (notably Singapore and Chile) have had low levels of it. But in nondemocratic states, leaders tend not to be accountable to ordinary citizens. Under these circumstances, whether corruption occurs and how pervasively depends to a large degree on the personal honesty of top leaders and their allies.[2]

Moreover, if the idea of corruption is to embody anything more than the interests of dominant elites, or the public's shifting views of particular politicians and groups, it must incorporate some sense of what we value in public life. As Susan Rose-Ackerman (1978, 90) argues, "Normative statements about corruption . . . require a point of view, a standard of 'goodness,' and a model of how corruption works in particular instances." In Dennis Thompson's view, "goodness" refers to a healthy political process in which freely chosen representatives openly debate important issues and must answer to their constituents for the decisions they make. He argues that corruption is bad not because money and benefits change hands but because it bypasses representation, debate, and choice (Thompson 1993). The vast majority of corrupt activities in any nation, and the politically manipulated meanings of corruption often found in undemocratic regimes, depart from these democratic values.

The concept of sustainable democracy has been defined in a variety of ways (see, for example, Buell and Deluca 1996; Przeworski 1995). Here, I use it to refer not just to the presence of liberal institutions and market economics (as much of an achievement as those embodied in many countries) but also to the existence of multiple and broadly balanced political forces. This means, first, a balance between the accessibility and autonomy of political elites, and second, a balance between wealth and power. The first envisions a relationship between state and society in which private interests have significant political influence but officials can formulate and carry out policies authoritatively.[3] The second refers to a situation in which both political and economic paths of advancement are numerous and open enough to reduce temptations to trade either wealth or power for each other.

Serious imbalances, by contrast, tend to foster corruption. Where

---

2. This works in both directions. An honest authoritarian leader can virtually eradicate corruption, as Lee Kuan Yew has done in Singapore, while a dishonest one can loot a country. It is said that under Ferdinand and Imelda Marcos, publicly owned Philippine corporations were like bath towels: "His" and "Hers."

3. I am grateful to Christopher Sabatini for his thoughts and comments on this issue.

access to elites significantly exceeds their autonomy, officials are vulnerable to private influence (legitimate and otherwise) and find it difficult to act independently. Indeed, if elites' hold on power becomes shaky, there is a temptation to take as much as one can as quickly as possible—Scott's (1972, 80-84) "hand-over-fist" corruption. If, on the other hand, elite autonomy exceeds accessibility, officials may be able to exploit private interests with impunity. As for wealth and power, Huntington (1968, 59-71) has argued that where political opportunities exceed the economic, people are likely to use power to enrich themselves; where economic opportunities exceed the political, people will tend to use wealth to buy political power. Particular combinations of imbalances among these forces give rise to characteristic corruption problems that differ in their nature and political implications and point to political and economic reforms that can aid both democratization and anticorruption goals.

Both kinds of balance are dynamic. They presume vigorous political contention. Where officials and private parties can influence each other but also resist exploitation by the other and where wealth and power interests are sufficiently balanced so that neither resource must chase the other, clear expectations and accepted rules governing relationships among them are more likely to be worked out. These rules—including boundaries and distinctions between state and society, public and private sectors, politics and administration, and individual and collective interests, and among market, bureaucratic, and patrimonial processes of allocation—have historically been drawn and have earned their legitimacy through political contention. Where they and the politics that define them are absent, corruption is very difficult to define and control by means other than coercion (Johnston and Hao 1995; Johnston 1993). Looked at this way, democracy—portrayed by the leaders of many coups d'état as vulnerable to corruption—has long-term anticorruption muscle. Ironically, coups against corruption, even if genuine in their intent—and most are not—preempt the political contention that could eventually forge boundaries to contain it. Corruption begets bad politics, and bad politics begets further corruption.

The sustainable democracy approach does not regard the state as a neutral referee or as a technical entity that merely processes demands from society. This approach is far from neutral in terms of the intrinsic value of politics. It asserts that some kinds of politics are better than others and joins political principles to the analysis of process. It draws on a classical republican tradition of thought in which morality and corruption are seen as properties not of particular actions but of whole societies and in which active citizenship, faithful representation, and free debate are valued in themselves quite apart from the utility of their results (Dobel 1978; Euben 1978; Moodie 1980; Philp 1987; Shumer 1979; Thompson 1993, 1995). Corruption in this view is a departure from a particular image of good politics. Quite apart from its role as a mechanism for who gets what, corruption is bad because it privatizes valuable functions of public life. We should not be reluctant to apply the sustainable democracy approach to a variety of settings. Not only do many people (though by no means all) in undemocratic and transitional regimes pursue similar goals themselves, but as we shall see, combatting corruption and encouraging open, competitive politics can also be closely allied reform goals.

Four Syndromes

The balance or imbalance between elite accessibility and autonomy and between political and economic opportunities will be difficult to measure; at best they are examples of long-term "moving equilibria." Short-term trends and events may alter both from time to time without necessarily producing major outbreaks of corruption. The focus here is on significant and lasting imbalances, combinations of which define four corruption syndromes, each marked by distinctive opportunities and dangers. In some of these syndromes, corruption will be significant but bounded in scope, serving more to limit the competitiveness of politics and the responsiveness of governments than to threaten their viability. In others, there are real dangers that corruption may spiral out of control (table 2).

The horizontal and vertical axes in table 2 are not precise demarcations but continua symbolizing relative relationships: the horizontal line, the balance or imbalance between elite accessibility and autonomy, and the vertical line, that between economic and political opportunities. These dimensions are ordinal, with imbalances greater toward the extremes. Countries located near the intersection of the two lines have a rough political balance on either dimension or both. The emphasis here is on relative imbalance: to say that economic opportunities are greater, for example, is not to say they are abundant in any absolute sense; the crucial fact might be the extreme scarcity of political opportunities. Moreover, I do not suggest that any scenario is the only one found in a country. This schema, and the four corruption scenarios, may be made clearer by focusing on each category in more detail.

Interest Group Bidding

In the upper-left quadrant of table 2, accessibility of elites exceeds autonomy, and economic opportunities are more plentiful than political ones. Where these imbalances are significant, interest groups are strong and political elites are vulnerable. These groups will represent many interests, only some of them economic in nature, but most will resort to economic resources (campaign contributions, other sorts of gifts, outright bribes) as they seek influence.

Table 2 Varieties of corruption as functions of political imbalance

State/society balance

Balance of opportunities	Accessibility of elites > autonomy	Autonomy of elites > accessibility
	A: Interest group bidding	**B: Elite hegemony (risk of extreme corruption)**
Economic > political	United States United Kingdom Germany	China Pre-IACC Hong Kong Military regimes (Nigeria at times) South Korea LDP Japan
Political > economic	Italy Russia Pre-Fujimori Peru Pre-Menem Argentina Early Tammany Hall Early civilian regimes in Africa **C: Fragmented patronage (*mafiyas*) (risk of extreme corruption)**	Mature Tammany Hall Indonesia Mexico Sicily **D: Patronage machines**

A: Interest group bidding is characterized by strong private interests, accessible elites, and political and economic competition. Wealth is used to seek political influence resulting in elite corruption but is largely nonsystematic and on an individual basis.
B: Elite hegemony is characterized by entrenched elites with limited political competition who sell political access and enrich themselves and their political and business allies.
C: Fragmented patronage is characterized by fragmented, politically insecure elites who build personal followings using material rewards. Followers are poorly disciplined and are vulnerable to interests and factions in society; some corruption linked to intimidation.
D: Patronage machines are characterized by strong elites who control mass participation, limit competition through patronage, and often capitalize upon mass followers' poverty. Parties are well-disciplined, hierarchical, and extend elite power into society. The result is often systematic corruption, perhaps accompanied by intimidation.

This corruption scenario is most typical of liberal democracies and is seen as a departure from procedural fairness and equity. It may be a serious problem but is unlikely to spiral out of control because bidding is open to many competing interests with relatively narrow agendas. Critics of the process can participate in politics too, creating a healthy tendency toward public scandals, and can win support from segments of the relatively decentralized, internally competitive political elite.[4]

4. Here I echo the argument by Markovits and Silverstein (1988) that scandal is most likely to be found in liberal democracies, although I would add that undemocratic societies also experience corruption-related political conflicts that, even if not focused on a set of accepted political values and principles, are significant for establishing new standards of behavior.

Some elites will engage in corruption, but elite syndicates and systematic shakedown operations will be rare.

The chief danger is that policymaking will become (or be perceived as) an auction, with favorable decisions going to the highest bidder. The American "iron triangle" metaphor (see, for example, Adams 1981) reflects this danger: it refers to long-standing alliances among economic interests, sections of the bureaucracy, and congressional subcommittees sharing an interest in a program or segment of the budget. Such preferential access will more likely produce policy stagnation than out-of-control corruption but can still be the focus of considerable resentment among those who see themselves as shut out by a corrupt process. Reforms in such systems are typically process-oriented and based on a market metaphor for politics. Many democracies' campaign finance laws and lobbying regulations, for example, are intended to protect political competition. Whether the results match the intentions is, of course, a different question.

Elite Hegemony

Different and more ominous corruption problems are outlined in the upper-right quadrant of table 2. Here, an entrenched political elite facing little political competition and few meaningful demands for accountability dominates and exploits economic opportunities, manipulating political access (a scarce and valuable commodity) in return for further economic gains. Boundaries between state and society, public and private interests, and politics and administration are likely to be weak or open to elite manipulation. In extreme cases such as China's, political figures, bureaucrats, and whole agencies go into business overtly or as partners with entrepreneurs. The Liberal Democratic Party (LDP) regime in Japan represented a somewhat different case. There, modified one-party politics with extensive state involvement in the economy and just enough electoral competition to persuade donors that they had a stake in keeping the LDP in power led to close links between party leadership and large corporations.

In undemocratic regimes in particular, corruption issues may become a vehicle for a broad range of grievances, but political and legal processes are manipulated from above, and the forces of reform are weak. Thus this sort of corruption may well become organized and systemic while facing little opposition, posing a danger of a hypercorruption spiral. Such political competition as does occur is likely to take place among elite political and economic factions. If it becomes intense, especially in a time of political or economic transition, political competition is more likely to produce extreme corruption, as officials take as much as they can as quickly as possible, than any sustained political check upon wrongdoing. Not surprisingly, reform efforts typically are sporadic, politically orchestrated crusades serving the political needs of top elites. Barring substantial opening up of politics, significant scandal, or meaningful demands for reform may require, and would very likely deepen, a serious political crisis.

Fragmented Patronage, Extended Factionalism

The lower-left quadrant of table 2 differs from the variety of corruption just discussed in terms of both state-society relationships and balance of opportunities but resembles elite hegemony in its danger of out-of-control corruption, especially in states undergoing systemic transformation with weak institutions and weak political leadership. Here, elites are not only accessible, but also seek power amid intense political competition and relatively scarce economic opportunities. The path to power consists of building a following, but because material rewards are relatively scarce and political alternatives are plentiful, patronage politics is fragmented. Elites build personal followings, not broad-based parties, and find them difficult to control because there is a chronic shortage of rewards and followers have political alternatives. Forces at play in such a setting may include not only political organizations but also more sinister groups such as Russia's *mafiyas* (Handelman 1995) or Colombia's drug cartels. Corruption may well be linked to intimidation and violence.

This is the most politically unstable of our four categories, and here the danger of extreme corruption is most pronounced. Elites are politically insecure and thus face temptations toward hand-over-fist corruption, but followers also contribute to the danger, for their loyalties may have to be purchased and repurchased in conflict after conflict, and patronage bidding wars may ensue. These splintered, shifting patronage groups marked the earliest phases of the rise of Tammany Hall (Shefter 1976). Orderly political competition will be difficult to establish as long as it is clear that playing the role of opposition is of little value for its own sake and that the real political opportunities lie in the scramble for spoils.

Apart from the use of corruption issues as a club against one's enemies, anticorruption reform is unlikely to be much more than a slogan; law-enforcement officials will be as politically vulnerable as politicians and bureaucrats, and neither side can count on much support from the other.

Patronage Machines

Finally, a well-entrenched elite can manipulate scarce economic rewards to control political competition even where there are significant political opportunities, via the sort of disciplined patronage organization once known in American cities as political machines. Indeed, as the evolution of Tammany Hall in New York illustrates (Shefter 1976), a patronage-wielding elite that gradually eliminates competing factions can control government, exploit economic interests, render existing political alternatives economically worthless (or nearly so), and create a disciplined patronage organization. Politics remains the path to wealth, but followers can be controlled through a monopoly over patronage; they need not be bribed again and again but must make do with petty rewards bearing a large political price. In effect, Tammany built this sort of machine out of the fragmented patronage politics found in the previous scenario.

Patronage machines are not totally harmonious internally (Johnston 1979), but they are unlikely to produce out-of-control corruption. The machine leadership profits, politically and economically, from the status quo; it is in business for the long term and will dole out patronage with an eye to maintaining its dominance rather than to looting the state. This is not to imply that the corruption involved is not serious or that it does not do economic and social damage. Machine-style corruption diverts wealth into the hands of the few; levies a "political tax" on business, investment, and many ordinary jobs; and maintains the poor in a state of political dependency (Johnston 1982, chapter 3). Damage to the political system, however, is more likely to come in the form of stagnation and postponed change than in the form of a short-term crisis or collapse. Machine leaders will occasionally put limited reform in place to preempt more serious political challenges. Chicago's Richard J. Daley was famous for this tactic, and Mexico's Partido Revolucionario Institucional (PRI) has accepted occasional losses in state elections and more extensive election reforms as the price of continuing power. But most corruption issues are likely to be raised by marginalized counter-elites, to little political effect.

Sustainable Democracy and Anticorruption Reform

The sustainable democracy argument suggests that serious corruption makes political systems less democratic. But is the converse true? Can democratization reduce corruption? As noted, I do not suggest that the more democratic countries are free from the problem. But if various kinds of corruption grow out of imbalances between state and society, and between wealth and power, efforts to restore (or institute) greater balance might contribute both to democratization and to corruption reform. That is a middle- to long-term approach and must be linked to more familiar political and administrative measures. Still, we can identify, conceptually at least, ways of smoothing out imbalances:

- where accessibility of elites decisively exceeds their autonomy, enhance official autonomy by regulating channels of private influence, improving internal bureaucratic management, and enhancing state capacity;
- where elites' autonomy outweighs their accessibility, open up channels of mass participation, accountability, and bureaucratic access;
- where economic opportunities outstrip political opportunities, enhance the depth and equality of political competition;
- where political opportunities greatly exceed economic opportunities, encourage broad-based economic growth.

The idea here is to identify ways of pursuing both democratization and anticorruption goals appropriate to the realities of differing situations and societies. American-style reforms, for example, with their emphasis on protecting elites and political competition from excessive private influence, are unlikely to work well in a setting marked by other sorts of imbalances. Just as each corruption syndrome is defined by two imbalances, the broad strategies suggested above for redressing them jointly suggest different reform strategies for each syndrome (table 3).

Interest Group Bidding

Although many of the states in this category are fundamentally democratic, they still face issues of sustainable democracy. Boundaries between state and society and between individual and public interests need to be protected and strengthened to preserve official autonomy and prevent policymaking from becoming an auction. Rules of access to political figures and bureaucrats may well need to be further specified and monitored through controls over contributions and lobbying; the real and perceived equality of political participation must be protected and, indeed, enhanced so that smaller and newer interests, noneconomic groups, and people with fewer resources can compete effectively. Supervision and accountability within the political elite must be considerably strengthened as well. Legislators who serve within a context of clear codes of ethics and who feel strongly their obligation to the legislative and representative process may be better able to resist economic temptations from interest groups. So may bureaucrats who are carefully recruited, well-paid, systematically trained and retrained, and given the proper mix of supervision, discretion, and protection from partisan pressures.

Good-government reform groups will be important to this agenda, but top bureaucrats must also insist on sound management and monitor paths of access to their agencies and staffs. The leadership, organiza-

Table 3   Strategies for controlling corruption arising from political imbalance

	State-society balance of elites	
	Accessibility > autonomy	**Autonomy > accessibility**
Balance of opportunities	**Corruption type** Interest group bidding	**Corruption type** Elite hegemony
Economic > political	**Anticorruption strategies** Strengthen and protect official autonomy, state-society boundaries, and internal bureaucratic accountability Protect equality of political competition	**Anticorruption strategies** Enhance mass participation Open up and routinize bureaucratic channels Emphasize legality and accountability Expand political competition
	Examples Campaign finance laws Lobbying rules Disclosure of assets and interests Civil service protection and professionalism	**Examples** Bureaucratic-judicial-press independence Competitive elections Stronger civil society Protect civil, political, and property rights Economic enterprises
	Strategic groups Political parties Lobby groups Reform groups Middle bureaucratic managers Individual legislators and staff Organizations in civil society	**Strategic groups** Economic interest and international trade partners Trade organizations Top jurists and bureaucrats Free professionals Potential opposition elites
Political > economic	**Corruption type** Fragmented patronage Extended factionalism *Mafiyas* **Anticorruption strategies** Strengthen and protect official autonomy and state-society boundaries Enhance state capacity Increase economic growth	**Corruption type** Patronage machines **Anticorruption strategies** Enhance mass participation and political competition Open up and routinize bureaucratic access Increase economic growth
	Examples Election laws (money and parties) Bureaucratic-judicial professionalism Law enforcement Broad-based economic growth	**Examples** Bureaucratic and judicial independence Press freedom and civil liberties Stronger civil society Clean-election laws Broad-based economic growth
	Strategic groups Political parties, interest groups, and individual bureaucrats Law enforcement and jurists International trade partners Potential opposition elites	**Strategic groups** Opposition elites and parties Independent groups in civil society Top bureaucrats and jurists International trade partners Foreign-educated technocrats and free professionals

tions, and mass support for political parties and legislative bodies will have to be strengthened, as will broad-based citizen participation. Interest groups can help check each other by guarding their own access rights. It will not be enough simply to change the rules regulating political money: the political action committees (PACs) created by American reforms in the mid-1970s were intended as a means for citizens and smaller interest groups to participate but are now widely (and, for the most part, inaccurately) seen as a corrupting force in their own right. The need, then and now, is to enhance political competition to even out the imbalance of economic and political opportunities while protecting the autonomy of representatives and decision makers.

Elite Hegemony

Both democratization and anticorruption efforts will require broader political competition and more accountability of and access to elites. Political pluralization and measures to strengthen civil society and broaden the range of groups that speak in and for it will be particularly critical. Indeed, such groups may already be gathering economic strength and searching for a political outlet; in the more undemocratic societies, this not only can make for more corruption but can also threaten a political crisis. Thus, opening or protecting channels of access to bureaucrats, the courts, and legislators and establishing the independence of those bodies from entrenched political elites will be particularly important (and particularly difficult in some regimes). Clarifying issues of property and ownership, protecting against political and bureaucratic exploitation of economic enterprises and market activities, and reaffirming principles of legality can strengthen the boundaries between public and private interests, individual and collective rights, and politics and administration, thus helping to limit elite exploitation and strengthen countervailing political forces.

Strategic groups and interests for such reforms would be the emergent economic interests of civil society and in particular any organizational base (trade associations and so on) they might possess. International business partners and investors will also have a stake in establishing and protecting channels of routine bureaucratic access and also possess valuable knowledge about the value of such links elsewhere. Any free professionals, particularly those educated abroad, and potential opposition elites can play similar roles. While they often will not have overtly political agendas, any social groups and civil associations can do much to establish the legitimacy of activities and interests beyond the reach of the state. In the more undemocratic cases, however, these reforms, by threatening elite hegemony and self-enrichment (as indeed they are intended to do), may be politically dangerous and could make a spiral of extreme corruption more likely in the interim.

Fragmented Patronage

In this scenario, fundamental reform would require an increase in elite autonomy and broad-based economic growth. The former entails a real commitment from both citizens and elites to the value and necessity of the state—not as a coercive force, and certainly not as a resource to be plundered, but rather as a guarantor of important processes and rights whose rules must be taken seriously. Clearly this will require a major change in attitudes in many transitional countries. More orderly interactions between officials and private interests—indeed, a clearer distinction as to which are which—stronger discipline and accountability within the elite, and enhanced professional standards and protections for jurists, bureaucrats, and law enforcement personnel would all contribute to a much-needed growth in state capacity. Consolidation of a limited number of strong, broad-based political parties—perhaps through representation and political finance laws encouraging such a party system— a proliferation of interest groups in civil society beyond the personal domination of political figures, and meaningful law enforcement and protection of civil liberties will be needed to persuade people they can deal with the state through official channels rather than personal connections. Broad-based, sustained economic growth is equally important in this reform scenario but must be coupled to the kinds of political reforms just discussed. Growth without an accompanying growth in elite autonomy and state capacity might well hasten the growth of out-of-control corruption.

Strategic groups for attacking corruption through democratization will include those with an interest in more orderly decision making and broad-based political competition. Parties, potential opposition elites, and interest groups will be important in such efforts, as will bureaucracies and their middle-level managers, court and law-enforcement personnel and regulatory staffs, and domestic and international businesses.

Patronage Machines

Reform when a political machine is in place will involve enhancing access to elites and expanding economic opportunities. The first would reduce the need to work through political patrons, and the second would reduce dependency on the machine's favors. Critical reforms include improvements in procedural democracy, particularly in elections but also in preserving parliamentarians' freedom from intimidation and civil servants' political independence; genuine protection of competing elites' and parties' rights; and open and nonpoliticized access for private interests to bureaucratic agencies and decision makers. So too will be strengthening of a viable civil society, politically and economically less dependent upon patronage, and of the organizations within it (overtly political or otherwise). Mass rights of expression and participation are critical to increasing political initiative and impetus for reform in society. Broad-based economic growth will be crucial to evening out the balance of opportunities and to reducing mass dependence upon the machine, but here again economic growth must be accompanied by political change. Growth alone might well move a nation from the lower-right to the upper-right quadrant of table 3, making its corruption more widespread and destabilizing. Mexico, for example, experienced an outbreak of more disruptive forms of corruption during its oil boom (Grayson 1980; Gentleman 1984; Riding 1985).

Strategic groups will be those with a stake in economic growth and in opening up political competition and access to an independent bureaucracy and judiciary. These would include opposition elites and parties, international business and its domestic partners, free professionals and technocrats (particularly those trained abroad), independent groups in civil society, and the courts.

Conclusion

Reform is thus complex and multidimensional. The balance between political reform—balancing elite accessibility and autonomy—and economic reform, which powerfully affects the balance of political and economic opportunities, is a critical issue. Indeed, an understanding of the implications of major imbalances can tell us a lot about the particular corruption problems of China, as one example, and the former Soviet satellites in Central Europe, as another. In China, economic reform was carried out in the absence of political reform, which led to a serious case of elite-hegemony (upper-right quadrant of table 3) corruption. In Central Europe, political reform outran economic change, at least in the first few years of the new political era, fragmenting patronage. In this discussion, I have tried to place such changes and contrasts in the context of an argument about the nature and significance of sustainable democracy, anticorruption reforms, and the positive relationships between the two. The argument may well be overly optimistic, particularly since I have deliberately emphasized the conceptual overlap between them. More common is the view that once corruption becomes a serious problem, it spreads like a fatal disease—the metaphor most frequently used in such discussions—until a political crisis or collapse occurs.

But the possibilities for more positive change are not just theoretical—they are supported by historical cases, too. There have been societies that have moved from serious episodes of corruption into eras of cleaner politics. Although careful administrative and institutional reforms are essential to any such process—and Hong Kong offers a particularly important success story here—in other cases, such as the United Kingdom and (to a lesser extent) the United States, vigorous political contention and the growth of civil society have also been critical. By itself, political reform is no cure for corruption, if only because corruption creates formidable incentives for powerful people and groups to resist reform. It is, however, essential if the benefits of more focused anticorruption reforms are to be sustained in the long run. Indeed, it is through democratization that resources other than wealth, connections, and personalized followings can be brought to bear upon the problem. Persuading citizens that they have a stake in such reform, however, and that short-term disruption will bring long-term benefits, is no easy task—particularly if political reform means that people must forgo the petty but tangible benefits they had been receiving under the old political dispensation. In addition, it is far from clear that a shift directly from particularly dangerous corruption scenarios to something resembling liberal democracy will be feasible in many cases. It may be that the best we can hope for, for a time, is to shift cases of elite hegemony and fragmented patronage in the direction of machine politics. This is not to suggest that machine politics is in itself a desirable state of affairs but rather that it may represent an alternative preferable to political crisis or out-of-control corruption.

But particularly in the transitional societies discussed above, we now have major opportunities for both democratization and anticorruption reforms. In the ways we work with partners and clients in those societies, we can create new expectations about how bureaucracies, the courts, and political officials should deal with private interests, and vice versa, and we can give major moral and organizational support to the people and groups within those countries who hope to pursue both kinds of reform. The four scenarios in the preceding section are offered as ways to begin to diagnose particular countries' problems—including those of our own—and to identify potential allies and targets for support. American businesses in particular can also set a useful example and protect their own interests and assets, depending on how they adapt to life under the Foreign Corrupt Practices Act, which is seen by some not just as an anticorruption "sword" but also as a "shield" for American businesses abroad (Givant 1994). A long-term commitment to good politics and good governance can be good business.

What I have tried to contribute to that process is a first step toward a more detailed assessment of the connections between politics and corruption, and of the nature and functions of democratic reform. With refinement and careful empirical application, this approach may eventually provide a guide to long-term reforms appropriate to particular countries. To reach that point, however, it would benefit greatly from the reactions and criticisms of the business, political, and international-policy professionals who know those situations best.

References

Adams, G. 1981. *The Iron Triangle: The Politics of Defense Contracting.* New York: Council on Economic Priorities.

Ades, Alberto, and Rafael Di Tella. 1995. *Competition and Corruption.* Institute of Economics and Statistics Discussion Papers 169. Oxford, UK: University of Oxford.

Buell, John, and Tom Deluca. 1996. *Sustainable Democracy: Individuality and the Politics of Growth.* Beverly Hills, CA: Sage.

Dobel, J. Patrick. 1978. "The Corruption of a State." *American Political Science Review* 72, no. 3 (September): 958-73.

Doig, Alan. 1984. *Corruption and Misconduct in Contemporary British Politics.* Harmondsworth: Penguin.

Euben, J. Peter. 1978. "On Political Corruption." *The Antioch Review* 36, no. 1 (Winter): 103-18.

Gentleman, Judith. 1984. *Mexican Oil and Dependent Development.* New York: Peter Lang.

Gibbons, Kenneth M. 1988. "Toward an Attitudinal Definition of Corruption." In A. Heidenheimer, M. Johnston, and V. T. LeVine, *Political Corruption: A Handbook.* New Brunswick, NJ: Transaction Press.

Givant, Norman. 1994. "The Sword that Shields." *China Business Review* 21, no. 3 (May-June): 29-31.

Grayson, George W. 1980. *The Politics of Mexican Oil.* Pittsburgh: University of Pittsburgh Press.

Hao, Yufan, and Michael Johnston. 1995. "Reform at the Crossroads: An Analysis of Chinese Corruption." *Asian Perspective* 19, no. 1 (Spring-Summer): 117-49.

Handelman, Stephen. 1995. *Comrade Criminal: Russia's New Mafiya.* New Haven, CT: Yale University Press.

Huntington, Samuel P. 1968. *Political Order in Changing Societies.* New Haven, CT: Yale University Press.

Johnston, Michael. 1979. "Patrons and Clients, Jobs and Machines: A Case Study of the Uses of Patronage." *American Political Science Review* 73, no. 2 (June): 385-98.

Johnston, Michael. 1982. *Political Corruption and Public Policy in America.* Monterey, CA: Brooks-Cole.

Johnston, Michael. 1986. "The Political Consequences of Corruption: A Reassessment." *Comparative Politics* 18, no. 4 (July): 459-77.

Johnston, Michael. 1993. "Political Corruption: Historical Conflict and the Rise of Standards." In Larry Diamond and Marc F. Plattner, *The Global Resurgence of Democracy.* Baltimore: Johns Hopkins University Press. Originally *Journal of Democracy* 2, no. 4 (Fall, 1991): 48-60.

Johnston, Michael. 1996. "The Search for Definitions: The Vitality of Politics and the Issue of Corruption." *International Social Science Journal* (English version) 149 (September): 321-36.

Johnston, Michael, and Yufan Hao. 1995. "China's Surge of Corruption." *Journal of Democracy* 6, no. 4 (October): 80-94.

Kameir, E., and I. Kursany. 1985. "Corruption as the Fifth Factor of Production in the Sudan." Research Report No. 72. Uppsala: Scandinavian Institute of African Studies.

Klitgaard, Robert E. 1988. *Controlling Corruption.* Berkeley: University of California Press.

Lambsdorff, Johann Graf. 1995. "Internet Corruption Perception Index: Ranking 1995." Available at [http://gwdg.de/~uwvw]. University of Goettingen and Transparency International.

Lambsdorff, Johann Graf. 1996. "Internet Corruption Perception Index: Ranking 1996." Available at [http://gwdg.de/~uwvw]. University of Goettingen and Transparency International.

Lampert, N. 1985. *Whistleblowing in the Soviet Union.* New York: Schocken.

Lasswell, Harold D. 1936. *Politics: Who Gets What, When, How.* New York: McGraw-Hill.

Leys, Colin. 1965. "What Is the Problem about Corruption?" *Journal of Modern African Studies* 3, no. 2: 215-30.

Lineberry, Robert L., and Edmund P. Fowler. 1967. "Reformism and Public Policies in American Cities." *American Political Science Review* 61, no. 3 (September): 701-16.

Lowi, Theodore J. 1968. "Gosnell's Chicago Revisited *via* Lindsay's New York." Foreword to the 2d edition of Harold F. Gosnell, *Machine Politics: Chicago Model.* Chicago: University of Chicago Press.

Markovits, Andrei, and Mark Silverstein. 1988. *The Politics of Scandal: Power and Process in Liberal Democracies.* New York: Holmes and Meier.

Mauro, Paolo. 1995. "Corruption and Growth." *Quarterly Journal of Economics* 110, no. 3 (August): 681-712.

Moodie, Graeme C. 1980. "On Political Scandals and Corruption." *Government and Opposition* 15, no. 2 (Spring): 208-22

Nye, Joseph S. 1967. "Corruption and Political Development: A Cost-Benefit Analysis." *American Political Science Review* 61, no. 2 (June): 417-27.

Peters, John G., and Susan Welch. 1978. "Political Corruption in America: A Search for Definitions and a Theory." *American Political Science Review* 72, no. 3 (September): 974-84.

Philp, Mark. 1987. "Defining Corruption: An Analysis of the Republican Tradition." Paper presented to the International Political Science Association research roundtable on political finance and political corruption, 15 May, Bellagio, Italy.

Przeworski, Adam. 1995. *Sustainable Democracy.* Cambridge: Cambridge University Press.

Riding, Alan. 1985. *Distant Neighbors: A Portrait of the Mexicans.* New York: Alfred A. Knopf.

Rose-Ackerman, Susan. 1978. *Corruption: A Study in Political Economy.* New York: Academic Press.

Sacks, Paul M. 1976. *The Donegal Mafia: An Irish Political Machine.* New Haven, CT: Yale University Press.

Sands, Barbara. N. 1990. "Decentralizing an Economy: The Role of Bureaucratic Corruption in China's Economic Reforms." *Public Choice* 65, no. 1 (April): 85-91.

Scott, James C. 1972. *Comparative Political Corruption.* Englewood Cliffs, NJ: Prentice-Hall.

Shefter, Martin. 1976. "The Emergence of the Political Machine: An Alternative View." In W. D. Hawley et al., *Theoretical Perspectives on Urban Politics.* Englewood Cliffs, NJ: Prentice-Hall.

Shumer, S. M. 1979. "Machiavelli: Republican Politics and Its Corruption." *Political Theory* 7, no. 1 (February): 5-34.

Simis, Konstantin M. 1982. *USSR: The Corrupt Society.* New York: Simon & Schuster.

Szeftel, Morris. 1982. "Political Graft and the Spoils System in Zambia: The State as a Resource in Itself." *Review of African Political Economy* 24 (May-August): 4-21.

Thompson, Dennis F. 1993. "Mediated Corruption: The Case of the Keating Five." *American Political Science Review* 87, no. 2 (June): 369-81.

Thompson, Dennis F. 1995. *Ethics in Congress: From Individual to Institutional Corruption.* Washington: Brookings Institution.

4

The Effects of Corruption on Growth, Investment, and Government Expenditure: A Cross-Country Analysis

PAOLO MAURO

The study of the causes and consequences of corruption has a long history in economics, dating back at least to the seminal contributions to the rent-seeking literature by Bhagwati (1982), Krueger (1974), Rose-Ackerman (1978), Tullock (1967), and others. However, empirical work in this area has been limited, partly because the efficiency of government institutions cannot easily be quantified. Corruption in particular is by its very nature difficult to measure.

Renewed interest in the topic has led a number of researchers to attempt to quantify, using regression analysis and indices developed by private rating agencies, the extent to which corruption permeates economic interactions. These indices are typically based on replies to standardized questionnaires by consultants in a variety of countries and therefore have the obvious drawback of being subjective. Nevertheless, the correlation between indices produced by different rating agencies is very high, suggesting a certain consensus on the ranking of countries according to their degree of corruption. In addition, the high prices that the rating agencies charge their customers (usually multinational companies and international banks) for access to these indices are indirect evidence that the information is useful.

At the same time, however, the consultants' judgments that form the basis of these indices may be influenced by the economic performance of the countries they monitor. Thus, researchers who use such indices must be extremely cautious in asserting a causal relationship between

Paolo Mauro is an economist at the International Monetary Fund, Washington. Helpful conversations with Andrei Shleifer and Vito Tanzi are gratefully acknowledged. The views expressed here are strictly personal. The author does not necessarily agree with the subjective indices relating to any given country.

corruption and any economic variables found correlated with it. One way of addressing this possible endogeneity problem is through the use of instrumental variables, as discussed later in this chapter.

An additional drawback of currently available indicators of corruption is their generality: they do not distinguish, for example, between high-level corruption (such as kickbacks to a defense minister for the purchase of expensive jet fighter aircraft) and low-level corruption (such as that of a minor official accepting a bribe to expedite issuance of a driver's license). Nor do they distinguish between well-organized and poorly organized corruption. In the latter, the required amount and appropriate recipient of a bribe are left unclear, and payment does not guarantee that the desired favor will be obtained. The uncertainty of poorly organized systems of corruption may make them the more harmful of the two (Shleifer and Vishny 1993). Yet, even with these limitations, the indices provide a wealth of information from which researchers have obtained a number of interesting results.

This chapter identifies a number of possible causes and consequences of corruption, with emphasis on those links that have been or that could, at least in principle, be investigated through the use of cross-country regression analysis. The chapter reviews and synthesizes the results of recent studies that have made use of such regressions. Although data limitations subject the empirical work to a number of difficulties, these studies provide tentative evidence that corruption may have considerable adverse effects on economic performance that merit the attention of policymakers. More interestingly, the identification of possible causes of corruption may suggest a number of ways to curb it. Although in some cases the distinction between causes and consequences is blurred, there are cases where such ambiguities about the direction of causality should not be overstated in drawing policy conclusions, as argued below.

This chapter also presents new results on the effects of corruption on investment and economic growth. These results were obtained by using a larger data set to expand the analysis of Mauro (1995). New evidence is also presented on the relationship between corruption and the composition of government expenditure. These results need to be interpreted with caution, but they do indicate that corruption lowers overall investment and economic growth and alters the composition of government expenditure, specifically by reducing the share of spending on education.

Causes and Consequences of Corruption

Causes of Corruption

Building upon theoretical contributions from the literature on rent-seeking behavior, recent empirical studies analyze the possible causes of corruption by regressing indices of corruption on a number of potential explanatory variables. Several of these causal variables are related to the extent of government intervention in the economy and, more generally, to variables (such as the level of import tariffs or civil service wages) that are determined by *government policy*. Where regulations are pervasive and government officials have wide discretion in applying them, private parties may be willing to pay bribes to government officials to obtain any rents that the regulations may generate. Identifying such policy-induced sources of corruption is obviously helpful in bringing it under control. The following paragraphs list some of the sources of corruption identified in the literature.

The original literature on rent seeking emphasizes trade restrictions as the prime example of government-induced sources of rents (Krueger 1974). For example, quantitative restrictions on imports make the necessary import licenses very valuable; importers may then be willing to bribe the relevant officials in order to obtain them. More generally, protection of domestic industries from international competition generates rents that local entrepreneurs may be willing to pay for, in the form of bribes. Ades and Di Tella (1994) find that greater openness in an economy, as measured by the sum of imports and exports as a share of GDP, is significantly associated with lower corruption.

Government subsidies can be a source of rents, as Clements, Hugounenq, and Schwartz (1995) have argued. Ades and Di Tella (1995) explain corruption as a function of *industrial policy*, showing that subsidies to manufacturing (measured as a proportion of GDP) are correlated with corruption indices.[1]

Price controls (which can be quantified on the basis of indicators such as those in World Bank 1983) are also a potential source of rents and therefore of rent-seeking behavior. For example, entrepreneurs may be willing to bribe government officials to maintain the provision of inputs at below-market prices.

Similarly, multiple exchange rate systems and foreign exchange allocation schemes (whose importance may be proxied by parallel exchange market premiums, such as those used by Levine and Renelt [1992]) lead to rents. For example, suppose that, in a given country, managers of state-owned commercial banks ration foreign exchange according to priorities they themselves establish; then the country's entrepreneurs may be willing to bribe the managers to obtain the foreign exchange necessary to purchase imported inputs.

Low wages in the civil service relative to private-sector wages or GDP per capita are also a potential source of (low-level) corruption, following

---

1. Ades and Di Tella (1995) also argue that, in evaluating the costs and benefits of industrial policies, it is necessary to take into account the fact that they may generate corruption as an unintended byproduct.

efficiency-wage mechanisms (Kraay and Van Rijckeghem 1995; Haque and Sahay 1996). That is, when civil servants are not paid enough to make ends meet, they may be obliged to use their positions to collect bribes, especially when the expected cost of being caught and fired is low. Countries should take such considerations into account when faced with the difficult choice of lowering an excessive civil service wage bill by cutting salaries or by reducing the number of staff. The International Monetary Fund's Fiscal Affairs Department (1995, 15) warns of the dangers of across-the-board civil service wage cuts, which could lead to a rise in corrupt behavior.

Other sources of rents or factors that make it more likely that rents will be exploited are due not to government policy but to certain underlying characteristics of an economy or a society. Policymakers need to be alert to the possibility of rent-seeking behavior arising from these factors, and attempts to evaluate the effects of government policy on corruption need to take them into account as well. The following are some of these nongovernmental causes of corruption.

Natural-resource endowments are a textbook example of a source of rents, since these resources can typically be sold at a price far exceeding their cost of extraction. Sachs and Warner (1995) argue that resource-rich economies may be more prone than resource-poor economies to extreme rent-seeking behavior. They find (although not at conventional levels of statistical significance) that a country's share of primary-product exports in total exports is associated with indices of bureaucratic efficiency.

Sociological factors may contribute to creating an environment in which the availability of rents is more likely to result in rent-seeking behavior. Shleifer and Vishny (1993) suggest that in countries populated by several ethnic groups one is more likely to find a less organized—and therefore potentially more harmful—type of corruption. This hypothesis is used in Mauro (1995), where an index of ethnolinguistic fractionalization is found to be correlated with corruption. Tanzi (1994) argues that public officials are more likely to do favors for friends and relatives in societies in which relationships are more personalized.

Consequences of Corruption

Corruption has a number of adverse consequences. In particular, recent empirical evidence suggests that corruption lowers economic growth. This may happen through any of a wide range of channels.

Where corruption exists, entrepreneurs are aware that some of the proceeds from their future investments may be claimed by corrupt officials. Payment of bribes is often required before necessary permits will be issued. Therefore, investors may perceive corruption as a tax—and one of a particularly pernicious nature, given the need for secrecy and the uncertainty that come with it—which reduces incentives to invest.

Mauro (1995) provides tentative empirical evidence that corruption lowers investment and economic growth. The observed effects are considerable in magnitude: in an analysis using the Business International (BI) indices of corruption, a one-standard-deviation improvement in the corruption index causes investment to rise by 5 percent of GDP and the annual rate of growth of GDP per capita to rise by half a percentage point. The evidence indicates that much of the effects on economic growth take place through the effects on investment. Using indices of institutional efficiency from the *International Country Risk Guide (ICRG)*, Keefer and Knack (1995) obtain broadly similar results, and in their estimates institutional variables have a significant direct effect on growth in addition to the indirect effect through investment.[2] Further evidence on these relationships is presented below.

Murphy, Shleifer, and Vishny (1991) argue that in situations where rent seeking provides more lucrative opportunities than productive work does, the allocation of talent will be worse: talented and highly educated individuals will be more likely to engage in rent seeking than in productive work, with adverse consequences for their country's growth rate.

Of particular relevance to developing countries is the possibility that corruption might reduce the effectiveness of aid flows, through the diversion of funds from their intended projects. The vast literature on aid flows has explored whether the fungibility of aid resources ultimately results in aid flows financing unproductive public expenditures. Perhaps as a result of this ongoing debate, many donor countries have focused increasingly on issues of good governance, and in some cases in which governance is judged to be very poor, some donors have scaled back their assistance (IMF 1995, 32-34).

Corruption may also bring about loss of tax revenue when it takes the form of tax evasion or the improper use of discretionary tax exemptions. Strictly speaking, these phenomena fall under the definition of corruption only when there is a counterpart payment to the tax official responsible.

By affecting tax collection or the level of public expenditure, corruption may have adverse budgetary consequences. Alternatively, where corruption takes the form of the improper use of directed lending at below-market interest rates by public-sector financial institutions, corruption may result in an undesirably lax monetary stance.

The allocation of public procurement contracts through a corrupt system may lead to inferior public infrastructure and services. For example, corrupt bureaucrats might allow the use of cheap, substandard materials in the construction of buildings or bridges.

---

2. One way in which the growth rate may be affected even for a given investment rate is through changes in the allocation of resources among sectors (Easterly 1990), perhaps including that between the formal and the informal sectors (Loayza 1996).

Finally, corruption may affect the composition of government expenditure. It is this possibility on which the empirical section of this chapter focuses. Corrupt government officials may come to prefer those types of expenditure that allow them to collect bribes and to keep them secret. Shleifer and Vishny (1993) suggest that large expenditures on specialized items such as missiles and bridges, whose exact market value is difficult to determine—lead to more lucrative opportunities for corruption. Opportunities for levying bribes may also be more abundant in connection with items produced by firms operating in oligopolistic markets, where rents are available. One might expect a priori that substantial bribes are easier to collect on large infrastructure projects or high-technology defense equipment than on textbooks and teachers' salaries. For example, Hines (1995) argues that international trade in aircraft is particularly susceptible to corruption. In other areas, such as health, the picture is less clear-cut: opportunities to collect bribes may be abundant in the procurement of hospital buildings and state-of-the-art medical equipment but more limited in the payment of doctors' and nurses' salaries.

Empirical work on the potential links between corruption and the composition of government expenditure is extremely limited. Among the few contributions, Rauch (1995) analyzes both the determinants and the effects of government expenditure composition in a sample of US cities. He finds that the wave of municipal reform during the Progressive Era increased the share of total municipal expenditure allocated to road and sewer investment, which in turn increased growth in manufacturing employment in those cities. To probe further into this relatively unexplored issue, this chapter analyzes data from a cross-section of countries and finds tentative evidence that corruption may lower government spending on education as a proportion of GDP.

Empirical Analyses

Description of the Data

This chapter uses indices of corruption drawn from two private firms: Political Risk Services, Inc., which publishes the *International Country Risk Guide* (*ICRG*), and Business International (BI; now incorporated into the *Economist Intelligence Unit*).

The *ICRG* indices are described in detail by Keefer and Knack (1995). The index used here, which was compiled by the IRIS Center at the University of Maryland, is the 1982-95 average from the *ICRG* and is available for more than a hundred countries. This index purports to measure for each country the likelihood that "high government officials [will] demand special payments" and that "illegal payments are generally expected throughout lower levels of government" in the allocation of import and export licenses, foreign exchange, tax assessments, credit, and the like (Keefer and Knack 1995, 23).

The full BI data set used in this chapter is provided, together with a more complete description, in Mauro (1995). The index used is the 1980-83 average and is available for 67 countries. This index attempts to measure "the degree to which business transactions involve corruption or questionable payments" (Mauro 1995, 684). Both the *ICRG* and the BI indices are scaled from 0 (most corrupt) to 10 (least corrupt), with similar distributions.

The corruption index used in this chapter is the simple average of the *ICRG* and BI indices, when both are available, and the *ICRG* index otherwise. The two indices are strongly correlated ($r = 0.81$) and, arguably, averaging them may reduce the errors in each. There are thus 106 observations in the Barro (1991) sample for which the corruption index is available. The sample statistics are as follows: mean = 5.85, standard deviation = 2.38, minimum = 0.59, maximum = 10.

On the argument that economic growth might contribute to improved institutional efficiency, I use instrumental variables in some estimates in this chapter to address potential endogeneity bias. The first of these, an index of ethnolinguistic fractionalization,[3] is a useful instrument because, as Shleifer and Vishny (1993) argue, more fractionalized countries tend to have more dishonest bureaucracies. The index correlates well ($r = 0.39$, significant at conventional levels) with the corruption index. The other instruments are two dummy variables specified to represent whether (following Taylor and Hudson 1972) the country has been a colony (since 1776) and whether the country achieved independence after 1945. These colonial dummies (data for which come from the *Encyclopedia Britannica*) are good instruments because they, too, are highly correlated with a country's corruption index ($r = 0.46$ and 0.38, respectively; both values are significant). In addition, these three variables may be valid instruments to the extent that ethnolinguistic fractionalization and colonial history are unrelated to economic growth, investment, or

---

3. The raw data from which this index is constructed refer to 1960 and come from the *Atlas Narodov Mira* (Department of Geodesy and Cartography of the State Geological Committee of the USSR, Moscow, 1964). This publication was the result of a vast project to provide an extremely accurate depiction of the ethnolinguistic composition of world population. The index is computed by Taylor and Hudson (1972) as

$$ELF = 1 - \sum_{i=1}^{I} \left(\frac{n_i}{N} \right)^2, i = 1, \ldots I$$

where n_i is the number of people in the ith group, N is the total population, and I is the number of ethnolinguistic groups in the country. The index measures the probability that two randomly selected persons from a given country will not belong to the same ethnolinguistic group.

the composition of government expenditure, other than through their effects on corruption.

This chapter uses three standard sources of data on the composition of government expenditure: Barro (1991), Devarajan, Swaroop, and Zou (1993), and Easterly and Rebelo (1993).

The Barro (1991) data set contains 1970-85 averages of government spending on defense, education, social security and welfare, public investment, and total government expenditure for over 100 countries. The primary sources are the International Monetary Fund's *Government Finance Statistics* (*GFS*) and UNESCO. All macroeconomic variables are also drawn from Barro (1991), since his data set provided the basis for much recent empirical work on the determinants of economic growth.

Data for the industrial countries were added to the Devarajan, Swaroop, and Zou (1993) data set of developing countries to obtain a larger sample of around 95 countries. The data ultimately come from the *GFS* and refer to 1985. The components of expenditure on education (primary and secondary, university, and other education) and health (hospitals, clinics, and other) are available for about 60 countries.

The Easterly and Rebelo (1993) data set consolidates the public investment expenditures of the general government with those undertaken by public enterprises for 96 countries. It provides data on the composition of public investment by sector (agriculture, education, health, housing and urban infrastructure, transport and communication, and industry and mining) for a sample of about 40 developing countries. Public investment data are also available by level of government (general government versus public enterprises) for about 50 countries. The primary sources are the World Bank's country reports, United Nations national accounts data, and the World Bank's annual *World Development Report*.

The Effects of Corruption on Investment and Economic Growth

Using cross-country regressions similar to those in Mauro (1995), this section examines a larger data set to provide further evidence that corruption may affect investment and economic growth.[4] Regression of the 1960-85 average investment rate alone on the corruption index shows an association between these variables that is significant at conventional levels (table 1, column 1). A univariate regression of the 1960-85 average

---

4. The analysis in this chapter relies only on cross-sectional regressions using averages of the data over the sample period, as a country's degree of institutional efficiency typically evolves only rather slowly. Mauro (1993) shows that the relationship between investment and corruption is significant in a fixed-effects panel.

Table 1 Results of regressions estimating the effects of corruption on investment-GDP ratios[a]

Independent variable	Univariate, OLS (1)	Univariate, 2SLS (2)	Multivariate, OLS (3)	Multivariate, 2SLS (4)
Constant	0.0780 (4.19)	−0.0025 (−0.05)	0.1226 (3.66)	0.0543 (0.47)
Corruption index	0.0187 (7.03)	0.0320 (3.93)	0.0095 (2.09)	0.0281 (0.99)
GDP per capita in 1960			−0.0062 (−0.91)	−0.0213 (−0.96)
Secondary education in 1960			0.1749 (2.95)	0.1241 (1.21)
Population growth			−0.8226 (−0.82)	−1.0160 (−1.05)
R^2	0.32	n.a.[b]	0.44	n.a.[b]

OLS = ordinary least-squares; 2SLS = two-stage least-squares; n.a. = not applicable.
a. There are 94 observations. The dependent variable is the average investment-GDP ratio for 1960-85. The corruption index is the simple average of indices produced by Political Risk Services, Inc. (compiled by the IRIS Center at the University of Maryland, for 1982-95) and Business International (for 1980-83). One standard deviation of the corruption index equals 2.38. A high value of the corruption index means that the country has good institutions in that respect. White-corrected t-statistics are reported in parentheses. In the 2SLS regressions the index of ethnolinguistic fractionalization from Taylor and Hudson (1972) was used as an instrumental variable.
b. R^2 is not an appropriate measure of goodness of fit with 2SLS.

Sources: Barro (1991); Business International; Political Risk Services, Inc.; IRIS Center, University of Maryland.

annual growth in GDP per capita on the corruption index (table 2, column 1) also produced a significant association. The magnitude of the effects is considerable: a one-standard-deviation (2.38-point) improvement in the corruption index is associated with over a 4-percentage-point increase in a country's investment rate and over a ½-percentage-point increase in the per capita growth rate. This means that if a given country were to improve its corruption "grade" from 6 out of 10 to 8 out of 10, its investment-GDP ratio would rise by almost 4 percentage points and its annual growth of GDP per capita would rise by almost half a percentage point.

The estimated coefficients become even larger when two-stage least-squares techniques, with the index of ethnolinguistic fractionalization as an instrument, are used to address possible endogeneity bias (tables 1 and 2, column 2). The relationships remain significant even in multivariate regressions that take into account the effects of other standard

Table 2 Results of regressions estimating the effects of corruption on growth of GDP per capita[a]

Independent variable	Univariate, OLS (1)	Univariate, 2SLS (2)	Multivariate, OLS (3)	Multivariate, 2SLS (4)	Multivariate including investment, OLS (5)
Constant	0.0035 (0.85)	−0.0284 (−2.12)	0.0012 (1.50)	−0.0404 (−0.81)	−0.0012 (−0.16)
Corruption index	0.0029 (4.74)	0.0081 (3.61)	0.0038 (2.95)	0.0175 (1.40)	0.0028 (2.01)
GDP per capita in 1960			−0.0075 (−4.49)	−0.01821 (−1.79)	−0.0069 (−4.78)
Secondary education in 1960			0.0401 (3.09)	0.0034 (0.09)	0.0217 (1.82)
Population growth			−0.4124 (−1.83)	−0.5192 (−1.29)	−0.3255 (−1.81)
Investment					0.1056 (3.09)
R^2	0.14	n.a.[b]	0.31	n.a.[b]	0.42

OLS = ordinary least-squares; 2SLS = two-stage least-squares; n.a. = not applicable.
a. There are 94 observations. The dependent variable is average annual growth of GDP per capita for 1960-85. The corruption index is the simple average of indices produced by Political Risk Services, Inc. (compiled by the IRIS Center at the University of Maryland, for 1982-95), and Business International (for 1980-83). One standard deviation of the corruption index equals 2.38. A high value of the corruption index means that the country has good institutions in that respect. White-corrected t-statistics are reported in parentheses. In the 2SLS regressions the index of ethnolinguistic fractionalization from Taylor and Hudson (1972) was used as an instrumental variable.
b. R^2 is not an appropriate measure of goodness of fit with 2SLS.
Sources: Barro (1991); Business International; Political Risk Services, Inc.; IRIS Center, University of Maryland.

determinants of investment and growth (tables 1 and 2, column 3).[5] The magnitude of the coefficients also rises when instrumental variables are used for the corruption index in the multivariate regressions (tables 1 and 2, column 4). Finally, when the investment rate is added to the list of independent variables in the growth regression, the coefficient on the corruption index falls by two-thirds (compare table 2, column 5, with table 1, column 3), although it remains just significant at the 5 percent

---

5. The specification chosen here is the base regression in Levine and Renelt (1992) and includes initial GDP per capita, the initial secondary education enrollment rate, and the population growth rate.

level. This result implies that much of the effect of corruption on economic growth takes place through investment, although it leaves open the possibility that some of the effect occurs directly.

The general result of these analyses—namely, that corruption may have large, adverse effects on economic growth and that investment may have important implications—has already received considerable attention elsewhere.[6] The following section focuses on a channel other than investment through which corruption may affect economic performance, namely the possible link between corruption and the composition of government expenditure.

The Effects of Corruption on the Composition of Government Expenditure

The potential effects of corruption on the composition of government expenditure remain largely unexplored, at least in the context of cross-country work. This section asks whether corrupt politicians choose to spend more on those components of public expenditure on which it may be easier or more lucrative to levy bribes. The appendix derives a generalization of the Barro (1990) model that shows that if corruption acted simply as though it were a tax on income, then the amount and composition of government expenditure would be independent of corruption. As a consequence, it seems reasonable to interpret any empirical relationships between corruption indices and particular components of government spending as tentative evidence that corrupt bureaucrats obtain more revenue for themselves not simply by increasing government expenditure and their share of it, but also by shifting the composition of government expenditure to those areas in which bribes can be more efficiently collected.

The question is interesting because, even though the empirical literature has so far yielded mixed results on the effects of government expenditure, and in particular of its composition, on economic growth,[7]

---

6. A number of additional robustness tests for similar regressions using the BI data set are reported in Mauro (1993, 1995).

7. Levine and Renelt (1992) show that the overall level of government expenditure does not seem to bear any robust relationship with economic growth. Previous work on the composition of government expenditure has been limited. Devarajan, Swaroop, and Zou (1993) find no clear relationship between any component of government expenditure and economic growth. Easterly and Rebelo (1993) do find some significant relationships: public investment on transport and communications is positively associated with economic growth, although not with private investment; public investment in agriculture is negatively associated with private investment; general government investment is positively correlated with both growth and private investment; and public enterprise investment is negatively correlated with private investment.

most economists seem to think that the level and type of spending undertaken by governments do matter for economic performance. For example, even though cross-country regression work has not conclusively shown a relationship between government spending on education and economic growth, it has gathered fairly robust evidence that school enrollment rates (Levine and Renelt 1992) and educational attainment (Barro 1992) play a considerable role in determining economic growth.

Perhaps part of the reason significant and robust effects of the composition of government expenditure on economic growth have proved difficult to find is that the quality of the available data may be relatively low, both because it is difficult to ensure that all countries apply the same criteria in allocating projects among the various categories of government expenditure and because each public expenditure component presumably contains both productive and unproductive projects. The relative noisiness of the expenditure data implies that this study must necessarily be exploratory and that one should not expect a priori to find significant relationships. Nevertheless, this section presents new, tentative evidence that corrupt governments may display predatory behavior in choosing the composition of government expenditure. In particular, government spending on education seems to be reduced by corruption.

Table 3 analyzes the relationship between each component of public expenditure (as a ratio to GDP) reported in the Barro (1991) data set and the corruption index.[8] Government spending on education as a ratio to GDP is positively and significantly correlated with lower levels of corruption (i.e., a higher ranking on the index). The magnitude of the coefficient is considerable: a one-standard-deviation improvement in the corruption index is associated with an increase in government spending on education by around half a percent of GDP. Taken at face value, this result implies that if a given country were to improve its "grade" on corruption from, say, 6 out of 10 to 8 out of 10, on average its government would increase its spending on education by about half a percent of GDP. Figure 1 shows that this result is not just driven by a small group of countries.

Other components of government expenditure (but, interestingly, not total government consumption expenditure) are also significantly associated with the corruption index at the conventional levels, most notably in the case of transfer payments, and social insurance and

---

8. The various components of government spending are analyzed as a share of GDP because the generalization of the Barro (1990) model that is derived in the appendix, which provides a useful theoretical benchmark, implies that if bribes could be levied just as easily on all income (rather than more easily on some government expenditure components than others), then the various components of government *as a ratio to GDP* should be unrelated to corruption.

Table 3   Results of regressions estimating the relationship between corruption and the composition of government expenditure, using the Barro data set[a]

Dependent variable (averages for 1970-85, as percentages of GDP)	Constant	Corruption index	GDP per capita (1980)	R^2	N
Regressions omitting GDP per capita as a variable					
Government expenditure on education	0.028 (7.48)	0.0023 (3.97)		0.13	103
Government consumption expenditure	0.213 (11.85)	−0.0047 (−1.70)		0.03	106
Government consumption expenditure, excluding education and defense	0.146 (10.69)	−0.0070 (−3.35)		0.10	93
Government expenditure on defense	0.032 (3.64)	0.0004 (0.28)		0.00	93
Government transfer payments	−0.039 (−2.22)	0.0208 (7.22)		0.45	73
Social insurance and welfare payments	−0.044 (−4.41)	0.0156 (7.94)		0.48	75
Regressions including GDP per capita as a variable					
Government expenditure on education	0.029 (6.85)	0.0020 (2.20)	0.0003 (0.43)	0.13	103
Government consumption expenditure	0.189 (10.20)	0.0052 (1.46)	−0.0094 (−4.88)	0.16	106
Government consumption expenditure, excluding education and defense	0.116 (7.79)	0.0049 (1.41)	−0.011 (−4.54)	0..25	93
Government expenditure on defense	0.030 (2.25)	0.0009 (0.25)	−0.0004 (−0.17)	0.00	93
Government transfer payments	0.013 (0.78)	0.0001 (0.03)	0.018 (5.60)	0.64	73
Social insurance and welfare payments	−0.015 (−1.70)	0.0041 (1.64)	0.010 (4.47)	0.59	75

a. The corruption index is the simple average of the indices produced by Political Risk Services, Inc. (compiled by the IRIS Center, University of Maryland, for 1982-95) and Business International (for 1980-83). One standard deviation of the corruption index equals 2.38. A high value of the corruption index means that the country has good institutions in that respect. White-corrected t-statistics are reported in parentheses. N is the number of observations.

Sources: Barro (1991); Business International; Political Risk Services, Inc.; IRIS Center, University of Maryland.

Figure 1 Correlation between corruption and government expenditure on education for 103 countries

Government expenditure on education as a share of GDP

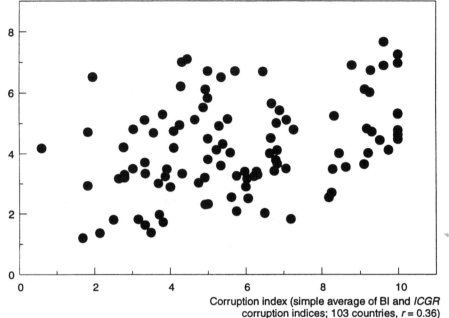

Corruption index (simple average of BI and *ICGR*
corruption indices; 103 countries, *r* = 0.36)

Sources: Barro (1991), BI, and *ICRG*.

welfare payments. However, it is important to take into account the well-known empirical observation—known as Wagner's law[9]—that the share of government expenditure in GDP tends to rise as a country becomes richer. When the level of income per capita in 1980 is used as an additional explanatory variable, education turns out to be the only component of public spending whose association with the corruption index remains significant at the 95 percent level.[10] The magnitude of the coefficient remains broadly the same as in the univariate regression.

Table 4 reports results obtained using *GFS* data, which are more finely disaggregated, although possibly at the cost of lower cross-country

---

9. Easterly and Rebelo (1993) review the literature on Wagner's law and show that, in a panel of countries, several components of public spending rise (as a ratio to GDP) as per capita income rises.

10. This analysis is a first pass at the data. Future research could introduce additional control variables, such as the demographic structure of the population (a higher share of the school-age population in the total population would usually imply a higher expenditure on education) and indicators of relations with neighboring countries (an increased possibility of war is expected to raise defense spending).

Table 4 Results of regressions estimating the relationship between corruption and the composition of government expenditure, using GFS data[a]

Dependent variable (1985 observation, as ratio to GDP)	Constant	Corruption index	GDP per capita, 1980	R^2	N
Total government expenditure	0.233 (4.16)	0.0043 (0.36)	0.0112 (1.59)	0.122 2	88
Government current expenditure	0.141 (3.33)	0.0124 (1.34)	0.0094 (1.64)	0.238 8	85
Government capital expenditure	0.081 (4.54)	−0.0064 (−1.61)	0.0011 (0.43)	0.118 8	86
Government expenditure on education	0.021 (3.95)	0.0030 (2.29)	−0.0020 (−1.93)	0.070 0	85
Government expenditure on schools	0.012 (2.01)	0.0028 (1.60)	−0.0022 (−1.69)	0.077 7	57
Government expenditure on universities	0.004 (2.71)	0.0008 (2.45)	−0.0006 (2.79)	0.074 4	56
Other government expenditure on education	0.007 (1.93)	0.0001 (0.01)	−0.0002 (−0.29)	0.003 3	54
Government expenditure on health	0.001 (0.13)	0.0027 (2.34)	0.0012 (1.27)	0.301 1	86
Government expenditure on hospitals	0.006 (1.62)	0.0006 (0.64)	0.0005 (0.69)	0.063 3	54
Government expenditure on clinics	−0.002 (−0.41)	0.0012 (1.02)	0.0003 (0.31)	0.093 3	28
Other government expenditure on health	0.001 (0.32)	0.0011 (0.83)	−0.0009 (−1.18)	0.042 2	44
Government expenditure on defense	0.034 (2.42)	−0.0009 (−0.24)	0.0010 (0.41)	0.003 3	82
Government expenditure on transportation	0.013 (4.13)	0.0009 (1.02)	−0.0003 (−0.39)	0.023 3	85

a. The corruption index is the simple average of the indices produced by Political Risk Services, Inc. (compiled by the IRIS Center, University of Maryland, for 1982-95) and Business International (for 1980-83). One standard deviation of the corruption index equals 2.38. A high value of the corruption index means that the country has good institutions in that respect. White-corrected t-statistics are reported in parentheses. N is the number of observations.

Sources: Government Finance Statistics (International Monetary Fund); Business International; Political Risk Services, Inc.; IRIS Center, University of Maryland.

comparability at the level of the more detailed items. Total government expenditure is again unrelated to corruption, and the results obtained when public expenditure is split by function are in line with those obtained using the Barro data set. In particular, when GDP per capita is controlled for, government expenditure on education is negatively and significantly associated with higher levels of corruption (a lower ranking on the index). Government expenditure on health is also found to be negatively and significantly associated with corruption. Finally, neither defense nor transportation displays any significant relationship with corruption. Of course, this does not mean that there is no corruption associated with spending on these items but only that this simple analysis does not find any significant evidence of it.

The link between corruption and the subcomponents of education and of health expenditure is more blurred. The association is significant only for spending on primary and secondary education and on universities, and then only at the 90 percent level.

Finally, table 4 shows the results of the test of a hypothesis often heard in popular debate—namely, that corruption is likely to lead to high capital expenditures by the government, perhaps on useless white-elephant projects. The data are consistent with this hypothesis but do not provide significant evidence in favor of it. In fact, an improvement in the corruption index does coincide with a decline in capital expenditure by the government as a ratio to GDP, but this relationship is barely significant at the 90 percent level. Similarly, an improvement in the corruption index is associated with an increase in current expenditure by the government as a ratio to GDP, but not significantly so. Therefore, these results are interesting, but only suggestive at this stage.

The impact of corruption on the level and composition of public investment were analyzed using the data from Easterly and Rebelo (1993), which unfortunately reduces the sample size sharply. Interestingly, most of the relationships are not statistically significant (table 5). In particular, although there is fairly robust evidence that corruption lowers total investment (and private investment—see Mauro 1995), no clear relationship emerges between corruption and public investment. A possible interpretation is that predatory behavior by corrupt governments may help sustain the level (although not the quality) of public investment as a ratio to GDP, even as private investment declines. In addition, none of the components of public investment (including the education component) is significantly associated with the corruption indices. In part, these findings may be due to the fact that the sample is relatively small and consists only of developing countries, yielding relatively little variation in the independent variables. However, it is also possible to speculate that bribes are difficult to levy on teachers' salaries but easier to levy on the construction of school buildings.

Finally, table 6 reports results from a number of simple tests of the

Table 5 Results of regressions estimating the relationship between corruption and the composition of public investment[a]

Dependent variable (1985 observation, as ratio to GDP)	Constant	Corruption index	GDP per capita, 1980	R^2	N
Public investment	0.110 (8.45)	−0.0041 (−1.95)		0.051	84
Public investment	0.098 (6.67)	0.0009 (0.29)	−0.0060 (−2.75)	0.121	84
General government	0.051 (4.76)	−0.0014 (−0.92)		0.021	51
General government	0.038 (2.34)	−0.0030 (0.85)	−0.0040 (−1.98)	0.126	51
Public enterprises	0.060 (4.93)	−0.0022 (−1.21)		0.028	42
Public enterprises	0.042 (3.83)	0.0052 (2.15)	−0.0079 (−4.21)	0.224	42
Agriculture	0.021 (2.15)	−0.0010 (−0.55)		0.013	44
Agriculture	0.023 (2.42)	−0.0007 (−0.37)	−0.0021 (−1.34)	0.033	44
Education	0.006 (2.58)	0.0001 (0.11)		0.001	42
Education	0.0058 (2.68)	0.0003 (0.49)	−0.0008 (−1.69)	0.035	42
Health	0.004 (2.59)	−0.0001 (−0.14)		0.001	37
Health	0.0046 (2.92)	0.0001 (0.19)	−0.0007 (−1.88)	0.038	37
Housing	0.004 (1.41)	0.0003 (0.57)		0.006	31
Housing	0.0049 (1.60)	0.0008 (1.16)	−0.0016 (−1.82)	0.056	31
Industry	0.011 (1.79)	−0.0001 (−0.10)		0.001	32
Industry	0.011 (1.88)	−0.0001 (−0.05)	−0.0003 (−0.28)	0.002	32
Transportation	0.018 (3.94)	0.0004 (0.45)		0.004	36
Transportation	0.019 (3.93)	0.0005 (0.55)	−0.0005 (−0.43)	0.007	36

a. The corruption index is the simple average of the indices produced by Political Risk Services, Inc. (compiled by the IRIS Center, University of Maryland, for 1982–95) and Business International (for 1980–83). One standard deviation of the corruption index equals 2.38. A high value of the corruption index means that the country has good institutions in that respect. White–corrected t–statistics are reported in parentheses. N is the number of observations.

Sources: Barro (1991); Business International; Political Risk Services, Inc.; IRIS Center, University of Maryland.

Table 6   Results of regressions estimating the relationship between corruption and government expenditure on education[a]

Dependent variable (average 1970-85)	Constant	Corruption index	GDP per capita, 1980	Government consumption expenditure as ratio to GDP	R^2	N
Ratio of government expenditure on education to GDP	0.010 (2.25)	0.0027 (5.48)		0.0863 (4.74)	0.278	103
Ratio of government expenditure on education to GDP	0.009 (2.15)	0.0014 (1.62)	0.0013 (1.75)	0.1042 (4.74)	0.318	103
Ratio of government expenditure on education to government consumption expenditure	0.103 (4.11)	0.0256 (5.40)			0.262	103
Ratio of government expenditure on education to government consumption expenditure	0.149 (6.49)	0.0056 (1.09)	0.0187 (5.00)		0.424	103
Ratio of government expenditure on education to GDP; instrument: fractionalization	0.036 (4.08)	0.0011 (0.74)			n.a.[b]	100

Ratio of government expenditure on education to GDP; instruments: fractionalization, colonial history, and postwar independence	0.033 (5.08)	0.0015 (1.36)	n.a.[b]	100
Ratio of government expenditure on education to government consumption expenditure; instrument: fractionalization	0.068 (1.11)	0.0318 (3.04)	n.a.[b]	100
Ratio of government expenditure on education to government consumption expenditure; instruments: fractionalization, colonial history, and postwar independence	0.059 (1.23)	0.0331 (3.95)	n.a.[b]	100

n.a. = not applicable

a. The corruption index is the simple average of the indices produced by Political Risk Services, Inc. (compiled by the IRIS Center, University of Maryland, for 1982-95) and Business International (for 1980-83). One standard deviation of the corruption index equals 2.38. A high value of the corruption index means that the country has good institutions in that respect. White-corrected t-statistics are reported in parentheses. N is the number of observations. "Fractionalization" is the index of ethnolinguistic fractionalization in 1960, from Taylor and Hudson (1972). "Colonial history" is a dummy for whether the country was ever a colony (since 1776). "Postwar independence" is a dummy for whether the country was still a colony in 1945.
b. R^2 is not an appropriate measure of goodness of fit with instrumental variables (two-stage least-squares).

Sources: Barro (1991); Business International; Political Risk Services, Inc.; IRIS Center, University of Maryland.

robustness of the relationship between corruption and government expenditure on education. This robustness is tested, first, by relaxing some of the previous estimates' assumptions on functional form and, second, by controlling for possible endogeneity problems by using instrumental variables. When the ratio of government expenditure on education is regressed on the corruption index and total government expenditure as a ratio to GDP, the relationship remains significant, but only barely so when GDP per capita is included in the specification. Government expenditure on education as a share of total government consumption expenditure is significantly correlated with the corruption index, but only when GDP per capita is *not* included in the regression. Thus, the relationship between corruption and government expenditure on education seems to be somewhat sensitive to changes in the specification, but not overly so.

To the extent that the direction of causality to be captured is that from corruption to government spending on education, it is interesting to estimate this relationship using instrumental variables (the index of ethnolinguistic fractionalization and the colonial dummies). The coefficient on corruption falls by about half in the regression of government expenditure on education as a ratio to GDP when instrumental variables are used (compare table 6, rows 5 and 6, with table 3, row 1). However, the use of instrumental variables raises the coefficient on corruption in the regression of government expenditure as a share of total government consumption expenditure (in table 6, compare rows 7 and 8, with table 3, row 3). Thus, there is some tentative support for the hypothesis that corruption *causes* a decline in government expenditure on education, but the results are somewhat mixed.

Overall, the evidence is suggestive, but by no means conclusive, that corruption is negatively associated with government expenditure on education and possibly on health. Despite some indications that the direction of the causal link may be at least in part from corruption to the composition of spending, the issue of the direction of causality remains unresolved. At the same time, the extent to which potential policy conclusions depend on the direction of causality should not be overstated—an issue that the next section explores.

The Direction of Causality—Is It Relevant for Policy?

For the sake of clarity, the above list of variables that might be related to corruption has been presented as though these variables could unambiguously be categorized as either causes or consequences of corruption. But in fact the direction of causality is blurred in some cases. For example, it is not clear whether the existence of regulations leads bureaucrats to ask for bribes to help entrepreneurs circumvent them, or instead whether corrupt bureaucrats are more likely to multiply regulations as a way of creating opportunities for bribes. The same is true for the empirical relationship on which this chapter focuses: just as the existence of corruption may cause a less-than-optimal composition of government expenditure, so it may be that high government spending on items where monitoring is difficult creates opportunities for corruption. The empirical section of this chapter has made some attempts to identify the correct direction of the causal links. But the issue of causality has not been—and may never be—fully resolved, since causality may well operate in both directions.

In general, the direction of causality has important implications for policy prescriptions, but in some cases policy conclusions are not entirely dependent on it. In the specific case of the composition of government spending, its observed correlation with corruption may constitute grounds for considering whether governments should be encouraged to allocate a larger proportion of their spending to those items that are less susceptible to corruption, subject to the following qualifications.

If a less-than-optimal composition of government spending causes corruption in the sense of creating opportunities for it, then encouraging governments to improve the composition of their spending might be an effective way of reducing corruption. If, on the other hand, it is corruption that causes a less-than-optimal composition of government expenditure,[11] then corrupt governments will attempt to circumvent any effort to encourage them to spend proportionately more on activities that are less susceptible to corruption. In fact, corrupt governments could thwart such pressure by substituting publicly unproductive but privately lucrative projects for publicly productive but privately unlucrative ones *within* a given expenditure category and still be able to show, for example, that their share of spending on education has risen. In such a case, would encouraging governments to improve the composition of their spending be an effective way of curbing corruption? The answer hinges on whether, as a practical matter, it is possible to specify the composition of government expenditure in a way that makes it difficult for corrupt officials to find scope for raising bribes while still appearing to adopt a more desirable composition of government spending.

Therefore, even if a priori considerations and the tentative evidence presented above suggest that any correlation between corruption and the composition of government spending reflects at least in part causality running from the former to the latter, encouraging governments to improve the composition of their spending may still be an effective way

---

11. The estimates in table 6 provide tentative evidence that the observed correlation between corruption and government expenditure composition may be due at least in part to this mechanism.

of curbing corruption. However, it is so only to the extent that the composition of spending may be specified so as to make substitution *within* its categories difficult.

Concluding Remarks

This chapter has analyzed a number of the causes and consequences of corruption. It has reviewed and synthesized recent studies that have estimated some of these links empirically, but others remain on the agenda for future research. In addition, the chapter has presented further evidence (which must, however, be interpreted with caution, given the data limitations mentioned) that corruption may have considerable adverse effects on economic growth, largely by reducing private investment, but perhaps also through a variety of other channels, which may include a worsening in the composition of public expenditure. Specifically, this chapter has presented new, tentative evidence of a negative and significant relationship between corruption and government expenditure on education. This evidence is reason for concern, since previous literature has shown that educational attainment is an important determinant of economic growth. A possible interpretation of the observed correlation between corruption and the composition of government expenditure is that corrupt governments find it easier to collect bribes on some expenditure items than on others. Although one policy implication might be that governments should be encouraged to shift the composition of their expenditure, an important issue is whether, as a practical matter, the desired composition can be specified in a way that corrupt officials could not circumvent by substituting publicly unproductive but privately lucrative projects *within* the various expenditure categories.

Appendix: A Generalization of the Barro Model as a Benchmark

This appendix develops a simple generalization of the Barro (1990) model, which may constitute a useful benchmark to analyze the relationship between corruption and the composition of government expenditure. It shows that if corruption acted simply as a proportional tax on income, the ratio of each component of government expenditure to GDP would be the same, no matter how corrupt or unstable the government.

Following Barro (1990), taxes are assumed to be levied as a proportion of income. The production function is assumed to be of the form:

$$y = A \, k^{(1-\alpha)} \prod_{i=1}^{N} g_i^{\alpha_i}, \quad \sum_{i=1}^{N} \alpha_i = \alpha, \quad 0 < \alpha < 1 \tag{1}$$

where y is income per worker, A is a technological parameter, k is private capital per worker, and g_i is the flow of public services from government expenditure of type i, per worker. This is the simple extension to N types of government expenditure of the production function in Devarajan, Swaroop, and Zou (1993).

Defining ϕ_i so that:

$$g_i = \phi_i g, \quad \sum_{i=1}^{N} \phi_i = 1 \tag{2}$$

where g is the total flow of public services from productive government expenditure per worker, the production function in equation (1) reduces to the Barro (1990) production function if $N = 1$.

Barro (1990) examines two extreme cases. In the first, a benevolent government maximizes the lifetime utility of the representative consumer, subject to the constraint that $\tau = g/y$; solving for the optimal τ yields $\tau^* = (g/y)^* = \alpha$. In the second, a self-interested government (of infinite duration in office) obtains consumption equal to $C_g = [\tau - (g/y)]y$; that is, corrupt bureaucrats get to consume the "budget surplus" (τ represents the sum of a proportional tax rate and a proportional bribe rate). The self-interested government maximizes the present value of the future flow of utility derived from C_g, subject to $\tau \geq g/y$.

To analyze the role of institutions in determining the composition of public expenditure, it is interesting to analyze the problem of a government that maximizes a weighted average of the lifetime utility of the representative consumer and of the lifetime utility derived from consumption by its self-interested members. The maximization program may be expressed as, choose τ and (g/y), subject to $\tau \geq g/y$, so as to maximize, $(1 - \psi) U + \psi U_g$, with $0 \leq \psi \leq 1$, and where U is the lifetime utility of the representative consumer and U_g is the lifetime utility of the self-interested government official.

Following Barro (1990), the lifetime utility of the citizen can be assumed to be:

$$U = \int_0^\infty e^{-\rho t} \left(\frac{c^{1-\sigma} - 1}{1 - \sigma} \right) dt \tag{3}$$

where ρ is the rate of time preference and σ is the inverse of the intertemporal elasticity of substitution. Similarly, the lifetime utility of the self-interested government official can be assumed to be:

$$U_g = \int_0^\infty e^{-\theta t} \left(\frac{c_g^{1-\sigma} - 1}{1 - \sigma} \right) dt \tag{4}$$

where θ is the sum of the government official's rate of time preference and of his probability of death (a metaphor for government collapse, for analytical simplicity).

Barro (1990) analyzes special cases (i and ii) of the above maximization program, where $\psi = 0$ and $\psi = 1$, respectively. The weight given to the lifetime utility of the self-interested government officials, ψ, may be taken to represent the degree to which the country is corrupt.

It can be shown that the more corrupt (higher ψ) and the more unstable (higher θ) the government, the higher is τ, and therefore the lower are private investment and economic growth. This result is consistent with the observation in this chapter that corruption reduces private investment and growth.

On the other hand, in this model it can also be shown that the optimal share of government infrastructure services is independent of corruption and political stability; that is, $(g/y)^* = \alpha$, regardless of the weights assigned to the two classes of people and regardless of the discount rate. A proof of this proposition can be obtained by simply taking derivatives of $(1 - \psi) U + \psi U_g$ with respect to τ and g/y. A few pages of algebra (not reproduced here) yield the result.

The following condition relating to the composition of productive government expenditure maximizes the lifetime utility of both the representative consumer and the self-interested bureaucrat:

$$\frac{\phi_j}{\phi_k} = \frac{\alpha_i}{\alpha_k}, \quad \forall j, k \tag{5}$$

As a consequence, any government would choose the composition of expenditure implied by equation (5), regardless of the degree of corruption and political instability. Therefore, under the assumptions of the Barro (1990) model, and most notably the assumption that corruption acts as a proportional tax on income, the ratio of each component of government expenditure to GDP would be the same, no matter how corrupt or unstable the government.

References

Ades, Alberto, and Rafael Di Tella. 1994. *Competition and Corruption*. Institute of Economics and Statistics Discussion Papers 169. Oxford, UK: University of Oxford.

Ades, Alberto, and Rafael Di Tella. 1995. "National Champions and Corruption: Some Unpleasant Competitiveness Arithmetic." University of Oxford. Photocopy.

Barro, Robert. 1990. "Government Spending in a Simple Model of Endogenous Growth." *Journal of Political Economy* 98, no. 5, part 2 (October): S103-25.

Barro, Robert. 1991. "Economic Growth in a Cross-Section of Countries." *Quarterly Journal of Economics* 106, no. 2: 407-43.

Barro, Robert. 1992. "Human Capital and Economic Growth." In *Policies for Long-Run Economic Growth*. Federal Reserve Bank of Kansas City.

Bhagwati, Jagdish. 1982. "Directly Unproductive, Profit-Seeking (DUP) Activities." *Journal of Political Economy* 90, no. 5 (October): 988-1002.

Clements, Benedict, Réjane Hugounenq, and Gerd Schwartz. 1995. *Government Subsidies:*

Concepts, International Trends and Reform Options. IMF Working Papers 95/91. Washington: International Monetary Fund.

Devarajan, Shantayanan, Vinaya Swaroop, and Heng-fu Zou. 1993. *What Do Governments Buy? The Composition of Public Spending and Economic Performance.* PRE Working Papers 1082. Washington: World Bank.

Easterly, William. 1990. "Endogenous Growth in Developing Countries with Government-Induced Distortions." In Vittorio Corbo, Stanley Fischer, and Steve Webb, *Policies to Restore Growth.* Washington: World Bank.

Easterly, William, and Sergio Rebelo. 1993. "Fiscal Policy and Economic Growth: An Empirical Investigation." *Journal of Monetary Economics* 32, no. 2 (November): 417-58.

Haque, Nadeem Ul, and Ratna Sahay. 1996. *Do Government Wage Cuts Close Budget Deficits?* IMF Working Papers 96/19. Washington: International Monetary Fund.

Hines, James. 1995. *Forbidden Payment: Foreign Bribery and American Business.* NBER Working Papers 5266. Cambridge, MA: National Bureau of Economic Research.

International Monetary Fund (IMF). 1995. "Official Financing for Developing Countries." *World Economic and Financial Surveys.* Washington, December.

International Monetary Fund (IMF), Fiscal Affairs Department. 1995. *Unproductive Public Expenditures: A Pragmatic Approach to Policy Analysis.* Pamphlet Series 48. Washington: International Monetary Fund.

Keefer, Philip, and Stephen Knack. 1995. "Institutions and Economic Performance: Cross-Country Tests Using Alternative Institutional Measures." *Economics and Politics* 7, no. 3 (November): 207-27.

Kraay, Aart, and Caroline Van Rijckeghem. 1995. *Employment and Wages in the Public Sector—A Cross-Country Study.* IMF Working Papers 95/70. Washington: International Monetary Fund.

Krueger, Anne. 1974. "The Political Economy of the Rent-Seeking Society." *American Economic Review* 64, no. 3 (June): 291-303.

Levine, Ross, and David Renelt. 1992. "A Sensitivity Analysis of Cross-Country Growth Regressions." *American Economic Review* 82, no. 4 (September): 942-63.

Loayza, Norman. 1996. "The Economics of the Informal Sector: A Simple Model and Some Empirical Evidence from Latin America." World Bank. Photocopy.

Mauro, Paolo. 1993. Essays on Country Risk, Asset Markets and Growth. Ph.D. dissertation, Harvard University.

Mauro, Paolo. 1995. "Corruption and Growth." *Quarterly Journal of Economics* 110, no. 3 (August): 681-712.

Murphy, Kevin, Andrei Shleifer, and Robert Vishny. 1991. "Allocation of Talent: Implications for Growth." *Quarterly Journal of Economics* 106, no. 2 (May): 503-30.

Rauch, James. 1995. "Bureaucracy, Infrastructure and Economic Growth: Evidence from U.S. Cities during the Progressive Era." *American Economic Review* 85, no. 4 (September): 968-79.

Rose-Ackerman, Susan. 1978. *Corruption: A Study in Political Economy.* New York: Academic Press.

Sachs, Jeffrey, and Andrew Warner. 1995. *Natural Resource Abundance and Economic Growth.* NBER Working Papers 5398. Cambridge, MA: National Bureau of Economic Research.

Shleifer, Andrei, and Robert Vishny. 1993. "Corruption." *Quarterly Journal of Economics* 109, no. 3 (August): 599-617.

Tanzi, Vito. 1994. *Corruption, Governmental Activities and Markets.* IMF Working Papers 94/99. Washington: International Monetary Fund.

Taylor, Charles L., and Michael C. Hudson. 1972. *World Handbook of Political and Social Indicators.* New Haven, CT: Yale University Press.

Tullock, Gordon. 1967. "The Welfare Costs of Tariffs, Monopolies and Theft." *Western Economic Journal* 5 (June): 224-32.

World Bank. 1983. *World Development Report 1983.* New York: Oxford University Press.

5

Comments:
Dani Rodrik and James E. Rauch

DANI RODRIK

The fascinating papers in part I of this book focus on the causes and consequences of corruption, primarily from a domestic perspective. We learn that corruption is a multifaceted and complex phenomenon, that it is often deeply rooted in the politics of a country, and that it is measurably costly in terms of foregone investment and growth opportunities as well as in terms of equity.

How we deal with corruption, however, depends very much on *why* we think it is a problem and which of its consequences we choose to deal with. The papers from this session tell us that corruption is first and foremost a domestic problem; that is, it is mostly the people of Indonesia, Haiti, or Zaire—to pick some nonrandom examples—who suffer from the presence of corrupt bureaucrats and leaders. The social price of corruption is largely paid in local currency by local people.

This is an important, if implicit, lesson because corruption owes its current salience as an international problem not primarily to a concern about what corruption does to the domestic economy and polity, but to a concern about what it does to foreign exporters and investors. Corrupt bureaucrats have always been around, and it seems unlikely that the problem somehow has become more acute in recent years. Rather, the developing countries in which these problems are rampant have now become more prominent on the radar screens of European and American businesspeople. Meanwhile, the Foreign Corrupt Practices Act

Dani Rodrik is Rafiq Hariri Professor of International Political Economy, John F. Kennedy School of Government, Harvard University.

(FCPA), which prohibits US-based companies from engaging in certain activities deemed corrupt while abroad, has put the United States at a competitive disadvantage relative to other industrial countries. Together, these two factors go a long way toward explaining why corruption has been transformed from an "economic development" problem into an "international trade and investment" problem. We in the industrial countries now care about corruption in the developing world because we believe "their" corruption hurts us.

One might say that the fact that people are paying more attention to this issue has to be a good thing. To some extent this is true. But I will be somewhat contrarian and argue that this shift in emphasis may have some unwelcome consequences if it is not complemented by efforts aimed at the deeper, developmental challenges posed by corruption.

The trouble with viewing corruption through the lens of international trade and investment rather than through the lens of development is that the issue becomes primarily one of redistribution—whether among the industrial countries or between industrial-country exporters and developing-country importers—and of confrontation. With this emphasis, the argument against corruption loses much of its efficiency rationale. Let me illustrate with a relevant example.

Suppose a developing country with a corrupt president invites bids for a large order of jet aircraft. Consider first the implications of the FCPA. Since the president and his entourage are determined to get a kickback, the Americans soon find themselves out of the running, and the Europeans get the order. But since the president now cannot play the Europeans off against the Americans, presumably his bribe (from the Europeans) is lower than what it would have been without the FCPA. Part of the cost of bribing the president, moreover, is presumably passed on in the final price of the European aircraft.

What are the implications of this from the perspective of global welfare? If the European jets are reasonably close substitutes for the American ones (which they are), the world as a whole is no worse off: whatever the Americans and the corrupt president lose, the Europeans gain, and the developed country still gets the same number of jets. A lot of money changes hands, but the global outcome is a wash and there is little or no efficiency loss.

Now consider what would happen if the Americans managed to get the Europeans on board and all exporters agreed to stop corrupt payments. Then the next time the developing country places an order for jet aircraft, the president does not get his bribe. His loss is the joint gain of the Europeans and the Americans. But if one assumes, as is likely, that there is no domestic manufacturing capability for the jets in the developing country, and that therefore the order has to be filled either by the Americans or by the Europeans, once again the world as a whole is no better off. The effects are purely redistributive.

Finally, consider what would happen if the corrupt president were overthrown and a clean government took over. Since the European and American exporters have already sworn off paying bribes, they are no better off. They may in fact end up worse off if the new regime, lacking a personal profit motive in the transaction, decides to order fewer aircraft. The primary beneficiaries, of course, are the people of the developing country.

This example suggests a number of things. First and foremost, the primary economic concern raised by corruption at the *international* level is often a distributive concern rather than an efficiency concern. This puts corruption as a trade issue in the same category as, for example, trade-related intellectual property rights (TRIPs) during the Uruguay Round and makes it quite different from the bread-and-butter concerns of the GATT/WTO system, such as reducing trade barriers. The example also suggests that the statement that I suspect we will now hear too often, namely—that "corruption is a tax on foreign exporters and investors, and hence acts as a trade and investment barrier,"—is misleading. For one thing, corruption is nondiscriminatory in a trade sense, in that domestic as well as foreign transactions are subject to it. In addition, as the aircraft example highlights, corruption need not be distorting in the sense that it reduces economic efficiency.

If we still wish to address corruption as an international trade and investment issue, a more appropriate justification may be found in terms of the fairness and morality of the practices and procedures that govern international transactions. Practices that violate ethical norms held within at least one of the countries party to trade undermine the legitimacy of trade itself and erode confidence in markets. This is a perfectly sound basis for international concern. Fairness and morality are not things that economists talk much about, but we should not lose sight of the fact that the FCPA itself was motivated by post-Watergate ethical concerns and that many (if not most) US, European, and Japanese businesspeople would agree that they would rather not engage in practices considered ethically repugnant in their home countries. This may be the more solid argument for cracking down on corruption in international trade and investment.

However, an ethics-based approach to corruption as an international problem opens a Pandora's box of complications, some of which may well end up embarrassing the same US and European businesspeople now advocating strict international controls on corrupt practices. Once it becomes legitimate to criticize developing countries for behavior that offends industrial-country businesses, what is to prevent other groups in the industrial countries from broadening the scope of the discussion to include similar matters of concern to them? Think, for example, of labor standards. Countless governments have signed the relevant International Labor Organization (ILO) conventions on child labor yet fail to enforce them rigorously and therefore are violating domestic laws as well as international obligations. Is there any real difference, one might ask, between extending WTO authority to goods produced by child labor and extending it to corrupt trade practices? What is the difference between the United States imposing trade restrictions on countries with labor practices that would be considered odious in the United States and imposing sanctions on countries with rampant corruption? Yet how many businesspeople would feel comfortable with the extension of the WTO's mandate or the use of the Super 301 for provisions of US trade law to address concerns over labor standards? On both these matters, the opposition of the Republicans in Congress leaves little doubt as to where the US business community stands.

I choose labor standards only as an example. A similar analogy can be drawn with respect to trade with highly repressive, authoritarian regimes. How many industrial-country businesspeople would want their own countries' trade policy (or the WTO) to meddle with trade and investment flows on the grounds that some political regimes deny civil and political rights to their citizens?

To recapitulate, I am as much against corruption as the next person. But I think corruption is a developmental problem, not a trade problem. The way to deal with it is through improved governance and better incentives in the developing countries themselves. I am all for corporate codes of conduct and legislation such as the FCPA that prevent home-country firms from partaking in corrupt practices wherever they do business. To the extent that international involvement is likely to be helpful, it is agencies such as the World Bank and bilateral aid groups that can and should make a difference.

But when I hear that corruption may be an agenda item for the next WTO ministerial meeting, or when the US trade representative starts talking of corruption as an unfair trade practice that could cost US companies $40 billion in foregone revenues, I become nervous. I fear that what drives these new demands is a battle for market shares rather than a genuine concern for global welfare. I worry that we will begin to confuse the huge developmental problem that corruption truly is with the problems that corruption causes for international commerce and that we will start to use the former as an excuse for the kind of trade initiatives I have just cited. The risk in viewing corruption through the lens of international trade and investment, in my view, is that doing so diverts attention from the serious issues raised in this book and turns the debate into an us-versus-them conflict between the industrial and the developing world. And I fear that this is much less likely to prove productive toward the ultimate goal of fighting corruption.

JAMES E. RAUCH

I will take as my point of departure Susan Rose-Ackerman's paper (chapter 2), although some of what I have to say will be closely related to the quantitative work of Paolo Mauro (chapter 4). I will first discuss bribery in the awarding of government contracts and then discuss my own research on the influence of bureaucratic career paths on bureaucratic corruption more generally.

Bribery in Awarding of Government Contracts

Bribery, or influence peddling, in the awarding of government contracts is common even in the most advanced industrial countries. There is often a fuzzy line between illegal bribery and legal political contributions. In the country with which I am most familiar, the United States, incidents of choosing contractors on the basis of campaign contributions (usually legal) can be observed all the way from municipalities up to the federal government.[1] A related form of influence peddling that does not involve bribery is the "revolving door" phenomenon, in which government officials leave office and join private firms that then bid on contracts from the government agencies for which the officials formerly worked. In the United States this practice is considered potentially corrupting, and laws attempting to control it include a "lifetime ban on all former executive branch employees from lobbying on matters in which they were 'personally and substantially involved' while in office" and "a two-year ban on matters that were 'under their official responsibility within the year preceding termination of government service'" (Congressional Quarterly 1991, 812). In Japan, on the other hand, the revolving door is virtually institutionalized, where it is known as *amakudari*, or "descent from Heaven." In the wake of threatened bank failures and financial scandals, however, the attitude in Japan has become more similar to that in the United States: "There is already a restriction preventing bureaucrats from taking jobs in such companies [that they used to regulate] until two years after their retirement. But some in the Finance

James E. Rauch is associate professor at the Department of Economics, University of California at San Diego.

1. The US Supreme Court recently ruled, however, that punishing independent contractors by revoking their contracts for failing to show political loyalty (e.g., by giving a campaign contribution to the other candidate) is a violation of their right to free speech. Justice Antonin Scalia dissented from the ruling, arguing that political favoritism is well-entrenched in American life and should not be ruled unconstitutional (*Washington Post*, 29 June 1996, A1).

Ministry have proposed making that five years" (*New York Times*, 5 May 1996, section 1, 8).

I would argue that, in general, this kind of influence peddling, whether through bribery or the revolving door, is often functional—and is extremely difficult to control in any case and thus should perhaps not be the main focus of anticorruption efforts. But in some cases influence peddling is not functional, and I would argue that reform should be aimed at deterring these cases.

The following anecdote, which concerns *private* business practices in Japan, illustrates my thesis. The entrepreneur of a small Japanese firm was convinced he had a superior input for the production of a large Japanese firm, but he was having trouble getting the attention of that firm's purchasing manager. He therefore sent a gift (the kind that comes in a box, not cash) and an invitation to dinner. The purchasing manager accepted, and over dinner the entrepreneur was able to explain the virtues of his product and win the contract.

Why do we observe this type of business practice? I believe that the incomplete and inadequate information provided by prices for differentiated products or services is a major cause. When a reputable producer of a simple commodity such as aluminum seeks new customers, all it has to do is offer a lower price than what the prospective customers are currently paying: the customers will either switch or demand that their current supplier meet the lower price. But when the item for sale is a sophisticated sewing machine for a garment factory, a cheaper price tells the buyer little. How does the new sewing machine compare with the model already on the shop floor? At a minimum, the buyer needs to see a sample and a demonstration, and probably not only the purchasing manager but also the production managers or engineers have to see it and must form an opinion on whether to buy. The buyer may judge that the expected payoff is not worth the trouble of even considering the new product. In such circumstances, a "gift" can tip the balance, making the effort to obtain the information worth the buyer's while.

Many of the things that governments buy, such as infrastructure projects and weapons systems, are likewise highly differentiated products for which the responsible bureaucrat cannot simply accept the lowest bid. How then does the bureaucrat choose? In the case of the revolving door, the contract often goes to the bidder whose capabilities the bureaucrat knows and trusts from their period of common government service. If the bureaucrat in question is an elected official, he may also have come to know and trust the bidder's capabilities through the access the latter has previously obtained in return for a campaign contribution.

This system of bribes as "access charges" ceases to be functional when corrupt favoritism leads to nonperformance—the bridge falls down or the plane does not fly. But then the problem is the nonperformance rather than favoritism. The appropriate reform may be to tie officials' pay and career advancement to the performance of the contracts they award. (Indeed, if officials are indifferent to performance, this is a problem whether or not they take bribes.) Putting such an incentive structure in place might not be as straightforward as it sounds, but it would surely be easier than trying to deter bribery-induced favoritism, which can be concealed in myriad ways. One avoids more welfare loss with less effort.

Bureaucratic Career Paths

The career paths that bureaucrats face may be an important determinant of whether they become corrupt. Rose-Ackerman makes the important point that "higher-ups are likely to have greater freedom to create extra rents than lower level functionaries." I would argue further that high-level corruption creates a climate favorable to low-level corruption. If the head of the Department of Transportation is devoting considerable time to making sure that a new highway runs past land that he owns, that official probably will not be paying much attention to subordinates who are fixing parking tickets. It would be nice if we could count on effective political oversight to reduce high-level corruption, but often we cannot, especially in the context of developing countries.

I have argued elsewhere that the degree to which top positions are filled by promotion from within the bureaucracy can influence the level of venality of high-level officials, and thus the level of low-level corruption as well (Rauch 1995). My argument is as follows.

Many civil servants care about power as well as money. The head of the Department of Transportation may have a vision of what kind of transportation system his country should have, as well as a desire for personal gain. He will have a hard time implementing that vision if the department is full of no-show jobs and deputies are busy working out kickback schemes and the like. Such a department head will therefore spend more time supervising his subordinates to make sure they do their jobs and do not waste the department's funds, and he will have less time to create extra rents for his own consumption.

If I am correct, society is better off if department heads place a high value on the exercise of power in the sense of imposing their preferences about collective goods on the public. Assuming that one cannot rely on politicians to appoint such people, I believe that a system of promotion to department head from within the deputy ranks will increase the odds of such people becoming department heads. Those deputies motivated only by desire for wealth will want to enjoy the low-level corruption currently available to them and will want to be promoted and enjoy high-level corruption. But a power-hungry deputy will want promotion even more and can be expected to take more actions to increase his chances. Those actions will include restraining his current low-level corruption. In a bureaucracy that promotes from within, deputies who care about exercising power are thus more likely to become department heads, and it follows that department heads in such a system are more likely to care about exercising power. This creates a virtuous circle, since such department heads spend more time supervising their deputies and are thus more likely to weed out corrupt ones, leaving only those who restrain their corruption available for promotion.

Work that Peter Evans and I are doing on the influence of bureaucratic structure on bureaucratic performance is in part motivated by this argument. We are collecting data from experts on various countries on bureaucratic structure as represented by the core economic agencies. Our questionnaires cover career paths, recruitment practices, and pay. The idea is to see whether variables representing bureaucratic structure can help explain performance, including the prevalence of corruption, as measured by the indices produced by various private country risk services, such as those used by Paolo Mauro (chapter 4). We control for other variables that might be expected to influence bureaucratic performance, in particular the income and average level of education of the country.

Our definitive analysis is not yet complete, but we have some preliminary results based on incomplete data for 25 of the 35 developing countries in our targeted sample. Of six performance measures, bureaucratic structure was found to have a statistically significant and positive influence on four. Career path variables, including not only internal promotion but also security of tenure, were the most influential for the corruption performance indicator derived from the International Country Risk Guide, whereas salary and meritocratic recruitment were the most influential variables for better performance on the Business and Environmental Risk Intelligence indicator of bureaucratic delay and the Business International red tape indicator.

References

Congressional Quarterly. 1991. *Guide to Congress,* 4th ed. Washington: Congressional Quarterly.

Rauch, James E. 1995. *Choosing a Dictator: Bureaucracy and Welfare in Less Developed Polities.* NBER Working Papers No. 5196. Cambridge, MA: National Bureau of Economic Research (July).

II

OPPORTUNITIES AND OPTIONS
FOR REFORM

6

International Cooperation
to Combat Corruption

MARK PIETH

In the summer of 1996, two events signaled a major breakthrough in the development of international instruments against commercial corruption. In May 1996, at a meeting convened by the Organization for Economic Cooperation and Development (OECD), ministers of 26 major industrialized nations agreed that tax deductibility of bribes to foreign public officials should be banned.[1] Ministers also maintained that the bribery of foreign public officials should be criminalized in an effective, coordinated manner. Then in June, the heads of government of the Group of Seven (G-7) strongly backed the OECD statement at their summit in Lyon.

Until recently, European and Asian countries were reluctant to respond to repeated US initiatives against transnational bribery in international forums. For example, when the United States suggested in 1989 that the OECD examine the feasibility of an international agreement on illicit payments in international commercial transactions, the reactions of other OECD members were at best reserved. Some country representatives thought the US proposal invited a replay of the debacle at the United Nations some 15 years earlier. Off the record, other delegates at the United Nations warned there must be a hidden trade agenda behind the

---

Mark Pieth is chairman of the Organization for Economic Cooperation and Development's Working Group on Bribery in International Commercial Transactions.

1. The more diplomatic wording of the communiqué of the OECD Ministerial Council is based on language developed by OECD's Fiscal Affairs Committee that calls on member states to reexamine tax treatment with the intention of denying deductibility.

US move. It was generally maintained that the United States had maneuvered itself into a competitive disadvantage on world markets with the Foreign Corrupt Practices Act (FCPA).

With the help of active, behind-the-scenes lobbying and a shift in the focus of external policy from East-West confrontation to consensus and the globalization of markets, attitudes have changed. OECD member states now generally accept that a worldwide anticorruption policy is in the general interest and that it is necessary for establishing a level playing field for commerce. Correcting market distortions has a new urgency. At the same time, many industrialized countries are uncovering extensive domestic networks of corruption, or even entire corruption cultures, and thus have come to realize that corruption is not restricted to their relations with developing countries.

Since 1994, when the 26 OECD countries initially vowed to take concrete and meaningful steps against bribery of foreign public officials, several other international organizations—including the Council of Europe, the European Union (EU), and the Organization of American States (OAS), as well as large money-lending institutions such as the World Bank—have been reviewing their policies and developing international instruments against corruption. The International Chamber of Commerce (ICC) and other business organizations are also working on guidelines and codes of conduct.

This chapter reviews past and current international initiatives against corruption, lays out the main issues at stake, and outlines how the various organizations' work could be combined in a coherent strategy.

The Risks of International Commercial Corruption

One might ask whether the international community should expend so much effort to control and reduce corruption. It used to be standard for business representatives in industrialized countries to refer to the endemic character of corruption in many developing countries and to claim that it was not up to them to intervene and change local customs. Especially in the 1970s, some economists even argued that corruption was actually helpful to development—"the oil that keeps the engine running smoothly." Another explanation heard frequently in business circles may be more honest: that the strains of globalization and increasing international competition are so considerable that they simply cannot forego bribery as a means of last resort to keep their products in some markets.

But what might be of short-term benefit to the individual business may be quite socially detrimental on a broader scale and over the long term. It is now widely accepted that corrupt practices distort market conditions. Those with access to vital information, connections, the necessary cash, and a certain amount of ruthlessness—not the best contenders—will prevail. These additional resources cannot be treated simply as market factors, as they regularly depend on a whole series of illegal acts: falsified statements, tax evasion, and sometimes fraud may be employed in the creation of "slush funds" that support corruption. Those who fail to take such preparatory measures often turn to suppliers of cheap money, who frequently are members of organized crime entities and are only too happy to filter their criminally obtained funds (e.g., drug money) through companies that generally operate on the licit and visible markets.

The effects on the recipient side, frequently in countries of the South, are no less harmful. As in the North, corruption adversely influences decisions, perhaps leading to the wrong choice among competitors. It may even be the only reason to enter into a contract at all. Rent seeking may be the motive to buy unnecessary or inadequate equipment. There are plenty of examples from past experience in the South in which huge projects that were organized and funded by bilateral or multilateral development agencies generated millions of dollars in bribes to government officials. This often not only resulted in an explosion of foreign debt to be paid off by the next generation under conditions of austerity dictated by the same development agencies but enabled an oligarchy to stay in power for yet another decade. Thus, grand corruption is detrimental not only to the public trust, but also to the functioning of a young democracy (see chapter 2 by Rose-Ackerman and chapter 3 by Johnston for examples of the economic and political consequences of corruption).

Of course, individual businesspersons might accept that corruption generates damaging effects on a macro level, but they would excuse themselves by referring to current practice, to local traditions, and to the difficulty of doing business if they were to abstain from corruption unilaterally. Nor can these individuals be held responsible for the collapse of an entire political system, as has been observed in Italy recently. In other words, there is a free-rider problem that makes an internationally coordinated response essential. In order to achieve this, it is necessary, first, to raise collective awareness and then to enact clear rules. An unambiguous statement, that it is forbidden to bribe a foreign official, would help a great deal. It is furthermore essential to detail possible sanctions and to enforce those rules. Such action, even if taken only by the countries of the North, will have great effects in the South as well, helping to dry up the "supply side" of bribe markets. Ultimately, however, controlling corruption will require both "donor" and "recipient" countries, as well as financial centers, to coordinate this action.

A Brief History of Early International Initiatives

Discussion of policy to combat international corruption has long been treated as taboo. Even codes of ethics of multinational enterprises tried to avoid use of the term corruption by all sorts of euphemisms. Undoubtedly the United States deserves credit for breaking the ice and introducing the first legislation to combat international corruption. A series of domestic and international corruption scandals in the 1970s led to passage of the US Foreign Corrupt Practices Act (FCPA) in 1977 (see Glynn, Kobrin, and Naím, chapter 1). The rationale and effects of the FCPA are complex. Apart from a moral element, the legislation also has economic and foreign policy implications. But the approach is essentially unilateral; it is intended to protect US interests, and foreign legislation is taken into account only on a secondary level, as a possible excuse.[2]

Early international efforts against corruption began at the United Nations in the mid-1970s. The United States pushed hard in the Economic and Social Council (ECOSOC) for an international agreement on illicit payments.[3] The drafts modeled after the FCPA were, however, caught in the crossfire between North and South, with developing countries maintaining that the concept of "illicit payments" should be understood in a broad sense, including payments also made to the apartheid regime in South Africa. The UN draft also met the stern opposition of other industrialized countries, which argued that it was another US effort to extend a unilateral policy choice extraterritorially. In an atmosphere of mutual distrust, heightened by the still prevailing Cold War, the project had to be abandoned in 1979.

Despite developed-country suspicions regarding US motives, the June 1976 OECD Declaration on International Investment and Multinational Enterprises included language on transnational bribery, but this initiative was never followed up.

Finally, in parallel with the UN initiative, a special commission appointed by the ICC drafted a report on the issue, including "Recommendations to Combat Extortion and Bribery in Business Transactions," that was released on 29 November 1977. Due to controversy over some of the recommendations, and without the backing of governments, the attempt at self-regulation remained a dead letter until 1996 when a new report was approved.

The OECD Initiative, 1989-96

US officials at the OECD launched a new initiative to combat bribery of foreign officials in commercial transactions in 1989. Finally, in the spring

---

2. A 1988 amendment to the FCPA allows firms to invoke as an affirmative defense evidence that a questionable payment is legal under the laws of the country in which it was made.

3. This occurred first in the ECOSOC's Commission on Transnational Cooperation, later in the Committee on an International Agreement on Illicit Payments.

of 1994, the OECD ministers agreed on a formal recommendation calling on member states to take "effective measures to deter, prevent, and combat the bribery of foreign public officials." Two years later, OECD ministers approved a second recommendation calling on members to review tax policy and, where permitted, to remove provisions for deducting bribes as a business expense.

It may astonish that it took five years and a considerable amount of pressure to agree on a nonbinding text as general and vaguely worded as the 1994 OECD Recommendation on Corruption in Business Transactions. On the other hand, this is the first international text in which the industrialized nations vowed to take concrete steps against corruption and agreed to follow up by discussing specific measures in greater detail and by mutually evaluating the progress made on a national basis.

The progress made between 1989 and 1994 was vital for the development of international instruments against commercial corruption, not least because it demonstrated that many of the skeptics realized that such an effort was in the genuine interest of their own business communities. The reasons for the change of attitude vary from country to country. Some still-hesitant countries may have felt embarrassed to oppose anti-corruption efforts. Others have realized that common action was not so utopian after all. In a third group of states, the recent flurry of scandals made politicians realize that the general public was fed up with both domestic and international corruption. The issue gained a far more prominent role in public discourse over these five years.

However, only the future will show if the commitments are backed by sufficient conviction to ensure effective implementation. This is where the follow-up procedures contained in the recommendations become important.

The 1994 recommendation, apart from the general commitment to take meaningful steps to combat corruption, listed specific items for domestic or international cooperative action. Thus, the real significance of this text lies in the process it initiated: a follow-up mechanism with regular reviews of the steps taken by member countries to implement their commitments.

Implementation Activity

Since adoption of the 1994 recommendation, several countries have begun revising relevant domestic legislation, especially on tax treatment of bribes and on the criminalization of the bribery of foreign officials. Others have realized that existing legislation already covers the same ground, or much of it, if interpreted accordingly.

Many countries have indicated that ancillary legislation, such as laws on unfair competition or on conspiracy, could be used to fight the brib-ery of foreign officials. Britain has notified the OECD that its 1906 legislation clearly covers bribery of foreign officials. The Netherlands and most Nordic states have already drafted legislation on criminalization of bribery of foreign public officials. Japan is considering extending its unfair competition legislation to cover Japanese bribing of foreign offi-cials both abroad and in Japan. In most countries, internal working parties are discussing the issue. In several countries, such as Great Britain, Switzerland, and Norway, tax deductibility of bribes is being banned. Other countries, such as Germany, have taken steps to toughen up national legislation on corruption and might eventually cover the criminalization of international corruption.

Such changes are being recorded as part of the follow-up procedures. At the same time, the OECD has the mandate to conduct in-depth stud-ies on specific items listed in the recommendations. In 1995 and 1996, four studies were launched on the following topics:

- tax deductibility of bribes;

- criminalization of bribery of foreign public officials and of the laun-dering of the illicit proceeds of corruption;

- adjustment of bookkeeping and auditing rules to prevent corruption;

- establishing a minimal standard on public procurement as well as using access to public contracts as an incitement or sanction.

Each close-up analysis starts with a hearing of experts, followed by a report detailing the problems encountered with existing legislation in various countries and a discussion of options for change. It finishes with a draft recommendation.

The working group has gone into great detail, especially on crimi-nalization. It has so far not attempted to draft a harmonized text for national adoption; it is concerned, rather, with defining a minimal standard for all industrialized countries. Substantial leeway for imple-mentation according to local legal traditions will remain. Still, many questions need to be resolved. For instance, when defining the catego-ries of bribe recipients, the OECD could refer to the "victim" countries' law or attempt an autonomous definition of public officials. So far, the OECD has concentrated on corruption of public officials, but in view of the privatization of official functions that is occurring around the world, discussion may need to be extended to the corruption of private opera-tors at a later stage. The formerly highly politicized issue of jurisdiction is now being discussed on a more technical level. In particular, some countries restrict application of their laws to crimes committed on their territory—even if the connection to the territory may be slight (such as a cross-border facsimile transmission). Other subissues at a similar level of detail are under discussion.

The idea is that in May 1997, when the text of the recommendation of 1994 is to be reviewed in the light of recent developments (a procedure agreed upon in the recommendation itself), elements for a substantially tougher recommendation will be readily available. The OECD has not yet decided whether to seek a more binding text on corruption. It may at some point be necessary to define the minimal standard in a convention. A convention has the advantage of precision, but it lacks the flexibility of soft law and is far more time-consuming to enact and to implement. Soft law is especially effective where political will needs to be generated, as long as it follows strict monitoring procedures.

An example of the effectiveness of this process is the Financial Action Task Force on Money Laundering. This group developed ideas for controlling money laundering in just half a year and achieved implementation over five years in all the major financial centers without drafting a formal treaty. The process started with the 1988 Vienna Convention Against Illicit Traffic in Narcotic Drugs and Psychotropic Substances. This text, however, covered only a small part of the money laundering problem. The detailed proposals for preventing money laundering were developed in the task force.

Implementation of the task force's recommendations on money laundering was supported by regional initiatives such as the Council of Europe's Convention 141 on Laundering, Search, Seizure, and Confiscation of the Proceeds of Crime, achieved in 1990. That same year, the European Union also approved a directive creating binding standards to discipline activities that facilitate money laundering.[4] The OAS's Inter-American Drug Abuse Control Commission (CICAD from the Spanish) in 1992 and the United Nations in 1995 also released model texts for the prevention of money laundering.

However, the actual motor driving implementation of the task force's 1990 recommendation on money laundering has been a tough, worldwide (but still voluntary) mutual evaluation scheme. Under this mechanism, members monitor not only changes in legislation but also current practices of each member country. OECD procedures also allow for such evaluations. The way forward on the issue of corruption does not have to replicate the task force process for combatting money laundering, but it certainly will be inspired by the experience.

The 1994 OECD recommendation on corruption contains another dynamic element that allows the organization to broaden the scope of

---

4. Convention 141 ensures mutual legal assistance in confiscation cases, even where national legal concepts diverge. The EU directive transposes the regulatory recommendations of the Financial Action Task Force—for monitoring the "know your customer" policy and awareness standards—into binding law for member states. The program has since been implemented by most EU members.

international cooperation on this issue. It asks the secretariat of the OECD to consult with international organizations and international financial institutions on a joint approach. It furthermore asks the secretariat to include nonmember states in the process. This clause is especially relevant to those doing business with, or in competition with, economies in transition, especially in Southeast Asia. As a first step, the OECD hosted a worldwide symposium in March 1995. In addition, the Council of Europe, the European Union, the OAS, and the World Bank regularly attend meetings of the OECD Task Force on Bribery as observers. Mexico, Hungary, and the Czech Republic have joined the OECD, and Korea's accession was approved in late 1996. Argentina is also interested in assisting the group. The issue of further broadening participation will be taken up below in the discussion of development of a worldwide strategy.

The 1996 OECD Council Recommendation on Tax Deductibility

In 1995 and 1996 a working group of the Fiscal Affairs Committee of the OECD examined the issue of tax deductibility of bribes to foreign public officials, one of the items raised in the 1994 recommendation. After some tough negotiation, the committee suggested that the council adopt a separate recommendation calling on member states to reexamine tax treatment with the intention of denying deductibility. The recommendation was approved by the OECD Council at its meeting in April 1996 and by the ministers in May. Even if the text sounds weak, it is the first straightforward international instrument—adopted by member states— asking for a ban on tax deductibility of bribes.

At the May 1996 meeting, the ministerial council also considered the issue of criminalization of transnational bribery, as well as the laundering of such funds. The working party on bribery has been invited to present detailed suggestions both in substance and on the choice of the right instrument (recommendation or convention) at the next ministerial meeting in 1997.

These two issues are of considerable symbolic significance to a worldwide approach to corruption. Their adoption would signal an important breakthrough. That will depend, however, on the willingness of members to take the domestic actions required to implement their commitments. Close monitoring will be necessary, especially since some countries needed much convincing to subscribe to the final document.

Other International Initiatives against Corruption

As described by Glynn, Kobrin, and Naím in chapter 1, anticorruption initiatives appear to be cropping up all over the globe. I will describe some of these initiatives below, focusing on the international financial institutions (IFIs), regional organizations, and nongovernmental organizations.

International Financial Institutions

Multilateral development agencies, especially the World Bank, have long been acquainted with the risk of corrupt schemes undercutting their aims. The traditional approach on a project level has been to insist on open, competitive bidding. This has been only a partial success, however, since many ways exist to evade the controls (Moody-Stuart 1994). The World Bank and International Monetary Fund have also tried more general approaches, especially making loans conditional on structural reforms with the goal of reducing corruption. With its recent emphasis on the importance of "good governance" in development, the World Bank often requires a wide range of public-sector reform activities to increase transparency, accountability, and participation in lending countries.

As some critics point out, however, the effects of many structural reform programs have been ambiguous regarding corruption. Often the required reforms have resulted in the reduction of public servants' wages, actually pushing them into illicit means of meeting their costs of living. Bank and Fund conditionality also usually requires some degree of austerity, which is felt heavily by the population, but without always securing strict enough controls on the use of the loans. Under such conditions, corruption may undermine public support for structural reforms.

One barrier to greater IFI activism against corruption is the understanding some lending institutions have of their political neutrality. Recently, however, attitudes have begun to change, and there is currently an active discussion in the World Bank taking place on how best to prevent corruption in projects it funds. The recently revised World Bank Guidelines on Procurement reserve to the World Bank the right to declare a procurement null and void where a contract was awarded on the basis of corrupt practices (appendix 4, Guidance to Bidders, paragraph 3). The role of the World Bank in the prevention of corruption is absolutely vital. Current and expanded efforts will be a necessary counterpart to action by industrialized countries.

Regional Initiatives

Regional international organizations in Europe and the Western Hemisphere also are tackling the issue of corruption.

Following a request by the meeting of European Ministers of Justice in Malta in 1994, the Council of Europe is examining the drafting of an international convention on corruption aimed at creation of binding laws. The approach is very broad, with a definition of public and private corruption that addresses both national and international corruption. It is of special significance that this effort includes countries in Eastern Europe. The Council of Europe also has the right to invite other participants. So far, the United States, Canada, and Japan have been participating in the meetings. The secretariat has prepared two draft conventions: one conceived as a framework convention containing the general principles and another more specifically concentrating on aspects of criminal law. The group is currently working on the drafts. Further working parties of the Council of Europe have been discussing administrative and private law sanctions.

Separately, in December 1995, the European Union finalized a protocol to the Convention on the Protection of the European Communities Financial Interests that commits member countries to criminalize the corruption of European officials and of officials of the other member states. This initiative is restricted to the context of "community fraud." The approach is binding but limited *inter partes* to members. A more general convention on internal EU corruption was initiated by Italy during its presidency of the European Union in the spring of 1996.

At the regional level, the OAS has made a most impressive attempt to harmonize rules against corruption. The Inter-American Convention against Corruption was adopted at an OAS conference on 29 March 1996 in Caracas. In contrast to an earlier draft, it goes beyond a mere multilateral treaty on extradition and mutual legal assistance. It calls on member states to criminalize both national corruption and transnational bribery and makes both extraditable offenses, subject to each member's constitutional and other fundamental legal principles.

Nongovernmental Organizations

Several NGOs have also been intensifying their work on international corruption. The International Chamber of Commerce (ICC) recently reviewed its 1977 guidelines, and in March 1996 the executive board approved a revised and updated set of recommendations (see Heimann, chapter 8, for a description of the new ICC recommendations). While reminding international organizations and governments of their role, it recommends specific rules of conduct for enterprises, toughening up the language of the 1977 report. The rules are meant to be adopted in company codes, applicable also to subsidiaries. Special attention is given to handling agents to prevent them from corrupting foreign government officials.

The Interparliamentary Union at its conference in Bucharest on 13 October 1995 adopted a resolution for controlling corruption and calling for international cooperation in this field. Among other points, it recommends criminalizing the bribery of a foreign official as well as cooperation in preventing the laundering of illicit corruption proceeds.

Transparency International, the specialized NGO concentrating on the prevention of corruption, has been rather active in its brief existence. It has founded chapters all over the world, organized conferences, edited a comprehensive source book on corruption, and, above all, has developed a *renomé* as a reliable partner: it fulfills an essential liaison role between international organizations, governments, and the business communities. One of its most original ideas is the creation of "islands of integrity," in which all participants in an area or a specific market or even a large project (officials and privates) are invited to formally declare that they will not engage in corrupt practices.

Future Developments

Of course, the essential question is whether all these initiatives and activities fit together and how best to pursue a coherent strategy to reduce international corruption in a business context worldwide in the near future.

Starting from the perspective of the businessperson, I am convinced that we have to take the anxieties of the business communities seriously, especially the problem that huge public procurement contracts may be lost due to corrupt payments. To submit individual competitors to a prohibition of corruption under current circumstances means to inflict a trade disadvantage on them. Therefore, the expansion of actions against corruption has to bind all major competitors simultaneously. Orchestrating such coordinated action is what international organizations can offer in this field. I would, however, like to advocate a flexible approach—one might call it the principle of "joining the club." It involves three stages:

- securing the political determination;
- broadening the geographic scope;
- integrating the business community.

Securing the Political Will

It may seem inadequate to concentrate on the corruptors of foreign public officials, predominantly to be found in multinational companies based in the North. Such an approach is for the time being favored by the OECD, since that reflects both its membership and its mandate. I would not maintain that corresponding action is not necessary on the recipient side, both in the North and the South. However, an approach focusing on the supply side of corruption seems more feasible in the short run, given the relatively smaller number of actors.

Political resolve to combat international bribery in business trans-actions is growing. The G-7 leaders' declaration in June 1996 to support OECD efforts is a breakthrough in efforts to establish coordinated standards—at least in industrialized states. The commitment of formerly reluctant states such as France, Germany, and Japan has been essential. But a consensus on exactly what to do and how to implement it still needs to be achieved. Here, the work done in a regional context—through the OAS, the European Union, and the Council of Europe—will be very valuable because this work has generated first solutions to some difficult technical problems. Furthermore, the acceptance of multilateral measures to prevent international corruption will grow when there are regional concepts in place. There is still a certain risk in delay: some states insist on the drafting of a treaty, especially on criminalization. If the forum chosen is too regional (for example, the European Union), it will not reach the decisive markets (i.e., Southeast Asia). If, on the other hand, the forum is too wide, a replay of the UN debacle of 1979 must be anticipated. The main political challenge of the near future will be to keep up the momentum and still do some very concrete and relevant work.

It may be added at this point that backsliding into unilateralism would be detrimental to the results already achieved. It is a matter of honor for some self-respecting nations to join the efforts on their own terms. They also join because they are convinced that concerted action is preferable to blackmail. Too much pressure from one country or a group of countries could derail collective efforts.

As for the OECD, the organization's role will be to build political will and apply indirect pressure through peer review and follow-up procedures. The next step will be creation of a concrete, formal recommendation against which members, observers, and potentially other countries may be evaluated.

Broadening the Geographic Scope

Again, simultaneous efforts should be made both on the donor and recipient sides of the bribe transaction. There is no longer a clear-cut distinction between North and South, since corruption seems to be universal. Still, there are marked differences between forms of bribery limited to a specific industry (for instance, the construction industry in a Western European country) and an endemic corruption culture that affects all aspects of public life.

Even if it makes sense to coordinate actions of development and lending agencies, regional organizations such as the OAS, and economic organizations such as the OECD and WTO, there is an argument for keeping efforts by the countries of the North relatively independent of wider circles until the concepts are firmly accepted. To establish links between the OECD and WTO makes sense. As a first step, the United States suggested including commercial corruption on the agenda of the first WTO ministerial in Singapore in December 1996.

Of course, timing is key. On the subject of money laundering, the Financial Action Task Force maintained that a standard could be submitted to a much larger circle for new discussion as soon as it had been accepted by the smaller group. But the standards on corruption stand a much greater chance of being accepted by the large countries of the South if the North demonstrates its own commitment and readiness to take responsibility, part of which is the resolve to implement its own standards. This step has yet to be taken.

Integrating the Business Communities

I regard it as fundamental to include the business communities when developing a broad concept for combatting international corruption. It is a common experience in talks with responsible businesspeople to find that they strongly favor stiff sanctions against corrupt practices, provided they are applied universally, effectively, and in a coordinated way. Concepts should not be developed without consultation and without the support of the private sector. In this spirit, the OECD held a joint meeting with representatives of business organizations and of active businesspeople in its member states in the fall of 1996.

The recent ICC recommendations also clearly signal the corporate interest in cooperating with international organizations and governments. The elementary contribution by the business communities and each individual company is not only the development of company codes but of the actual compliance programs for day-to-day work.

Final Remarks

This paper has placed a special emphasis on the rationale for maintaining or creating a level playing field for commerce. It has furthermore concentrated on initiatives suggested for and by industrialized countries. This is certainly only a partial perspective. The approach has been chosen predominantly for strategic reasons. With the cooperation of industrialized countries as well as the business communities, an internationally coordinated approach could be feasible in the near future.

References

Moody-Stuart, George. 1994. *The Good Business Guide to Bribery: Grand Corruption in Third World Development.* Washington: Transparency International.

7

The Importance of Leadership in Fighting Corruption in Uganda

AUGUSTINE RUZINDANA

Africa is now the world's top development problem, and the role of corruption in development has been much debated. Uganda has undertaken significant economic and political reforms over the past decade and is showing that Africa's problems are not insurmountable. But what Uganda has done is just to stop sinking. It is not yet safely afloat; the actual conditions facing the country are still miserable and the immediate future still looks bleak. The measures the government has taken were designed to arrest the sinking process, but whether they are enough to keep the country afloat and take us to dry land is another matter. We must, therefore, be modest about our achievements; otherwise we may fail to appreciate the tremendous tasks and hurdles still facing us.

The key to success in Uganda has been a leadership that has brought political stability and peace. This has made it possible to initiate and implement a series of programs and policies for the country's economy, politics, and governance that have made democracy and a constitutional order possible. As a result, there is a new constitution that incorporates a bill of rights, a political system that does not gag anyone, the rule of law, freedom of expression, and regular elections. Full-fledged political party activities have been shelved for the time being, but democracy does not depend mainly on political organizations, which come and go. Democracy depends on the rights and freedoms enshrined in a

Augustine Ruzindana is a member of the Ugandan Parliament and serves as chairman of its Public Accounts Committee. He is also vice chairman of the Center for Basic Research's board of trustees, Kampala, and was Uganda's inspector general of government (from 1986 to 1996).

133

constitution and on how fully they are enforced and respected. In 1996 a series of elections were held: presidential elections on 9 May, parliamentary elections in June, and local government elections later in the year. By the end of 1996 Uganda could call itself a democracy, but it was not yet a developed country in any sense, despite the tremendous progress made in the last 10 years. Corruption is definitely one of the problems that impedes Uganda's rapid development.

The Roots of Corruption in Uganda

Without a short summary of the genesis of corruption in Uganda, my comments would lack reference or context. Uganda became a protected colony of the British in 1894 and gained political independence on 9 October 1962. During the colonial period, there was no possibility that the indigenous people employed in the public service could be seriously involved in corruption, as all the major decisions were made by the colonial officials. Colonialism, being based on coercion and subjugation of one people by another, was not the best school for democratic rule. Therefore, representative institutions that could criticize, exert public control, and demand accountability from public officials never developed. After independence, the new rulers took over a colonial system that was controlled by excessive use of force, and they perpetuated this colonial system rather than modifying it and making it responsive to the people. In addition, soon after independence, Uganda's leaders used the army and the police to overthrow the democratic process. The Independence Constitution was abolished and a new one was illegally promulgated, postponing elections for five years. Corruption therefore soon emerged, reflecting not merely economic greed but also the realities of political survival, since the continued support of the rulers was based on patronage, which can only be sustained by a continuous flow of favors to one's followers.

Soon after independence, many projects were initiated to fight what were considered the greatest enemies of the time: namely, poverty, ignorance, and disease. The projects required that contracts be awarded, with the attendant power to dispense favors for personal gain. Before independence, the awarding of contracts was a monopoly of colonial officials; now the holders of public office became aware of the favors they could bestow. These contracts involved the construction of roads, schools, public buildings, radio and TV stations, hotels, and so forth. The other relevant aspect of these development projects was the expansion of the public sector through the formation of numerous parastatal organizations, whose number was further increased by the expropriation of Asian properties after the expulsion of Asians in 1972 by Idi Amin.

Systems of control, accountability, and management broke down during the periods of dictatorship and chaotic rule. Instability and insecurity of job tenure resulted from the political upheavals of the time. Corruption was also exacerbated by a population expanding while the economy contracted and standards of living deteriorated. Thus within a short time after independence, corruption permeated every sphere of public life, and the population became resigned to it as inevitable. "Man eateth where he worketh" became the cynical biblical rationalization of corruption. But, in fact, corruption extended even to eating where one did not work, through supply of "air": in other words, getting paid for goods not supplied or services not rendered.

By 1986, when the government under President Yoweri Museveni came to power, corruption was generally considered to be one of the primary problems facing the country, and the population had been yearning for a clean government for a long time. In the 1980 election manifesto of the Uganda Patriotic Movement (UPM), "clean leadership" was a primary objective, distinguishing the UPM from the other political parties contesting the elections. When the leaders of the old UPM formed a new government in 1986, the public therefore expected it would implement the principles of "clean leadership" by putting in place strong measures against corruption. In fact, point 7 of the 10-point program of the new government concerned the "elimination of corruption and misuse of power" (Museveni 1985, 64):

> Africa, being a continent that is never in shortage of problems, has also the problem of corruption, particularly bribery and misuse of office to serve personal interests. Corruption is, indeed, a problem that ranks with the problems of structural distortions that we have been talking about.
>
> We have just referred to the way in which corruption can neutralize any disease-elimination programs as the medical staff invariably ensure that government drugs are diverted for private sale. Consequently the patients get underdoses which render some of the microbes resistant to those drugs and create many chronic cases.
>
> In development planning or trade, a cheaper option can be ignored in preference to a less efficient one, because the officials concerned see a chance of making a 10% illegal commission by adopting the less useful options. These types of decisions can cause distortions of great magnitude. Therefore, to enable the tackling of our backwardness, corruption must be eliminated once and for all.

Clearly, tackling the problem of corruption, which had assumed gigantic proportions, was a major priority in the government's program. Corruption had become the main channel of contact between public officials and those they supposedly served. It had totally undermined the rights of the people. Everything had become a privilege to be paid for; there were no rights. This mainly affected the poor and the financially weak, who make up the majority.

Corruption affected recruitment and promotion patterns, to the extent that the best people could not be recruited at all. Employees shunned the more socially valuable activities in favor of areas in which corruption was possible. Professionally competent officials were frustrated, intimidated, and terrorized into silence. The result was a considerable brain drain of the more qualified people, who sought areas in which they could work with satisfaction, find appreciation of their skills, and preserve their personal dignity.

Deleterious Effects of Corruption

The Museveni government had other good reasons to make fighting corruption one of its main objectives. Corruption's harmful effects have been observed for a long time in Uganda and other African countries. Several of these will be summarized here.

First, corruption leads to economic waste and inefficiency because of its effects on the allocation of available resources, whether from local or external sources. Corruption causes discriminatory dispensation of government services and the distortion of the economy through misallocation and wastage of resources. The least efficient contractor with the greatest ability to bribe may receive government contracts. Corruption, therefore, lowers the general welfare of the people by raising prices, damaging the structure of production, and reducing consumption. The economies of the countries of Africa suffer unnecessarily high prices for goods and services because the prices are inflated by the corrupt activities of political leaders and bureaucrats. When corruption determines who supplies capital investment or consumer goods and services, the cost of the bribes, "commissions," or kickbacks are usually added to the prices of the goods supplied or services rendered. If the goods, works, or services are externally funded, then corruption increases the external debt burden of the country. Furthermore, these goods, works, or services may be of a lower quality or a smaller quantity than specified because of the collusion between officials and the corrupter. Corruption may also misdirect investment or goods and services sourcing toward foreign suppliers rather than local ones because the former may be more discrete or more able to pay bribes.

Second, corruption contributes to the persistence of underdevelopment and poverty in countries that are richly endowed with natural resources and with hard-working, enterprising populations. When government diverts resources to useless, nonpriority projects that are not related to the real needs of the people, it ensures that the country concerned remains underdeveloped and poor. Corruption also quite often involves the transfer or diversion of resources or services from public to private use. The diversion sometimes entails transferring funds to foreign countries, thus causing harmful leakages from the domestic economy that further impede economic development. The fundamental needs of the people—food, shelter, health, and education—remain neglected. As a result, an artificial need for external assistance is created to make up for the corrupt, irresponsible mismanagement of locally available resources. When the external assistance received is also misused or mismanaged, the situation deteriorates further and the expected alleviation of poverty and underdevelopment is not achieved.

Third, as corruption stunts development it also exacerbates poverty. In many African countries, those who gain power for the first time are often poor, and when poor people are suddenly surrounded by the trappings and perks of power, particularly access to financial resources and the discretionary power to award contracts and favors, the resistance to corruption sometimes collapses. Having tasted the fruits of corruption, the newly corrupted rulers endeavor to make corruption systemic and self-perpetuating so that, even when a political change occurs, the new people will soon assume the legacy of those they have just replaced. In this situation, the best preventive measure is the empowerment of the ordinary people, as they are the only ones who have no stake in the continuing existence of corruption.

Fourth, corruption is an impediment to foreign investment and foreign assistance. That is why countries where corruption is endemic and institutions nonfunctional often attract only adventurers, rejects, or failures in their own societies and not the more respectable investors. All businesspeople want to make money, but they look for countries where the conditions are stable and predictable. Where everyone is grabbing, corruption cannot be calculable, and even the most money-hungry will find the situation unbearable and leave. Similarly, foreign aid will gradually be reduced until it disappears, as the donor states will not keep throwing their taxpayers' money into a bottomless pit.

Fifth, corruption distorts official decisions. The development priorities of a country may thus be neglected in favor of projects that the officials and the bribers find more personally rewarding. This is what accounts for the many projects in African countries that never got finished or that should never have been built in the first place. For example, all over Africa there are abandoned roads, factories, schools, and hospitals; there is machinery and equipment that was never installed or that does not work when installed; and there are factories and other businesses that will never be used to their optimum capacity because they were either unsuitable or far outstrip the demand for their products or services. All these unprofitable operations and transactions, which vividly testify to the harmful effects of corruption, are quite often rationalized with spurious arguments about protecting infant industries, the need for economic independence, or the national interest. It is high time that these white elephants are exposed for what they are: unfortunate miscarriages of management induced by corruption.

Thus, corruption impairs political and economic development as well as undermining administrative effectiveness and efficiency. Corruption undermines the legitimacy of political leaders and political institutions, since it brings the leadership of a country into disrepute and contempt and makes the government less able to rely on the cooperation and support of the public. Because of this loss of confidence in the political system, the government is compelled to resort to force and coercive measures to maintain public order. Corruption is an impediment to democracy because it subverts the democratic process of elections, government administration, law enforcement, and the judiciary. The resultant political instability and social unrest hinder development and may lead to violent reactions. In Africa, virtually every change of government, whether peaceful or violent, is rationalized as necessary to get rid of corrupt governments.

The Importance of Leadership and a Strong Civil Society

The period before Uganda's current government took over was a period of decay, in which systems of accountability, rule of law, independence of the judiciary, and constitutional order had broken down. It was a period of lawlessness, in which laws were applied capriciously. Government was for a long time characterized by the arbitrary actions of political leaders, military personnel, and other public officers who engaged in unlawful arrests and detention, torture, robbery, and looting with impunity. The administration of justice, law enforcement, and the judicial process was routinely interfered with. Perhaps the most important change that has taken place since the Museveni administration came to power in 1986 has been the creation of a political environment that has facilitated the success of anticorruption activities.

The views of the new leadership regarding the evils of corruption led the administration to include the elimination of corruption and abuse of power as one of its primary objectives right from the start. This is important because corruption cannot exist without the connivance—even if only passive—of the political leadership. By tolerating or even encouraging corruption, for example, or by lacking a strong will to punish those who are corrupt within its own group, the political leadership will foster corruption, and it will become uncontrollable. The backing and the political will of the leadership are required for any anticorruption strategy to succeed.

Equally important, the new government formed by the National Resistance Movement in January 1986 introduced a democratization program that in October 1995 culminated in a new constitution, which has entrenched the democratic order on a firm footing. There is now freedom of the press, and, as a result, corruption and other malpractices are exposed in numerous newspapers. Corrupt officials are also exposed in public meetings and memorandums addressed to government offices, especially that of the inspector general of government (IGG). Accountability and transparency within public administration have gradually been established over the past 10 years.

Accountability and transparency are central to good governance, and where they are lacking, corruption and misappropriation of public funds become rampant. Thus the important measures taken to curb corruption include the formation of the office of the IGG and the reactivation of the auditor general's office and the Public Accounts Committee of Parliament. Now that both the auditor general and the committee are active again, the accounting officers in the different ministries and departments are every now and then called before them to account for the funds entrusted to their management.

In addition, the Prevention of Corruption Act of 1970 confers on the director of public prosecutions, in conjunction with the police, powers of search, seizure, arrest, and interrogation of people suspected of corruption. The Penal Code also specifies penalties for different corruption offenses such as fraud, embezzlement, false accounting, and abuse of office. However, until the current administration took over, the law against corruption generally remained unenforced. These laws are now being implemented, and a number of officials have been charged in court with corruption.

The other necessary measure that has been put in place is the leadership code. The necessity for a leadership code in Uganda has been realized for a long time, but former regimes had a stake in the persistence of corruption and so they could not countenance its enactment. Such a code now provides for the annual declaration of income, assets, and liabilities by leaders. It details a minimum standard of behavior and conduct for leaders regarding gifts and other benefits in kind; possible conflicts of interest with respect to contracts and tenders in which a leader may have an interest; and the use or abuse of public property. The code also specifies the legal sanctions that may be taken against a leader who violates the provisions of the code. The aim of these measures is to emphasize the separation of public offices from private business interests.

The determination of the political leadership to fight corruption earned it the cooperation and support of the public, which is also essential to a successful anticorruption effort. When the people woke up and understood the dangers posed by corruption, they began to dictate the pace of the anticorruption activities. For example, in 1989, 121 civil servants were dismissed as a result of the outcry of the press and the public, which forced the cabinet and the Public Accounts Committee to act decisively. About half of those dismissed were customs officials. Numerous senior officials have also since been dismissed or prosecuted in response to public pressure; political leaders also have been relieved of their appointments. As long as the problem of corruption persists, the public remains dissatisfied and keeps on pressing for harsher punishments for those deemed corrupt. However, the lopsided legal machinery still greatly favors the corrupt, and this therefore is the next important area to be tackled: enacting appropriate laws to reinforce the efforts against corruption.

When the Museveni administration was formed, among the first steps taken to ensure the accommodation of different views and interests was the formation of a government of national unity. This broad-based government brought in virtually all shades of political opinion, including organizations involved in armed conflict against the previous and current governments. This was done to create a climate for peace and security, without which there cannot be democracy, there cannot be respect for human rights, there cannot be good governance, and there cannot be development. Peace and security are essential for economic development, for democracy, and for healthy politics. This is why achieving them is a top priority of this government.

Also among the first steps taken was the formation of elected local government councils, from village, urban, and city levels upward to the national level. These councils and committees are democratic structures elected by the people and are not part of the central government machinery. They select and change their own governing committees without government interference. They can object to a government official, and the government will feel obliged to remove the official. Any adult citizen is eligible for office. These councils also enjoy judicial powers in some local matters, which has helped reduce the backlog of cases in the lower courts of law. There is national consensus on the value and desirability of creating these democratic structures. Even some political organizations that were initially against them have changed their views because they realized that these councils were popular among the people.[1]

At the same time, other social groups within civil society have been encouraged to organize. Youth and women's organizations have sprung up in large numbers. Theater, arts, and drama groups have formed all over the country. Farmers, traders, industrialists, academics, students, and anybody that can be organized have all been encouraged to freely form their own associations. A vigorous Uganda Manufacturers' Association has been formed. The Bankers' Association is very active, and the number of banks and other financial institutions has more than

---

1. I have heard of some opposition from Ugandans abroad, but perhaps that is because they are not properly informed about the situation within Uganda.

doubled in a short time. Importers and exporters have organized themselves. Private human rights organizations have been formed, and they are actively exposing human rights infringements and are educating the public about their rights. Civil society is getting stronger, and therefore a sound foundation for sustainable democracy, as well as the diminution of corruption, is being laid.

The government has also embraced freedom of the press, which has led to a mushrooming of newspapers representing different views. Foreign papers, magazines, and journals freely circulate in the country. Open debate on democracy, human rights, and corruption has been taking place in the press, public meetings, schools, churches, and seminars and in clubs, bars, and other social gatherings.

Democracy cannot be simply decreed; it is a way of life in which the dignity of the individual is respected by fellow citizens and the government. But certain institutional structures, both civil and governmental, are a prerequisite for democracy to take root and thrive. This is why institution building has been taken to be one of the most important tasks in ensuring sustainable democracy and good governance. Thus, appropriate institutions to promote democracy and the type of behavior and practices that are part and parcel of a democracy have been put in place, including the Human Rights Commission, the IGG, a strengthened and more independent judiciary, and a free press.

Economic and Political Reforms

Besides the problem of rampant corruption, the Museveni government found a shattered economy and a lawless society. After independence, the economy initially thrived on coffee, cotton, tea, tobacco, copper, and tourism, but by 1986 the economy depended solely on coffee. Production in agriculture, industry, and services was very low because of lack of investment, coupled with the prevailing environment of insecurity and mismanagement. Roads, railways, and telephone services were in disrepair, and hospitals and schools lacked basic supplies. Income per capita had fallen between 1969 and 1986 by about 50 percent, and inflation was running at an annual rate of over 300 percent. The living standards of the people were very low throughout the country. This was very fertile ground for corruption; therefore, policies and strategies formulated to address the economic situation would inevitably also make the conditions less conducive to corruption.

The government responded with the following policies and strategies:

- rehabilitation of physical and social infrastructure and industrial capacity, focused on upgrading roads, railways, and industries and purchasing commercial vehicles and locomotives;

- elimination of government marketing boards, thereby allowing the introduction of producer incentives through appropriate pricing policies, the improvement of the marketing system, and increased reliance on market mechanisms;

- improved capacity utilization in industrial and agricultural processing units;

- better mobilization and allocation of public-sector resources;

- restoration of price stability and a sustainable balance of payments position;

- restoration of discipline, accountability, transparency, and efficiency in the public sector.

To implement this recovery program, the government had to address the problem of resource mobilization, in particular local and foreign financial resources. This in turn required the government to formulate policies consistent with current international economic development trends. The key reforms adopted are summarized below.

First, it was necessary to liberalize trade and foreign exchange transactions. In addition to suffering bottlenecks caused by poor infrastructure, the economy was bogged down by numerous marketing boards. Trade monopolies have since been dismantled in coffee, cotton, tea, and other products. Price subsidies have been removed, and exporters are allowed 100 percent retention of the proceeds from exports. The government also removed restrictions on the buying and selling of foreign exchange and allowed the formation of foreign exchange bureaus, thus removing the problem of accessibility to foreign exchange, which had limited commerce and industry.

Second, public enterprises had become a burden on the treasury because of their incessant need for subsidies. The government therefore decided to privatize most public enterprises, and although still in its early stages, the privatization program has made significant progress. Since its start in 1992, 36 enterprises have been privatized, 22 of them in 1995 alone. By the end of 1997, 85 percent of public enterprises will have been privatized. The privatization efforts will be further enhanced when the stock exchange becomes operational.

A third economic policy reform involved the disposition of the expropriated (nationalized) Asian properties. In its determination to protect the right to property and also to build confidence among foreign investors, the government has taken measures to resolve the issue of Asian properties expropriated by Amin. Most of the properties have been returned to their owners. For those that will not be returned, the owners will be compensated when the properties are sold. As of 10 April 1996, out of 7,226 properties that had been expropriated from Asians, 3,908 had been repossessed by previous owners, 809 had been sold, 1,181 had been found problematic (investigations are proceeding on how to handle them), and 1,328 had not yet been dealt with. It is clear, therefore, that the process of returning these properties is quite advanced, and the agency charged with managing them will soon be winding up.

Fourth, in order to overcome the problem of insufficient domestic saving, to reduce the dangerously high level of dependence on foreign assistance, and to improve the poor technological base of the country, the government enacted an Investment Code. The code eases and simplifies the regulations and procedures for investment in the economy, by both local and foreign investors. The Uganda Investment Authority (UIA) was established as a "one-stop shop" to administer the code and spare investors the problems associated with getting approvals from various ministries and agencies. The UIA has licensed new investments worth over $1 billion, and about half of these projects are in different stages of implementation. The Investment Code is under review so that some of its negative aspects—for example, revenue losses due to tax evasion by recipients of special incentives—can be ironed out.

Fifth, a number of measures have been taken to improve the performance and managerial capacity of the civil service so that policies are implemented more effectively. The public service is being strengthened through training and by appointment and promotion on merit. Other measures have included restructuring and retrenchment, reducing the civil service from around 300,000 to about 150,000. The result should be improvement in management and real increases in salaries and wages of the remaining civil servants. Indeed, from July of this year, the government is expected to pay a "living wage," provided that the efforts to mobilize domestic resources continue to be successful.

The final key reform involved decentralizing local government. For a long time, power and resources were concentrated within the central government. Central government officials at the district level were rarely supervised by their line ministries, and this led to corruption and a decline in the delivery of services, as well as a decay of physical infrastructure. The remedy has been decentralization of powers, responsibilities, functions, and resources from the central government to the districts to enable local governments to become more efficient, more accountable, more transparent, and more sensitive to the people's needs. Democratic participation and control are now possible because of this devolution of power from the center to the districts. The shift in power also reduces the opportunities for corruption at the center, because in central government there are fewer officials and diminished resources.

All of these reform measures taken together have led to significant improvements in the economy. High growth rates have occurred in agriculture, industry, tourism, transportation, and communications. Inflation has been reduced from around 300 percent in 1986 to about 5 percent currently, and the value of the Uganda shilling has been relatively stable for quite some time. GDP has been growing consistently at an average rate of 6 percent in the last 10 years. Expenditures have been targeted to key economic and social sectors, including agriculture, physical infrastructure, water, power, basic health care, and primary and secondary schools. Fiscal discipline has generally been maintained by keeping expenditures within the budget limits. Foreign exchange reserve levels are relatively healthy due mainly to the stable macroeconomic environment, which has encouraged private transfers into the country. The Uganda shilling is freely convertible, and there are no significant foreign exchange restrictions.

New Plan of Action against Corruption

Over the years the IGG has pursued an anticorruption strategy with three components: raising public awareness on the dangers and effects of corruption, preventing corruption, and receiving and investigating allegations of corruption. To enhance these efforts, a new anticorruption program covering one to three years has been worked out in conjunction with a number of other offices. The essence of this program is to strengthen and enhance ongoing efforts, not to replace them. Let me highlight some of these efforts, which correspond to the tripartite anticorruption strategy.

The public awareness program aims at educating the public about the damage caused by corruption and making them aware of their rights to government services without paying bribes; it also is intended to make officials aware of their responsibilities to the public. This program includes seminars and workshops for ministers, senior civil servants, senior local government officials, judicial officers, the police, prosecutors, and prison officials. It also makes readily available certain publications and material providing useful information: for example, standing government orders regulating the civil service, the leadership code, and relevant statutes; training materials for schools, media, and religious institutions; and radio and TV programs, theatrical performances, posters, and so on.

The preventive measures in the program include strengthening compliance within the existing systems and simplifying management procedures by reducing red tape. Senior government officials must declare their assets, as part of the supervision and enforcement of the leadership code. Effective prosecution must be followed by publicizing the successful convictions in order to show that corruption is a risky business.

The enforcement program includes applying existing laws against the corrupt, irrespective of who they are. This requires specifying a court to handle corruption, fraud, and embezzlement cases; permitting the IGG's staff to prosecute expeditiously cases investigated by the office; and random checking of public officials in order to ensure compliance with laws, rules, and regulations. It will also be necessary to review and strengthen laws relating to corruption, with respect to freezing, seizing, and confiscating the proceeds of corruption and fraud, and modification of the rules of evidence.

The success of these measures is predicated on the strengthening of relevant institutions and on better coordination and cooperation among the institutions. To this end, a National Coordinating Committee, led by the IGG and comprising departments and institutions involved in anticorruption activities, has been formed to develop and implement this anticorruption strategy. The committee should make it easier for agencies involved in similar or complementary activities to cooperate more effectively. Already, a coordinating desk has been set up in the IGG's office, and several seminars to sensitize journalists on investigative methods have been organized.

In the long run, however, the best way of guaranteeing accountability and transparency is by placing government business under public control. Control is implicit in a democratic government because government is responsible to the people. The greater the involvement of the people in public affairs, the more control is exerted on government. A leader in a nondemocratic system may be personally honest, and in fact in a democracy there may be many corrupt officials, yet democracy in general is the best guarantee of accountability, transparency, and good governance.

References

Museveni, Yoweri. 1985. *Selected Articles on the Uganda Resistance War*. Kampala: NRM Publications.

8

Combatting International Corruption: The Role of the Business Community

FRITZ F. HEIMANN

International Corruption in Perspective

Why Corruption Is Difficult to Control

To evaluate the role of corporations in combatting corruption, we must consider first why corruption is so difficult to control. Corruption is clearly a worldwide problem. It afflicts advanced industrialized economies as well as developing economies, market economies as well as government-controlled economies, states with long democratic traditions, states with authoritarian regimes, and states in transition to democracy. Scandals in Europe, Japan, and South Korea have demolished the notion that corruption is primarily a disease of the developing world.

We must also recognize that the benefits of corruption to the participants are often huge. Corrupt officials can make vastly more money by taking bribes than by being honest. For corrupt companies, paying bribes is an effective way to win orders. Bribery provides a way to beat competitors who have better technology or lower costs. The cost of bribes can often be built into selling prices. Bribes can be treated as tax-deductible business expenses in the home countries of many multinational corporations. The damage done by corruption hurts others, not the corrupt parties.

Fritz F. Heimann is Counselor to the General Counsel, General Electric Company (GE), Fairfield, CT. He is a founding member of Transparency International and is chairman of its US chapter (TI-USA). The views expressed are the author's and should not be attributed to Transparency International or to GE.

The risk of getting caught has traditionally been low. Bribes are always paid in secret, and they are usually channeled through middlemen. Governments whose leaders take large bribes rarely prosecute bribe payers. The home countries of bribe-paying companies disregard what their companies do abroad. Currently, only the United States makes bribery of foreign officials a crime.[1] Bribes are often deposited in states with bank secrecy laws. Prevailing legal systems are ill-equipped to deal with an economic world in which a company from country A bribes an official in country B using an agent from country C, and the funds are deposited in a bank in country D.

Finally, it must be recognized that Gresham's law applies to the morality of the international marketplace. Without strong deterrents, the rules of competition will be influenced by the conduct of the least scrupulous participants.

Need for Comprehensive Countermeasures

Because combatting corruption is such a difficult undertaking, there are no simple solutions. To make progress requires action on many fronts. Corruption must be attacked from both the demand side and the supply side: by private-sector initiatives, such as corporate codes of conduct; by public-sector reforms, such as more transparent procurement rules, deregulation, and privatization; by better enforcement of existing laws prohibiting bribery of domestic officials and by passage of new laws prohibiting bribery of foreign officials; by ending tax deductibility of bribes; by stricter auditing, accounting, and corporate disclosure rules; by changes in bank secrecy laws; by providing easier access to government information and greater freedom to criticize government officials; and by defining clearer conflict-of-interest and ethics rules.

The length of the anticorruption agenda appears daunting. However, as will be discussed below, different reforms reinforce each other. Once several reforms have been enacted, there will be synergistic effects that can rapidly improve conditions even in societies in which corruption has been pervasive. This is illustrated by the experience of the Hong Kong Independent Commission against Corruption. After a very difficult start, the cumulative effects of a series of reforms built on one another to transform a deeply flawed governmental system into a clean one. There appears to be an analogy to the "tipping point" phenom-

---

1. The Inter-American Convention against Corruption, signed in March 1996, calls on member states of the Organization of American States to make it a crime to bribe government officials of states that ratify the convention. Ratification and enactment of implementing laws is likely to take several years. A number of states, including the United Kingdom and Sweden, have broadly worded antibribery laws that arguably could be applied to foreign bribery. However, that has not been the practice.

enon in epidemic diseases. Efforts to control epidemics often make little progress for long periods until suddenly a tipping point is reached. Thereafter, the incidence of the disease declines rapidly.[2]

To carry forward a comprehensive reform agenda will require a broad coalition involving national governments, corporations, and international institutions such as the Organization for Economic Cooperation and Development (OECD), the Organization of American States (OAS), and the World Bank. Support will also be required from civic groups and from the media.

What to Avoid

Now that the many steps needed for an effective anticorruption strategy have been listed, it is worth noting two things to avoid. Debates about original sin or about cultural diversity lead nowhere. Both issues should be avoided by those interested in moving forward with reforms.

The argument over who is to blame for corruption derives from two irreconcilable beliefs. In one, the developing world was innocent and pure until multinational corporations brought bribery into the garden of Eden. The second sees previously upright corporations succumbing to extortion by venal officials in the developing world. But debating whether extortion came before bribery, or vice versa, ignores the obvious. Corruption, like other illicit practices performed by consenting adults, requires two willing parties. Unless both sides are willing, the illicit act will not be consummated. There is enough guilt to spread around. Such arguments not only are a waste of time, but they are also counterproductive. Attitudes are polarized, and it becomes impossible to develop consensus behind proposals for reforms, as happened when the United Nations tried to deal with corruption in the late 1970s and early 1980s.

The second mistake is the attempt to justify corruption by citing cultural diversity. Some defenders of the status quo claim that prohibiting foreign bribery is a misguided effort to impose Western moral standards on countries with different cultures and traditions. But so-called respect for cultural diversity is usually an excuse for continuing corruption, offered by those who benefit from it. There is no country in the world where bribery is legally or morally acceptable. Bribes must be paid

---

2. The program of the Hong Kong Commission initially met with strong opposition and widespread public cynicism. Only after overcoming a police riot and carrying out several successful prosecutions was public confidence established. This led to greater willingness to report abuses, which in turn resulted in improved enforcement (B. E. D. de Speville. Presentation at Transparency International's annual meeting, Mweya Lodge, Uganda, 23 April 1996).

secretly everywhere; officials resign in disgrace when their acceptance of bribes is disclosed. Clearly, bribery violates moral standards in Africa, Asia, and Latin America, just as it does in Europe or the United States.

A variation of the cultural diversity theme is the argument that standards regarding the acceptance of gifts differ greatly around the world, and that the line between gifts and bribes is hard to draw. This is partly true, but it misses the key point. The level of acceptable gifts does vary. (Pentagon officials can no longer accept inexpensive pocket calendars from contractors!) However, as General Olusegun Obasanjo, the former president of Nigeria and chairman of Transparency International's (TI) Advisory Council, has observed, the distinction between gifts and bribes is easily recognizable: a gift can be accepted openly; a bribe has to be kept secret (Olusegun Obasanjo. Presentation at Transparency International's annual meeting, Quito, Ecuador, 27 February 1994).

Corporate Codes of Conduct

There are differences of opinion about the value of corporate codes of conduct. Many in the business community believe that self-regulation is the right solution and that it is preferable to government regulation. Antibusiness groups argue that self-regulation is a sham—that only government action can be expected to curb corruption.

In my view, corporate codes are an important component of a comprehensive anticorruption program, but they are not a substitute for government controls. Both are needed, and each reinforces the other.

The New International Chamber of Commerce Rules of Conduct

In 1977 the International Chamber of Commerce (ICC) issued a report, "Extortion and Bribery in Business Transactions." This was the work of a commission chaired by Lord Shawcross, a former attorney general of Great Britain and Nuremberg prosecutor; Lloyd Cutler was the US representative. The report called for action at three levels: an international treaty to be drawn up by the UN, proposals for actions by national governments, and rules of conduct to serve as a basis for corporate self-regulation. It set an ambitious agenda, much of which remains relevant after two decades.

In one respect, the 1977 report was overly ambitious. It called for the establishment by the ICC of a panel to consider allegations of infringement of the rules of conduct. This recommendation aroused much controversy, and the panel was never established. This controversy, and the general decline of interest in corruption in the 1980s, limited the impact of the ICC program.

In response to the wave of bribery scandals in the 1990s, the ICC established a committee in 1994 to review the earlier report and make new recommendations. François Vincke of Belgium, who is general counsel of Petrofina, served as chairman; Charles Levy of Wilmer, Cutler & Pickering and I were the US participants, representing the US Council for International Business, the American affiliate of the ICC. The committee's recommendations were adopted by the ICC's Executive Board on 26 March 1996.

The 1996 report confirms the basic approach recommended in 1977: the need for comprehensive action by international bodies, by national governments, and by corporations. In key respects, the recommendations have been sharpened and strengthened. The focus for international action is shifted from the UN to the OECD. The ICC urges all governments to implement promptly the May 1994 OECD recommendation to take steps to combat international corruption (see Pieth, chapter 6). The report notes that action relating to the tax deductibility of bribes is of particular urgency. It recommends that the OECD establish close liaison with the WTO. The 1996 report also calls on the World Bank and other international financing institutions to play an active role in reducing extortion and bribery.[3]

The ICC calls for more transparent government procurement procedures, including disclosure of payments to agents. The ICC recommends that bidders on government contracts be required to provide undertakings to refrain from bribery and comply with corporate codes barring bribery. Governments are also urged to regulate the conditions under which political contributions can be made. Where contributions are permitted, legislation should be enacted requiring that payments be publicly recorded by the payers and accounted for by the recipients.

The 1996 report takes a more flexible approach on the issue of extraterritoriality. The 1977 report had urged national governments to act "within the limits of their territorial jurisdiction." The 1996 report urges governments to act "in conformity with their jurisdictional and other basic legal principles." This brings the language in line with the OECD's May 1994 recommendation.

The revised rules of conduct prohibit extortion and bribery for any purpose. This is a change from the 1977 rules, which prohibited payments only in connection with "obtaining and retaining business." Thus, corruption in judicial proceedings, in tax matters, and in environmental and other regulatory proceedings are now clearly covered by the rules.

The prohibition of bribery has been broadened to bar not only kickbacks but also other techniques, such as subcontracts and consulting agreements, that channel payments to government officials, their

---

3. At the World Bank's annual meeting in September 1996, Bank President James Wolfensohn announced that fighting the "cancer of corruption" has become a high-priority issue.

relatives, or their business associates. The provision dealing with the use of agents has been sharpened to provide that payments to agents be limited to "appropriate remuneration for legitimate services." The restriction on agents' compensation is important because large payments to agents are the most common way to channel bribes to officials. Companies are also required to take steps to ensure that agents do not pay bribes.

The financial provisions of the rules prohibit the use of "off the books" or secret accounts and call for the establishment of independent auditing systems to expose any transactions that contravene the rules of conduct. Boards of directors are to establish and maintain proper systems of control, to conduct periodic compliance reviews, and to take appropriate action against any director or employee contravening the rules. The rules also specify that political contributions may only be made in accordance with applicable law, that all requirements for public disclosure shall be fully complied with, and that all such contributions must be reported to senior corporate management.

The ICC has established a Standing Committee to promote widespread use of the rules of conduct and to stimulate cooperation between governments and world business. The committee will work with ICC national committees in 62 countries to encourage their companies to adopt the rules of conduct. The committee will also serve as an information clearinghouse and will conduct seminars designed to promote the rules of conduct. The Standing Committee will work with the OECD, the WTO, and other international organizations. It will also encourage ICC national chapters to work with their national governments to enact or strengthen legislation combatting extortion and bribery.

The new rules of conduct eliminate the panel to investigate infringements of the rules, called for in 1977 but never activated. It was concluded that such a role could not be performed effectively by a nongovernmental organization.

In promoting widespread international adoption of the rules of conduct, the ICC can make a critical contribution to the fight against corruption. Business leaders around the world would like to see an end to corruption. However, many companies are reluctant to adopt antibribery rules unilaterally as long as they believe their competitors continue to pay bribes. For that reason, the ICC program to promote widespread acceptance of the rules of conduct is crucial. Only by developing a broad consensus can the reluctance of individual companies be overcome.

Requisites for Effective Codes of Conduct

The ICC rules are a general statement of the key elements of corporate codes of conduct. The ICC recognized that individual companies must formulate codes specifically tailored to their own circumstances, including type of business, system of organization, and applicable legal rules. The US chapter of TI has recently completed a "best practices" study of anti-bribery codes of conduct and compliance programs used by American companies.[4] My discussion is based on this study.

One fundamental point needs to be stressed. Whether a code of conduct is only a fig leaf or whether it effectively governs corporate behavior depends on the compliance program the company uses. Unequivocal commitment by top management is essential. The prohibition of bribery must be more than the policy of the legal or financial department. Without strong involvement from the CEO, the policy will be undermined by cynics who prefer to believe that it is just an exercise designed to shield top management from responsibility when bribes are paid.

Prohibition of bribery At the heart of the policy must be a clear statement that the company prohibits employees, and third parties representing the company, from offering anything of value, directly or indirectly, to a government official to influence or reward an action.

Gifts and entertainment The policy should provide detailed guidelines regarding gifts and entertainment. They must conform with applicable laws and regulations, including policies of the recipient's organization and of institutions funding the transaction. Gifts and entertainment should also meet an "ordinary and reasonable" standard. This will vary for different categories of customers. One useful criterion is the newspaper test: how would it look on the front page?

Travel expenses Only reasonable and bona fide travel expenses of government officials should be reimbursed. They must be directly related to the work, and they must conform with applicable laws and regulations. Here, too, the newspaper test provides a guide to screen out frolics and diversions, such as trips to resorts and casinos.

Political contributions The starting point must be strict compliance with applicable laws and regulations regarding corporate political contributions, including disclosure requirements. These, of course, vary from country to country. In addition, the policy should prohibit arguably legal political contributions when made to influence or reward

---

4. This effort was led by Howard Aibel, who was general counsel of ITT for over two decades and is now a partner at LeBoeuf, Lamb, Green, and MacRae. Also actively involved were Jay Singh of Coopers & Lybrand; Don Zarin of Dechert, Price & Rhoads, a leading authority on the Foreign Corrupt Practices Act (FCPA); and Scott Gilbert of GE.

specific governmental acts or decisions. Circumstances and timing are likely to be critical.

Facilitating payments   The Foreign Corrupt Practices Act (FCPA) does not apply to facilitating payments: that is, small payments to low-level officials to expedite routine approvals. Most laws prohibiting bribery make no exception for such payments, yet in many places there is a wide gap between legal theory and actual practice. This poses a dilemma for corporate policymakers. Arguments can be made for a consistent, no-exceptions approach. However, it is questionable whether compliance with such a policy can realistically be expected. In places where making facilitating payments is the customary practice, it may be better to provide some administrative flexibility than to ignore the problem.

At this stage in the fight against corruption, the major objective should be to stop large bribes to politicians and senior officials. When extortion and bribery at top levels are curbed, governments can be expected to take steps to clean up petty corruption.

Internal controls and record keeping   The policy should require a system of internal controls and record keeping to ensure that company books accurately reflect its transactions. An audit committee, composed of outside directors, should oversee the structure of internal controls, the internal audit function, and the retention of outside auditors.

Sales representatives and other agents   Because bribes are customarily channeled through middlemen, the process for selecting, training, and monitoring the work of foreign sales representatives, consultants, and other agents is one of the most critical parts of a corporate compliance program. Because agents are more difficult to control than company employees, the first question should be: is it necessary to hire a sales representative? If an agent is needed, great care should be exercised in selecting someone reputable and qualified.

Written agreements   These should be signed by the agent and should explicitly prohibit bribery. It is often difficult to get the message across that the company "really means it." Many sales representatives abroad have the mind-set that codes of conduct are a charade, that the company is building a paper record to support denials of responsibility, that the agent's job is to do what it takes to get the order. It is essential that such attitudes be overcome.

Compensation arrangements   This is the key factor. Excessive payments to agents are a common way to fund bribes. The test should be whether the agent's fee represents reasonable compensation for legitimate services. Where percentage commissions are used, a sliding scale is appropriate, reducing the percentage as the value of the order increases. For example, a 5 percent commission on a $1 million order may be appropriate; 5 percent on a $1 billion order should raise red flags. Large payments to agents should require review and approval by senior management. Procurement agencies can help control abuses by requiring disclosure of all commissions paid to sales representatives and other agents.[5]

Reporting mechanisms Employees should be encouraged to report any possible violations of the antibribery policy. This must be coupled with assurances against retribution. Even though whistleblowers are well-regarded by the media and the general public, they are rarely popular within an organization.

Decision making Even a well-drafted policy will not answer all questions. There will inevitably be difficult judgment calls. Higher levels of management must become involved when such issues arise. It must be made clear that management does not want to be shielded from responsibility for controversial decisions.

The Corporate Interest in Prohibiting Foreign Corruption

Foreign bribery is contrary to the best interests of corporations because toleration of foreign bribery has an insidious effect on a company's moral climate. Even when bribing foreign officials is not a crime in the company's home country, it is a crime in the country whose officials are bribed. Therefore the bribe has to be kept secret, and subterfuges, such as off-the-books "slush funds" and masking book entries, must be used to avoid exposure.

Bribery requires all kinds of moral compromises and deceptions. Who in corporate management participates in the decision-making process and who is kept in the dark? How much is told to top officers, to corporate lawyers and accountants, and to outside auditors? Because normal corporate controls are usually bypassed, abuses are likely to occur, such as diversion of funds by middlemen or even by company employees.

There is also the risk that distinctions between foreign and domestic bribery will be ignored and slush funds for foreign bribery will be used at home. The Watergate investigation in the 1970s uncovered widespread use of US companies' foreign slush funds in the United States. This was

---

5. The World Bank, for example, now requires disclosure of all commissions paid on projects it finances.

the driving force for the passage of the FCPA. There have been recent cases involving similar practices in Germany.

Beyond the risks involved in a particular transaction, there are often unpleasant aftereffects, such as blackmail threats. Can the company terminate relations with a sales representative who paid bribes? Can the employees who were involved be laid off or denied promotions?

The epidemic of well-publicized bribery scandals during the last five years shows that the risks of getting caught have increased. Corporate and political leaders, who previously operated above the law, have been exposed and forced to resign. Corruption is no longer an area in which it pays to take chances. It behooves all responsible companies to adopt and enforce codes of conduct prohibiting bribery.

Synergy between Corporate Codes and Government Programs

In evaluating the role of corporate antibribery codes, their interplay with government programs must be considered. The effectiveness of corporate codes is enhanced by governmental measures. Similarly, corporate codes reinforce the effectiveness of government antibribery programs.

Relevant government programs include such measures as criminalizing bribery of foreign officials, ending tax deductibility of bribes, and procurement reforms. Also important are the effects of actions by international financing institutions, accounting reforms, and the role of the media.

Criminal Laws

The United States made bribery of foreign officials a crime almost 20 years ago. The widespread adoption of corporate codes of conduct prohibiting bribery was the direct result of enacting the FCPA. Corporate compliance programs have, in turn, had a multiplier effect on criminal law enforcement. For every Justice Department employee involved in enforcing the FCPA, there are scores of corporate lawyers and financial people working on compliance programs.

Anyone familiar with corporate compliance programs knows that the threat of criminal penalties has a potent influence. Even cynical managers are concerned about their personal exposure to large fines and prison terms. In any organization there will be tensions between those whose job is to get the next order and those whose job is to protect the company against unreasonable risks. The position of the latter group is clearly strengthened by the existence of criminal sanctions.

The existence of the FCPA has also provided American companies with a credible basis for rejecting extortion. Refusing to pay a bribe may result in losing an order. However, foreign officials who want to deal with American companies are prepared to accept the fact that criminal sanctions under US law effectively bar the payment of bribes.

The synergy between government enforcement and corporate compliance programs is further enhanced by the Justice Department's sentencing guidelines. These provide more lenient treatment for companies that conduct proper compliance programs. The sentencing guidelines provide a strong incentive for companies to establish compliance programs.

Tax Deductibility of Bribes

The tax treatment of bribes can also make a major difference in corporate behavior. When the tax laws treat bribes as tax-deductible business expenses, they send both a moral and a financial message.

The moral message of tax deductibility is that foreign bribes are considered legitimate business expenses. From the financial standpoint, tax deductibility means that bribery is subsidized by the government. The financial importance of tax deductibility was made clear at a June 1995 hearing in Bonn, in which I participated. A prominent German tax lawyer argued that it would be unfair to German corporations to end tax deductibility of foreign bribes because German corporate tax rates were much higher than those in the United States and in other major exporting countries. He was very upset by the idea of losing a 65 percent subsidy from the German government. It seems clear that there will be less bribery without tax subsidies.

Ending tax deductibility of bribes also introduces internal corporate constraints. Corporate tax returns must normally be signed by a company's chief financial officer (CFO), and filing a false return exposes both the company and the CFO to liability for tax fraud. This means that the company's financial people must undertake to distinguish between proper business expenses and bribes. For example, they must scrutinize payments to foreign sales representatives to determine whether the amounts can be justified as legitimate business expenses.

It has been suggested that tax deductibility of bribes should only be denied when there has been a criminal conviction of bribery. It is argued that the line between bribes and legitimate business expenses is unclear and that the tax authorities could not distinguish between the two. This argument is specious. Tax authorities constantly make distinctions between legitimate and improper business expenses—for example, in the closely related area of business entertainment deductions. When a company makes huge payments to a sales representative in connection with a contract award, and only a small fraction can be shown to have been used for legitimate activities, the conclusion is obvious.

Government policy regarding the tax treatment of bribes can have a significant effect on corporate conduct. Deductibility encourages bribery. Nondeductibility discourages bribery. The action of the Ministerial Council of the OECD on 22 May 1996 urging all OECD member countries to deny tax deductibility of bribes paid to foreign public officials is an important step forward. It should be implemented promptly by national governments.

Government Procurement Policies

There is a clear reciprocal relationship between corporate codes of conduct and government procurement practices. The use of corporate codes and compliance programs will reduce corruption in procurement. This will result in cost savings and the acquisition of better products and services. Government procurement agencies can in turn increase the use of corporate compliance programs by making their use a condition of bidding.

To accelerate government procurement reforms, Transparency International is promoting the use of "antibribery pacts," an idea proposed by Robert McNamara, former president of the World Bank. McNamara recommended that government leaders convene meetings of procurement officials and prospective bidders to develop understandings designed to prevent bribery. The objectives of these antibribery pacts are to make clear that all bidders will play by the same rules, and that there are serious risks and no rewards for briber payers. These pacts would include the following elements:

- Procurement agencies would commit to follow transparent procurement procedures and to adopt strict measures preventing extortion by government officials.

- Bidders would commit not to pay bribes and to adopt compliance programs covering their employees and agents.

- Monitoring procedures would be established with sanctions for violations, including debarment.

- Only companies signing an antibribery pact would be allowed to bid.

The detailed provisions of antibribery pacts would be tailored to meet the conditions of particular industries and of national procurement systems. Such pacts could be developed for individual projects, for all procurement by a single agency, or for all government procurement in a country. International financing agencies and organizations representing civil society could participate in developing the pacts.

International Financing Agencies

The World Bank could do the most to accelerate the widespread adoption of corporate codes of conduct if it were to require the use of such codes as a condition for bidding on the thousands of projects the Bank finances annually. The multiplier effect of this action could be further augmented because the Bank's procurement rules serve as a model for the other multilateral development banks, including the Inter-American, European, Asian, and African development banks. The Bank's practices also influence bilateral funding agencies.

The OECD's Development Assistance Committee can play a similar role, and their recent actions should be welcomed.

Accounting, Auditing, and Disclosure Requirements

Because bribery can only be conducted in secrecy, accounting rules can play a key role in curbing corruption. Under US law, the failure to maintain proper records and controls can itself become a basis for prosecution. As noted previously, the ICC rules require all financial transactions to be properly recorded and specifically prohibit secret accounts. There is also increasing pressure from corporate governance groups for independent auditing to improve public disclosure.

Financial recording and reporting requirements clearly affect the supply side of the corruption equation. They cause corporate accountants and auditors to exercise greater internal discipline. They also make prosecution easier by providing clearer accounting tracks.

The Media and Civic Society

Civic society and a free press reinforce the demand for public accountability for corruption. Otherwise, corruption is successfully swept under the rug (as occurred after the corruption scandals of the 1970s). A freer press and a more conscientious civic sector provide the best protection against that danger. Their function can be improved by providing freer access to government information and by removing restrictions on criticism of government officials.

US Role: Strengths and Limitations

The United States has gone further in combatting corruption than any other country. Tax deductibility of bribes was terminated in 1958. Bribery of foreign officials became a crime in 1977. American procurement agencies use elaborate systems to prevent corruption. These steps were taken unilaterally, in order to regulate the conduct of US companies. Even though US companies lose billions of dollars in orders each year to foreign companies that continue to pay bribes, there is no support for repealing the FCPA.

An ironic result of unilateral US reforms is that when Americans promote similar reforms abroad, our motives are called into question. It is alleged that the real motive is to promote the interests of American corporations in obtaining a level playing field. Indeed, that is clearly a motive. However, much more important interests are at stake: preventing corruption from undermining the growth of democratic institutions and market economies around the world. Opponents of antibribery initiatives also argue that the United States is engaging in moral imperialism, seeking to impose puritanical American values on people who have more tolerant traditions and enjoy giving and receiving large gifts. Even some European supporters of antibribery reforms worry whether their political effectiveness will be compromised if they are perceived as closely allied with US interests.

There are undoubtedly a range of motivations behind European concerns about the US role in combatting international corruption. However, when sincere proponents of reform express concern, it means there is a trouble spot that should not be ignored. The United States must remain a leader in the fight against corruption. But the United States must exercise discretion, evaluating carefully which US actions will promote international reforms and which will be counterproductive.

The central point is that corruption is an international problem that requires action by many countries. Progress will be made only if others agree that it is in their own interest to take action. In pounding the table about how much business American companies are losing, government and corporate leaders Americanize the problem. Only by internationalizing the problem can the United States promote solutions.

The most important reforms, including criminalization of foreign bribery and ending tax deductibility of bribes, require legislation by national governments in the major exporting states. This is best achieved through a combination of multilateral initiatives by organizations such as the OECD, the OAS, and the World Bank, as well as active support by local groups such as national chapters of Transparency International. Increased adoption of codes of conduct by foreign companies can be more effectively promoted by the ICC than by unilateral US action.

The dilemma is that international action by its nature will take time, and patience is not a common American trait. Failure to produce quick results then generates pressure for unilateral US moves to punish countries that fail to act. Some US actions, such as proposals for a more active CIA role, would almost certainly be counterproductive. Foreign opponents of reform will use allegations of CIA involvement to shift the debate from the need to curb corruption to charges of improper US interference. Foreign supporters of reform—who generally come from liberal, social democratic, church, and academic groups—would clearly be turned off by CIA involvement.

Similarly, creation of new legal rights of action in US courts with extraterritorial application will predictably stir up a hornet's nest, as it has in the Cuban context by the Helms-Burton law. Are we creating rights that are practically enforceable in US courts? What kind of counter-measures may be taken against US companies?

Conducting a successful international effort to curb corruption will re-quire political skill, persistence, and patience. Encouraging progress is being made at the OECD, the OAS, and elsewhere. The corruption issue has been successfully internationalized. Unlike the corruption scandals of the 1970s, which were uncovered by US investigations, the much more widespread scandals of the 1990s result from local investigations in many countries.

The difference in the origins of corruption scandals reflects funda-mental changes in the post-Cold War world:

- The growth of independent judiciaries has resulted in magistrates with the power to track down corrupt ministers, business leaders, and party chiefs.

- The breakdown of rigidly controlled political systems has led to dis-closures that would previously have been suppressed.

- Freedom of the press, and the accompanying investigative journal-ism, has become much more common.

- The corporate governance movement is spreading abroad and is press-ing for greater accountability.

- Whistleblowers are no longer rare birds seen only in North America.

- Transparency International has grown in just four years to a move-ment with chapters in over 60 countries.

- Perhaps most important, civil society in many countries is fed up with corruption and supports reform.

These are the reasons we now have a realistic opportunity to achieve lasting reforms. Let's not spoil it by trying to Americanize what by its nature must be an international effort.

9

Comments:
Vito Tanzi and Jules Kroll

VITO TANZI

Some years ago, the department I supervise in the International Monetary Fund (IMF), the Fiscal Affairs Department, was asked by the Ugandan government to assist it in the reform of its tax administration. The experts from the Fund soon came to the conclusion that it would be very difficult, or even impossible, to reform the existing tax administration, which was considered quite corrupt. It thus made the radical recommendation of replacing the tax administration with a totally new one. The government acted on this recommendation. It was simply easier to replace than to reform. Occasionally this same advice has been given to other countries—for example, Peru—which have followed the same strategy with good results. For customs administrations, where problems of corruption are often rampant, several countries have come to the same conclusion and some have asked private foreign companies to take over, for a period, the functions of a customs administration. This route has not yet been followed for tax administrations, which continue to rely on domestic personnel.

Augustine Ruzindana's paper reminds me of a conversation, a couple of years ago, with two senior officials from China, one of them from the tax administration. During a luncheon conversation, I had asked him whether the people I had seen driving Rolls Royces in Beijing were foreigners. He seemed a bit annoyed by my question and stated, proudly, that they were Chinese. I then asked if these people were major payers

Vito Tanzi is director of the Fiscal Affairs Department at the International Monetary Fund (IMF).

of income tax—since I had just been told of the difficulty encountered by the tax administration in identifying people with high incomes. He replied that probably they weren't. When I inquired why, I was told that it was difficult to prove that these people had an income. I then asked why the tax administration couldn't check whether they had declared incomes in past years. I was told that this was irrelevant, because they could have bought the Rolls Royces with inherited money. This anecdote supports the importance of a point made by Ruzindana, that public officials must disclose their assets when they join the government and the government must check what assets they accumulate while they have official positions. If this system works, it may identify cases in which public officials become mysteriously rich during their tenure in office. However, the system often does not work, because there are various possibilities for hiding accumulated wealth.

Some of this book's authors ask why there is so much interest in corruption now. Glynn, Kobrin, and Naím in particular discuss this issue at length and mention several reasons (chapter 1). One is globalization, which brings people from different countries into frequent contact and makes foreigners more interested in the issues of other countries. This interest is sharpened when corruption plays a role in the selection of foreign firms for domestic contracts so that the firms that do not play the game are left in the cold. This is the aspect that attracts most of the attention in the chapters by Mark Pieth and by Fritz Heimann and that has been attracting the attention of the Organization for Economic Cooperation and Development (OECD) and other organizations. Reportedly, US firms have lost tens of billions of dollars in contracts because they were prevented from giving bribes.

Globalization also contributes to the development of a more efficient market economy. The distortions created by corruption are more difficult to identify and have less of an impact on the functioning of markets when the markets are already much distorted by bad domestic policies. But in markets that are becoming more efficient and where the playing field becomes more level, the effects of corruption become more apparent. Also, because orthodox or market-oriented economics is more fashionable and more accepted now, there is much more interest in the effects of corruption on the allocation of resources and on competition. And as globalization proceeds and international competition increases, the international community becomes much more concerned with the potential for corruption to distort the playing field of international competition.

There has been some discussion about the costs and the benefits of corruption. I must confess that I have little patience for those who try to find benefits in corruption. These individuals are often addressing artificial or very unusual situations. Unfortunately, when corruption exists, it is often widespread. It affects not just some decisions or sectors but many decisions and most sectors. In these circumstances, public officials may even create the conditions (such as additional regulations) that will allow them to extract extra rents. Thus, in reality, corruption is likely to distort markets and to impose major costs on the economy.

Let me illustrate with an example. A few days ago I got a call from an acquaintance of mine from the south of Italy. This person wanted me to "recommend" her grandson for a vacant position as a musician on the provincial orchestra. She obviously believed, as many in the south of Italy do, that most public positions are allocated not through merit but through personal endorsements. Just think of an environment in which such "recommendations" and not ability could determine whether somebody is chosen to play in an orchestra! Assume that the same attitude could influence the allocation of positions not just as flutists but, say, as surgeons. In this case, the cost of corruption would not be measured just in missed musical notes but in botched operations.

The point is that once corruption becomes prevalent, it becomes impossible to confine it to areas in which it does the least damage or in which it even "oils the mechanism." It may extend to the choice of surgeons, to appointments to key official positions, to decisions regarding the safety of particular activities, to allocation of credit, and so on. In some countries, government positions are sold to the highest bidder, who can then recover the cost of getting the job once he is in the position. If a corrupt inspector, because of a bribe, approves an unsafe building or an unsafe bridge or if, because of corruption, unsafe equipment is used in sensitive activities, corruption will impose major costs on society. The same will happen if public works are undertaken just to generate bribes or if the quality of the work is very poor.

Corruption also distorts the role of the government. Elsewhere I have argued that corruption distorts the government's role in income distribution because the benefits from corruption tend to go to the better connected, who often are in the higher percentiles in the income distribution (Tanzi 1995). It certainly affects the stabilization role of the government because it tends to reduce tax revenue and to increase public spending. This happens when corrupt tax inspectors collude with taxpayers to reduce tax revenue and corrupt officials assign public benefits to individuals who are not entitled to them. Corruption also distorts the allocation of resources in other ways. In Italy, and especially in the south, before *tangentopoli*[1] some school buildings were built but were never used. And in many countries often roads are built that lead to nowhere or that benefit some important personality. The whole point of building these schools or roads is to give an opportunity to somebody to get a bribe related to the building contracts. In some cases the project may be

---

1. *Tangentopoli* means "bribe city" and is the name given to the corruption scandal that rocked Italy in recent years.

economically justified but may become much larger or more complex than it needs to be to allow a percentage of the larger cost to be transferred to some of those who authorized the work. Thus public spending not only grows, it is also unproductively spent.

In Italy and elsewhere, corruption must have had a positive impact on the size of public investment. My observations over the years in many countries have convinced me that corruption tends to swell public investments while reducing private investment. However, the increase in public investment is largely an illusion. Part of the expenditure classified as investment is, in fact, a transfer to those who have the power to make decisions.

Corruption comes in many forms. There is corruption at the highest level, including heads of state, ministers, and other senior policymakers. But there is also corruption at the bureaucratic level. Sometimes little attention is paid to the latter, although bureaucratic corruption may be prevalent even when there is little corruption at the top. (The converse is not true: it is unlikely that there are situations where corruption exists only at the top.) Corruption depends on many factors, and some of these continue to play a role even when corruption may have stopped at the highest levels. An interesting point made by Ruzindana was that in Uganda, while particular legal institutions were being created to combat corruption, there was also major reform of the economy. He has described some of these reforms. This is an extremely important aspect. If a country enacts anticorruption laws but does little else to alter the environment that promotes corruption, not much will change. There is a demand and a supply aspect to corruption. When there are many regulations and policies that are not fully objective and transparent, corruption will tend to flourish, or at least continue, even when institutions to combat it are being created.

In Italy, the political or high-level corruption originated in part from the fact that, according to some estimates, the political parties (and there were several of them) were employing tens of thousands of people to do their political work. This work involved doing favors for individuals —such as helping them in getting government jobs, pensions, scholarships, public housing, and job transfers—thus assuring their political support for the party. There was a small civil service working for the parties and somebody had to pay the cost. It could not be financed with the fees of the members of the party, which were small. So funds had to be generated in other ways. Public enterprises were pushed to make under-the-table "contributions." Those who won government contracts for public works were also pushed to "contribute," and so on. Some of these funds went to the parties; some found their way into the pockets of officials. This may imply that a system that subsidizes political parties with public funds may reduce the scope for corruption. Although campaign finance reform may not be amenable to international cooperative action, comparative international research on the relationship between corruption and the way political parties are financed would be useful.

The relationship between public-sector intervention in the economy and corruption is an aspect of the problem that has not received much attention, though Ruzindana touched on this. If the government controls financial markets, foreign trade, access to foreign exchange, and access to many goods provided at subsidized prices (such as telephones, water, electricity, credit, and imported goods), bribes will often play the role in allocating scarce goods and resources that prices are not allowed to play. An Indian official recently told me that in some parts of India, households frequently experience the loss of electricity. A few dollars "contributed" to the right employee in the electric company solves the problem immediately. The difficulty is that electricity provided at too low a price creates an extra demand and makes it possible for some employees of the electric companies to extract some rents.

There is also the problem of low wages. Wages are often mentioned as a reason for corruption or for the lack of corruption. Singapore is cited as a country in which the salaries of public officials (ministers and heads of departments) are very high to discourage corruption. At the other extreme, at the beginning of the 1980s I remember the minister of finance of Ghana telling me that the monthly wage of ministers was extremely low and not much above that of their drivers. Conditions such as these must contribute to both corruption and to attitudes that tolerate corruption. At the same time, it is important to avoid the mistake of assuming that simply changing the level of wages, without changing anything else, is enough to reduce corruption. If wages are increased but jobs are still assigned on the basis of nepotism and cronyism, and job security remains regardless of circumstances, raising the wage level will do nothing to reduce corruption. Singapore sharply raised the level of wages, but it also introduced many other changes—increasing public-sector transparency and accountability—that together sharply reduced the level of corruption. Today it is considered one of the world's least corrupt countries.

There is something that bothered me about some of the other papers in this book. My concern is similar to one that Dani Rodrik expressed. Corruption is a widespread phenomenon that generally happens *within* countries. But these authors discuss mainly the corruption that involves contracts between foreign companies and countries. This latter form of corruption is important, and I certainly do not wish to minimize it. It is good that work related to these corrupt contracts is going on. However, we should not have the illusion that eliminating this form of corruption would do much about corruption in general in these countries. At best, such elimination will solve a problem of particular relevance to industrial countries. Thus, all aspects of corruption should receive the same attention.

The last point I want to make, and a point that has been made but probably is worth repeating, is that the changes taking place in transition economies and in several developing countries undergoing structural reforms create conditions in which, in the short run, there are many possibilities for corruption on a large scale. Thus, corruption may have increased because of these changes. Maybe that is one additional reason we have become more interested in the issue of corruption. In these countries, much corruption is taking place, which, unfortunately, will give a bad name to market reform. But the changes taking place are those that reduce the opportunities for corruption in the long run.

References

Tanzi, Vito. 1995. "Corruption, Arm's Length, and Markets." In Gianluca Fiorentini and Sam Peltzman, *The Economics of Organized Crime*. Cambridge, UK: Cambridge University Press.

JULES KROLL

I would like to focus on just two points. First, it is impossible to review here all the collective wisdom this volume represents, so I would like to discuss my own experience and then try to distill one thought from that. Second, I have been preaching for a few years now about the danger in the increased activity on the part of the secret services and intelligence agencies of various countries. The intelligence community is looking for new markets, and that presents a tremendous danger that has not been focused on sufficiently. Unlike many of the other problems confronting us, this is something I believe those concerned about these corruption issues may actually be able to do something about.

The first point I would like to address is, why now? Corruption is not exactly new. Why suddenly are policymakers, academics and policy analysts, corporate affairs people, and brand-new organizations such as Transparency International involved in this noteworthy cause? This issue was raised by Moisés Naím, Patrick Glynn, Mark Pieth, and almost all the other authors.

There are three reasons, and I think we can build on those. First, when the economies of countries go through difficult times or crises—such as the savings and loan scandal in the United States, the bubble bursting and subsequent financial crisis in Japan, or the absorption of the costs of reunification in Germany—the water level in the stream gets lower, and the rocks that were always there emerge. And no one likes what they see because there is nothing to like.

In particular, where you have a free media and a democratic political system, people get very upset when these things come out. In many countries recently, governments have fallen, in part because of dissatisfaction on this issue. You find this also in countries in transition where people's hopes are dashed, or even in authoritarian political systems where people simply become fed up.

Let me give you some examples from my own experience. In the last 10 years, we have conducted investigations of "Baby Doc" Duvalier after he fled to France, Brazilian President Fernando Collor de Mello and his campaign manager, who were accused of malfeasance soon after taking office, and also the old Soviet regime to try to identify illicitly acquired assets hidden in foreign bank accounts. I could go through a litany of similar cases. Generally, the corruption was going on for a long time. And until there was either a transition to a democratic system or people simply got fed up because economic conditions were so terrible, no one was willing to do anything about it.

Jules Kroll is founder of Kroll Associates, Inc., New York, an international corporate investigations and risk management firm.

Increasingly, however, I think conditions are improving for fighting corruption. But there is another reason this issue is so prominent on the US trade agenda. Why are certain companies backing this meeting? Why are very smart, very capable people focusing on this issue now? Above all, US companies have gotten their brains beaten in over the years because of the "genius" of the Foreign Corrupt Practices Act (FCPA), which has many problems that I will not review here. As American companies have increased their global activities, particularly in the "big emerging markets" identified by the Clinton administration for special marketing attention, they are increasingly running into situations where they are not able to win contracts in certain countries—either because they're inept, inexperienced, or afraid of going to jail for violating the FCPA. As a practitioner advising clients on how to deal with corruption, I must tell you that I have seen very few benefits to my American clients of the FCPA. The gymnastics they go through, trying to stay in business and keep up with their competition, are really quite something.

But progress is being made and will continue to be made only when it is unacceptable politically for the heads of state to engage or acquiesce in this sort of behavior. You can only solve this problem, in my view, on a top-down basis. Heads of state have to take the lead in combatting corruption. That, to me, is the clearest message to come through in part II of this book. Augustine Ruzindana talked about the importance of leadership and how that made the reforms in Uganda possible. If the leadership had not changed, no change would have been possible.

Next, what is needed is focus on the part of governments, companies, and nongovernmental organizations (NGOs) interested in this subject. Fred Bergsten was able to get us all in this room—at great expense in time and money—because this is a subject whose time has arrived. I believe some organization—whether it is the Organization for Economic Cooperation and Development (OECD), Transparency International, or someone else—needs to take charge and build on the achievements that have been made.

Most important, with respect to combatting corruption in developing countries and the economies in transition, everyone else is in 14th place after the International Monetary Fund (IMF) and the World Bank. If those organizations get tough on this issue, if there is serious auditing of loans, and if the crooks that run these countries are told they will not receive any more money unless they cooperate, then this corrupt behavior will stop. It is the World Bank and the IMF that have the resources to make it work; the rest is largely symbolic from my point of view.

Let me go to my second major point. My firm employs a number of people from around the world who came out of intelligence agencies. I have enormous respect for many of these agencies around the world, including our own. But I see a very dangerous activity that has been increasing for a number of years.

As one of the authors has already pointed out, the end of the Cold War has changed the world on a number of fronts. It has permitted democracy to emerge in some countries. It has also had some, I hope temporary, negative effects. When a totalitarian regime is toppled, corruption typically does not decrease: it increases. It's every man and woman for themselves.

Also, with the end of the Cold War, in a number of intelligence agencies, employees are seeking desperately to keep their jobs. Whether it is in Russia or elsewhere in Eastern Europe, there are many smart, capable people who have done some interesting things during their lives and are now looking for work or looking for new activities so they can keep their current jobs. The CIA is looking for new "markets." Such searches are even more dangerous in countries with state enterprises. When you combine state enterprises with a secret service, with bureaucrats and politicians—and it's a closed circle—look out.

Intelligence agencies should be kept out of this business. They should be focused on other, more serious problems. I am concerned about the possibility of their activities turning into "econo-war," with countries engaging in tit-for-tat games of spying, revelation, and scandal. This could then spill over into other, more serious issues.

Those are the two basic points I wanted to make: that the time is ripe for real progress in the battle against corruption but that intelligence agencies around the world, including the US Central Intelligence Agency, should stay out of the fight.

Let me conclude by reiterating that the problem can only be solved with leadership. We have to move beyond codes and lectures on ethics. We know what has to be done. The leadership in the countries where corruption is most prevalent have to stand up against it. We ought to focus our resources on what is achievable, and, while I think what the OECD has done is wonderful, I am getting too old to wait around for the year 2020 before they pass three more amendments. What we need is more focus.

SUMMARY AND CONCLUSIONS

10

Corruption as an International Policy Problem: Overview and Recommendations

KIMBERLY ANN ELLIOTT

In just a few months in early 1997, Mexico fired its top drug-enforcement official for accepting bribes and ultimately closed the agency because it was so ridden with corruption; Ukraine's president once again declared war on corruption; Chinese Prime Minister Li Peng lamented that his country was losing ground in its war on corruption; President Kim Young Sam deplored endemic corruption in South Korea; Russian Interior Minister Anatoly Kulikov pledged to crack down on corruption and the gray economy; Pakistan's voters, disillusioned by perceptions of widespread corruption, stayed away from the polls in droves; and public schools in Washington were alleged to be rife with cronyism and nepotism.

Corruption scandals in recent years have also contributed to the downfall of governments in Ecuador, Brazil, Italy, and India. Long-entrenched ruling parties have been weakened, including Japan's Liberal Democratic Party and Mexico's Institutional Revolutionary Party. In the United States, two decades after the Watergate scandals prompted new rules regarding political contributions and the passage of the Foreign Corrupt Practices Act (FCPA), campaign finance reform has reemerged as a major political issue.

The number, variety, and importance of countries experiencing corruption scandals highlight both the complexity of this phenomenon and its prominence as a global issue. When it is pervasive and uncontrolled, corruption thwarts economic development and undermines political legitimacy. Less pervasive variants result in wasted resources, increased inequity in resource distribution, less political competition, and greater distrust of government. Creating and exploiting opportunities for bribery at high levels of government also increases the cost of government, distorts the allocation of government spending, and may dangerously lower the quality of infrastructure. Even relatively petty or routine corruption can rob government of revenues, distort economic decision making, and impose negative externalities on society, such as dirtier air and water or unsafe buildings.

The spread of democratization and market reforms should reduce corruption in the long run. In the short run, however, the opening of political systems may expose previously hidden corruption and create a perception of increased corruption, or it may allow newly empowered citizens to voice disgust more openly. Imbalances in the pace and scope of political and economic reforms may also introduce new forms of corruption or allow more virulent forms to take hold. The privatization of state-owned enterprises, for example, is thought to have been distorted by bribes or favoritism in many countries. Real or perceived increases in corruption during times of transition often threaten to undermine support for difficult reforms. Thus, whether the political and economic opening that is occurring around the world is sustained may depend on the ability of governments to do something about corruption.

Of course, corruption is not just a problem for developing countries and countries from the former Soviet bloc. The fund-raising scandals in the United States, the demise of the Christian Democratic Party in Italy, and the dissatisfaction with politics as usual in a number of Western European countries and Japan demonstrate the need for continued vigilance if democracy is to be sustained.

Increasing global integration has also elevated the importance of corruption as an international issue. The impact of corruption on economic development and political stability within countries sometimes spills over to neighboring countries or the international community more broadly. In an essay for the *Financial Times* (31 January 1997, 18), Grigory Yavlinsky warns of an extreme case in which the potential consequences of corruption and a failure of reforms in Russia could spill far beyond its borders, including "loss of control over nuclear weapons [and] nuclear materials . . . development of a breeding ground for terrorism . . . [and a] high probability of large-scale environmental disaster." The recent dismissal and arrest of General Jesús Gutiérrez Rebollo as head of Mexico's drug control agency is an all too familiar—if still shocking—example of the deep connections between corruption and international drug trafficking.

More broadly, as economic globalization grows, so does the potential impact of corruption on international flows of goods and capital. International financial institutions and bilateral assistance agencies are concerned that resources intended to assist development in poor countries be used as efficiently as possible. Developing countries are concerned that the perceptions of corruption will cause them to lag as private capital increasingly displaces official finance in many emerging markets. Government procurement, particularly related to large infrastructure projects in developing countries, has been a focus of several recent international anticorruption initiatives. Finally, US policymakers are concerned that US firms will become increasingly handicapped in international markets if their competitors continue to use bribery as a tool to win business.

This discussion underscores the difficulties facing analysts and policymakers alike in addressing corruption problems. The first task in this overview chapter is to summarize the key analytical lessons elsewhere in this volume and in the literature with particular regard to patterns of corruption that are most damaging to the domestic economic and political development of countries. This chapter also examines the potential international consequences of corruption in an increasingly integrated international economy, before turning to policy options. It examines how trends toward democratization and economic liberalization affect corruption and what types of institutional reforms may be needed to supplement these broader systemic reforms. Next comes an assessment of the international initiatives being pursued in a variety of forums, including the Organization for Economic Cooperation and Development (OECD), the international financial institutions, the Organization for American States (OAS), and the World Trade Organization (WTO). Despite the high-level attention recently given to anticorruption movements around the world, there is a danger that the momentum may flag as it did after a brief spurt of interest in the 1970s. The chapter concludes with priorities for international action to keep that from happening again.

The Many Meanings of Corruption

> Graft is what he calls it when the fellows do it who don't know which fork
> to use.   —Jack Burden in *All the King's Men*

The challenges facing corruption analysts begin with how to define it. Most people know corruption when they see it. The problem is that different people see it differently. The most commonly specified definition is something along the lines of *the abuse of public office for private gain* (Klitgaard 1991, 221; Transparency International 1995, 57-58; Shleifer and Vishny 1993, 599). But, as Johnston notes in chapter 3, the meaning of each of the elements of the definition—abuse, public office, private gain—is subject to debate. And "contention over who gets to decide what those terms mean is [often] the most important political dimension of the [corruption] problem." Ultimately, defining corruption is a social and political process, although certainly some lines may be drawn and some behaviors universally condemned.

What is clearly excluded from this definition is identical behavior that occurs entirely within the private sector. Insider dealing, bribes to secure private contracts, and other practices that might be considered corrupt are ignored in this analysis, not because their economic effects are small, but because the topic is already complex, and it need not be made even more unwieldy.[1] Both the private and public sectors may also at times be plagued by "internal" corruption—theft or fraud that is perpetrated on a firm or public agency by its employees without the involvement of an outside actor. Although graft in the public sector clearly represents "abuse of public office for private gain," it is not a major focus of this analysis, which looks more closely at corruption arising from the interaction between the public and private sectors.

Figure 1 illustrates this nexus, dividing the actors in a country into three groups: private actors, elected politicians, and nonelected public officials identified as bureaucrats and the judiciary.[2] The figure highlights the fact that sectors often expected to behave autonomously within their separate spheres in fact interact extensively. As emphasized by Johnston (chapter 3), the key difficulty lies in balancing access and autonomy so that public officials have both the information and independence necessary to promote the public interest.

In this stylization, petty corruption occurs when private actors interact with nonelected government officials, particularly lower-level, administrative bureaucrats. These transactions involve taxes, regulations, licensing requirements, and the discretionary allocation of government benefits such as subsidized housing, scholarships, and jobs. It is at the highest levels of government, where political leaders, the bureaucracy, and the private sector all interact, that grand corruption may occur. This consists of government decisions that typically cannot be made without high-level political involvement. Examples include the procurement of big-ticket items such as military equipment, civilian aircraft, or infrastructure or broad policy decisions about the allocation of credit or industrial subsidies. Distortions at both levels can arise from either economic influ-

---

1. The multibillion dollar bailout of failed savings and loan (S&L) associations in the United States in the late 1980s is a striking example of the potential public costs of private-sector corruption. Although economic forces, regulatory laxness, and the incentives for S&L executives to take excessive risks were the major factors in the crisis, the Congressional Budget Office (CBO) (1992, 12-13) cites estimates by others that fraud accounted for anywhere from 3 percent to 25 percent of the government costs of the bailout. With a total estimated cost of $180 billion, the lowest estimate of taxpayer losses due to fraud would be nearly $5.5 billion, although it may actually be much larger (CBO 1993, 6). The role of deregulation in contributing to the crisis should also serve as a cautionary note to those who would emphasize it as a remedy for corruption. The environment in which deregulation occurs is crucial.

2. This stylization ignores the fact that judges in some countries, including in some US states, are elected.

Figure 1   Types of corruption

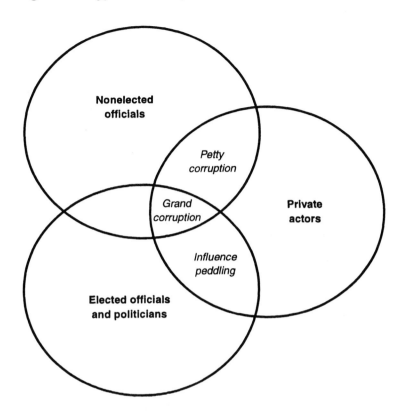

ences, such as bribes, or from personal allegiances, such as ties of family, tribe, or friendship.

At times the line dividing the licit and illicit interactions of private agents and politicians becomes blurred, as illustrated so vividly by the debate in the United States over campaign finance reform. Noonan (1984, chapter 19) discusses the difficulties in distinguishing between bribes and legal campaign contributions and the degree of reciprocity expected. He offers seven hypothetical situations ranging from a case in which a contributor gives to candidate X because he does not like candidate Y—meaning he is not rewarding X and expects nothing from him—to a case in which the contributor gives to candidate X with the expectation that X will vote a particular way on a particular piece of legislation—meaning full reciprocity is expected. In the latter case, Noonan notes that the "distinction between bribe and contribution is close to collapsing" (1984, 623). Situations like the latter, especially where contributions to top political leaders or their parties are intended to influence specific decisions, for example on defense procurements, can be labeled grand corruption. In general, however, because of the complexities involved and because campaign finance reform does not lend itself to international coordination, what is often called electoral corruption is largely ignored in this discussion.

The final area of overlap in figure 1 is between elected and non-elected government officials. The variety of interactions occurring here prevents the use of a handy shorthand for the illicit activity that might arise. One possibility is "bribe sharing," if politicians pass on proceeds from a bribe in order to influence how legislation is implemented by bureaucrats or vice versa. Similarly, a high-level elected official might share bribe proceeds with lower levels of the bureaucracy in order to fulfill an understanding arising from a bribe. Another possibility is that either bureaucrats or politicians might bribe a judge in order to avoid prosecution or reduce a penalty. Less direct exchanges might also occur, such as appointments of "friendly" judges—even relatives—with the expectation that they will treat the leadership's friends with leniency.

In each of these spheres, lines must be drawn between legitimate and illegitimate interaction. Kjellberg (1995, 342-43), for example, distinguishes four types of corruption depending on whether the transgression flouts legal, ethical, or social norms, and whether the transaction involves a direct or indirect exchange. Bribes of public officials fall into the category that is easiest to define because they are illegal in most countries and typically involve a direct exchange of money for favors. An illegal transaction involving indirect exchange, perhaps over a period of time, may be more difficult to police and to prosecute in court than a bribe, which is already difficult enough to detect given the secrecy involved. Questionable transactions in which the exchange is indirect and does not run afoul of the law will be the most difficult to discipline. An example of the latter might be the high-level attention given to a trade dispute between the United States and the European Union over bananas, following large campaign contributions by Carl Linder, head of Chiquita Bananas, to both the Democratic and Republican Parties.

In political terms, what is ultimately being sought in all these cases is influence. Each society will, through the process of political give-and-take, draw a line somewhere between licit and illicit public-private interactions. Though the divide may vary across countries and over time, both Klitgaard (1991) and Noonan (1984) note that legitimate gifts can usually be distinguished from illegitimate bribes: gifts can be given openly, bribes cannot. Similarly, Heimann (chapter 8) suggests that corporations unsure about where to draw the line should use the "newspaper test": if it would cause discomfort on appearing in tomorrow's newspaper, then don't do it.

Figure 1 illustrates just one possible set of arrangements; many alternative configurations with different implications for the predominant type or volume of corruption are possible. The relative size of the areas of overlap will vary with the relative size of government and the balance of power between the executive and legislative branches of government. The size of the overlaps reflects the potential volume of illicit transactions, but it is not necessarily indicative of the magnitude of the impact. Ideally, the figure would be three-dimensional, illustrating depth or density as well. It is possible for some forms of corruption, such as influence peddling, to be widespread but relatively shallow in impact, while others such as grand corruption may occur less often and yet have a deeper impact. Other concrete factors determining the prevalence of corruption are discussed below.

Sources of Corruption

The temptation to engage in corrupt behavior may arise whenever a public official has control over something valued by the private sector and the discretion to determine how it will be allocated (Rose-Ackerman, chapter 2). And since every government in the world spends money and taxes and regulates its citizens to one degree or another, "[w]hatever size and type of state a country chooses, the threat . . . remains" (Klitgaard 1993, 231). But as suggested in figure 1, the incidence of corruption and the predominant forms that it takes across countries might be expected to vary with the size, structure, and type of government as well as the types of activities in which it engages.

Klitgaard (1988, 75) summarizes the "basic ingredients of corruption" in the following formula:

$$\text{Corruption} = \text{Monopoly} + \text{Discretion} - \text{Accountability.}$$

Rose-Ackerman (chapter 2) discusses in detail the factors that determine the incidence and size of bribes. The aim here is to use what empirical evidence is available to look for general patterns across countries.

First, a measure of corruption across countries is needed. Since 1995, Transparency International (TI), a Berlin-based nongovernmental organization (NGO) established in 1993 to combat corruption around the world, has released rankings of countries according to how corrupt they are perceived to be. The ranking, which starts at zero for the most corrupt and goes to ten for the least corrupt, is based on a survey of surveys compiled by Professor Johann Graf Lambsdorff and is available on the Internet. Because it includes only 54 countries, however, I have added corruption ratings from a second source that covers more than 100 countries (see appendix B for more details).

As for evidence on the sources of corruption, it is difficult to measure bureaucratic discretion across countries. But quantitative indicators of potential monopoly—government size and the importance of industrial policies, trade restrictions, and other state interventions in the economy—are available for many countries. Accountability of public officials, which determines the likelihood that corruption will be punished, is more difficult to measure objectively. But accountability is derived in part from the political structure in which officials operate, and qualitative indicators of relative political openness are also available for a large number of countries.

One simple measure of the role of the state in an economy is its size. LaPalombara (1994, 338) argues that the larger the government, as measured by its share of GDP, the higher the level of expected corruption. A large government share of GDP could indicate a large bureaucracy and a lot of regulation and red tape; it might also be expected that the larger the share of national income that passes through government hands, the greater the opportunities for malfeasance. But, as LaPalombara notes, the experiences of Norway and Sweden show that high levels of government spending do not necessarily lead to higher levels of corruption. In fact, for 83 countries for which data are available, there is a strong positive correlation between low levels of corruption and the level of central government expenditure (table 1). Moreover, in the 16 most corrupt economies for which data are available, the average share of government expenditure is 21 percent of GDP, well below the 32 percent average for the sample as a whole.[3]

More important than the size of government are the types of activities in which it engages. Most obviously, a government that restricts economic competition—for example, through maintenance of trade restrictions or monopolistic state-owned enterprises—will create economic rents (profits in excess of a normal return in competitive markets) and thus greater incentives and opportunities for rent-seeking corruption.[4] Table 1 presents evidence on the correlation between corruption and the share of state-owned enterprises in nonagricultural GDP and between corruption and the openness of economies as measured by trade shares. Though simple correlations do not demonstrate causality, both coefficients offer at least some support for the hypothesis that more direct government intervention in the economy will tend to produce more corruption. By far the strongest of the correlations shown in table 1, however, is the qualitative measure of economic freedom developed

---

3. LaPalombara argues that this problem will be worse in developing countries where "the institutions of civil society that might serve as watchdogs against and brakes on corruption are very weak" (338). But there is also a positive correlation between the size of government and the relative honesty of government when higher-income countries are excluded from the sample.

4. As noted above, however, in sectors that are imperfectly competitive, collusion and rent-seeking can occur whether ownership is private or public. Similarly, fraud and white-collar crime are problems that can involve private as well as public managers.

Table 1 Quantitative and qualitative indicators of potential sources of corruption

Indicator	Number of countries for which data are available	Value of simple correlation coefficient[a]
Central government expenditure as a percentage of GDP	83	0.428
Share of state-owned enterprises in nonagricultural GDP	61	−0.299
Share of exports and imports of goods and services in GDP	98	0.240
Freedom House ranking of economic freedom	66	0.676
Freedom House ranking of political freedom	111	0.534
Per capita GDP	107	0.653

a. The coefficient measures the degree to which the indicator is correlated with the combined corruption ranking for 111 countries described in appendix B. Recall that the corruption ranking runs from 0 for the most corrupt to 10 for the least corrupt. Thus, for example, there is a positive relationship between a country's income level and how "clean" it is and a negative correlation between the role of state-owned enterprises and how clean a country is.

Source: See appendix B.

by Freedom House, which is a subjective index designed to measure in 66 countries the freedom to hold property, earn a living, operate a business, invest one's earnings, and trade internationally.[5]

Ades and Di Tella (1994) provide further evidence that the less competitive the economy the greater the opportunities for corruption. They conclude that in 55 economies in the early 1980s there was a significant negative correlation between corruption and the share of imports in GDP. They also find higher levels of corruption to be associated with qualitative measures of market dominance by a few firms and with lax antitrust enforcement in a sample of 32 countries. In a subsequent work, Ades and Di Tella (1995) find evidence that various measures of government industrial subsidies are correlated with relatively more corruption,

---

5. The Freedom House scoring of economic freedom also includes the freedom to participate in the market economy, but that part of the index is excluded because it includes a judgment on how pervasive corruption is and the degree to which it interferes with market forces. The construction of the particular form of the ranking used here is described in more detail in appendix B.

but they suggest caution in interpreting the results, again because of the very small sample size (no more than 32 countries).

Although the level of potential rents created by the government's role in the economy may be an incentive for engaging in corrupt activities, holding public officials accountable for those activities will offset the temptation. Freedom House also gauges governments for the level of political rights and civil liberties permitted and protected. This index captures some elements of transparency (media freedom) and accountability (the degree to which citizens are allowed to express their opinion through protest and the ballot box) that one would expect to find positively correlated with cleaner government. Indeed, table 1 confirms a relatively strong correlation between political openness as measured by Freedom House and lower levels of corruption. This supports Johnston's conclusion that "combating corruption and encouraging open, competitive politics can be closely allied reform goals" (chapter 3).

Other factors that may affect the opportunities for corruption include the stage of economic and political development and how development interacts with cultural tradition. This is not to suggest, as is sometimes argued, that certain cultures are inherently corrupt. Rather, the argument is that broad environmental factors—history and culture—influence the evolution of political and economic institutions, their legitimacy in the eyes of the governed, and the capacity of government to deliver the services demanded of it. Moreover, in times of transition when values, standards, and institutions are undergoing change, countries may become particularly prone to certain forms of corruption.

Table 2 lists countries perceived as more and less corrupt according to the survey of surveys compiled by TI. It is immediately obvious that in the eyes of international business, for whom and by whom these assessments and surveys are compiled, relatively more developed and richer countries are perceived to be less corrupt than poorer ones. It is likely that the differences in relative levels of corruption between developed and developing countries are somewhat overstated because of the way corruption is usually defined and measured in these surveys. Nevertheless, there are a number of reasons that developing countries might be more vulnerable to corruption and that, in turn, corruption might help to keep them poor.

Low wages are frequently cited as a source of corruption (see Ul Haque and Sahay 1996, 761). When public sector wages do not even cover subsistence, the petty bureaucrat may be expected to supplement his salary with "tips." This situation recalls the European feudal era when "public" office typically was regarded as private property, with the proceeds of office serving as remuneration for services rendered (usually loyalty to the sovereign) (Heidenheimer 1970, 10-12). Poverty is also often accompanied by illiteracy, which may make it easier for relatively more literate bureaucrats to exploit their clients. In addition to inadequate pay

Table 2 A partial profile of corruption around the world (1996 rankings)

Least corrupt (in descending order)	Most corrupt (in descending order)
New Zealand	Nigeria
Denmark	Pakistan
Sweden	Kenya
Finland	Bangladesh
Canada	China
Norway	Cameroon
Singapore	Venezuela
Switzerland	Russia/USSR
Netherlands	India
Austria	Indonesia
Ireland	Philippines
United Kingdom	Uganda
Germany	

Note: As Transparency International makes clear, these rankings should not be interpreted as saying that Nigeria is the most corrupt country in the world. The rankings are subjective assessments of business and others; they do not include all forms of corruption and they cover only 54 countries.

Source: See appendix B.

and illiteracy, other factors identified in a cross-country study of seven developing countries in East Asia were: inadequate management controls and lack of adequate technology for monitoring, poor recruitment and selection procedures, including nepotism, poor working conditions and facilities, lack of public information, and generally inadequate capacity to meet the demand for government services (Alfiler 1986, 66; Lee 1986, 101-03).

Social attitudes toward government institutions are also important. Colin Leys (1965) has argued that "new [post-colonial] states" were particularly vulnerable to corruption because "the idea of the national interest is weak . . . [because] the 'state' and its organs were identified with alien rule and were proper objects of plunder," and because corruption is easier to conceal where the rules are unclear, the commitment to them is weak, or the enforcement institutions themselves are weak (the police and judiciary, in particular). It may be that these factors put in motion a vicious cycle whereby initial, supposedly transitional, conditions facilitate corruption that further undermines the state's legitimacy and capacity, and evokes yet more corruption. This could help explain why many "new" states suffer from pervasive corruption 30 years or more after independence.

Domestic Economic Consequences of Corruption

[S]ure, there's some graft, but there's just enough to make the wheels turn without squeaking.
—Willie Stark, All the King's Men

Corruption leads to loss of much needed revenue and human talent for development, distorts priorities for public policy, and shifts scarce resources away from the public interest . . . . [P]olitical instability, corruption, and underdevelopment are mutually reinforcing.
—Stephen Ouma, Corruption in Public Policy and Its Impact on Development

While positive effects in certain situations have been claimed for corruption, most scholars agree with Ouma that widespread corruption is detrimental to economic and political development. As detailed in the papers in this volume, higher levels of corruption may lower total investment (and thus growth) and skew the allocation of government spending, particularly away from public education (see Mauro and Ruzindana). Even when relatively contained, corruption can cause inefficiency in the allocation of resources, greater inequities in income distribution, and the loss of savings and investment due to the flight abroad of proceeds from bribes (see Rose-Ackerman). In general, the consequences of corruption depend on

- the degree to which economic incentives are already distorted by government policy;

- the degree to which economic incentives are distorted or social objectives undermined by corruption; and

- the prevalence of corruption and the ability of the government to control it.

Corruption as a Second Best

Some analysts and observers argue that corruption need not be inimical to economic development. When facing an inept or understaffed bureaucracy or inefficient regulators, corruption may be a rational second-best response (see Bayley 1970, Leff 1970, and Nye 1970). Also, where the rule of law is weak, as in Russia and China today, corruption may serve as an alternative means of contract enforcement. Samuel Huntington said, "In terms of economic growth, the only thing worse than a society with a rigid, overcentralized dishonest bureaucracy is one with a rigid, overcentralized, honest bureaucracy" (1968, 498-99). In this context, bribes are often called "speed money" or "grease" and are viewed not only as reasonable but as enhancing efficiency in situations where red tape or state control of the economy may be strangling economic activity. As suggested below, however, the conditions under which corruption has positive economic effects appear to be fragile.

When the demand for government services exceeds the bureaucracy's ability to keep up, speed money, in the form of a "voluntary tax" or "tip," may be offered to a public official in exchange for faster or more efficient service.[6] This second-best solution has net positive effects for the economy as a whole, however, only if the official is constrained—by limits on discretion or political power or by careful monitoring—from introducing new delays or regulations to increase bribe collections (Rose-Ackerman, chapter 2; Alam 1990). Empirical evidence suggests the net effects are often negative. The Santhanam Committee found in its investigation of corruption in India many years ago that the "custom of speed money has become one of the most serious causes of delay and inefficiency," because bureaucrats will do nothing until paid off (cited in Myrdal 1970, 541). In Ecuador, under allegedly corrupt ex-President Abdala Bucaram, the processing time for import shipments in the port city of Guayaquil reportedly increased from two days to a month (Washington Post, 16 February 1997, A36). More broadly, Mauro (1995, 695) found in a statistical analysis of more than 60 countries that corruption is negatively correlated with investment even in the presence of large amounts of "red tape"—when corruption in the form of grease money would be expected to be most beneficial.

Corruption may also be a second-best response when a bureaucrat is bribed to ignore official duties that entail enforcement of regulations that are inefficient, duplicative, or simply unnecessary. In this case, there may also be a welfare gain. Edward Banfield (1975, 595, 23n) offers the example of the New York City construction industry, which at the time was governed by an 843-page building code that required as many as 130 permits from a variety of city departments for large projects. Banfield cites a city commission study that found that most builders typically applied for only the most important permits, often bribed officials to get those permits quickly, and then paid off the police or inspectors to avoid harassment for not having the others. The commission concluded that none of the bribes they investigated ". . . resulted from a builder's effort to get around the requirements of the building code. What was being bought and sold, an official said, was time."

While corruption in particular situations may be efficiency-enhancing, it is difficult to restrict it to only those situations. Because these transactions are usually secret, it is difficult to monitor them to ensure that the public interest is not subverted. In a competitive market with reasonably honest enforcement agencies, especially the judiciary, Rauch's "perfor-

---

6. In this case, Tilman (1970, 62) argues that corruption may be seen as "a shift from a mandatory pricing model [for government services] to a free-market model"—what he dubs "black-market bureaucracy."

mance rule" might work to ensure generally efficient outcomes (see his comment in part I). Under this "rule," if the builder does not abide by essential safety regulations and the building collapses, he will go out of business or go to jail and the corrupt inspector will also be punished. With less competition and accountability, however, both parties will be more likely to escape punishment and more tempted to cross the line, skirting regulations or standards to cut costs in ways that affect quality and are not simply timesaving. And when government benefits are allocated, what ensures that a bribe only cuts through red tape and does not divert benefits intended for "worthy" individuals to those with the ability to pay?

Misallocation and Redistribution of Resources

The supply of bribes is often linked to a desire to influence the creation or distribution of scarce government benefits or of the economic rents that often arise when government intervenes in the economy.[7] Bribes that are extorted by government officials introduce distortions by raising the cost of doing business. Whether extorted or voluntary, the degree of distortion tends to rise with the rank of the official involved and the value of the bribe (or other exchange) (see figure 2).

The distinction between bribes that are voluntarily offered or extorted is similar to the distinction in Shleifer and Vishny (1993, 601-02) between corruption involving and not involving theft. In the latter case, the official turns over the full cost of the public good or service (for example, a license) to government coffers but is able to extract additional bribes, because he is in a position to withhold the service and in effect create an artificial shortage. In this situation, competition among suppliers of public services might reduce the probability that bribes will be extorted, because the applicant can go to another official. Among those most vulnerable to extorted bribes are firms with high fixed costs and without alternative production locations, producers or brokers of perishable goods, or uneducated taxpayers or other constituents in need of government services. Firms working under contracts with fixed deadlines and penalties for delays will also be vulnerable to bribe demands.

In the case of corruption with theft, the official accepts a bribe in exchange for lowering or waiving the price of the good (for example, by influencing a tax bill), thus depriving the government of its due. As Shleifer and Vishny note, "Corruption with theft is obviously more attractive to the buyers" and competition among buyers in this type of

---

7. See Krueger (1974) and Bhagwati (1982) for analyses of the inefficiencies and wasted resources arising from "directly unproductive" efforts to capture rents created by government interventions that restrict supply or artificially depress or subsidize prices.

Figure 2 Analyzing the consequences of corruption

Degree of distortion[a]	Voluntary bribes[b]	Extorted bribes
Petty ↑ | | | | | | | | | | | | ↓ **Grand**	Paying to expedite a building permit for which seeker is eligible (speed money). Paying a building inspector to overlook a missing permit although the building is in compliance with all regulations (grease). Paying to get offspring who is on waiting list admitted to university. Paying the tax collector to lower your assessment and the customs officer to allow you to import steel beams duty-free. Paying a building inspector to overlook deficiencies in building design or construction. Paying a minister in exchange for the award of a contract to build a new hospital despite contractor's lack of experience and higher bid than competitors'.	A licensing officer holds up building permit until a bribe is paid. The building inspector threatens to levy a fine for not having a permit that builder is unaware is needed, unless a bribe is paid. The tax collector threatens to audit a company unless a bribe is paid. When building is near completion, a high-level construction ministry official threatens to have it condemned as unsafe unless a large bribe is paid.

a. These examples are intended to be illustrative. Whether a particular situation involves petty or grand corruption depends not just on the type of transaction but also on the size of the bribe and the level of the public official, which are likely to be positively correlated.

b. Voluntary does not necessarily mean enthusiastically, and, in practice, there may be a fine line between bribes offered and extorted.

case will tend to increase the level of corruption (1993, 602; see also Klitgaard 1988, 87).

Petty corruption generally refers to the routine government transactions typically overseen by middle and lower-level bureaucrats, such as tax payments, allocation of permits, and regulatory enforcement. At higher levels of the bureaucracy and among the political leadership, officials and politicians will tend to control more valuable assets or opportunities and have more discretion in their allocation. At this level, decisions are made regarding major procurements (including airplanes, military equipment, power-generating equipment, and telecommunications infrastructure) and major investment projects (including roads, irrigation projects, and dams). The greater the concentration of political power (i.e., the less

Table 3 Opportunities for and consequences of corruption

Opportunities for corruption	
Vying for government benefits Government procurement contracts, ranging from routine purchases of supplies to large infrastructure projects	Access to government services or subsidies, such as scholarships, health care, or subsidized housing
Purchases from or sales to state-owned enterprises	**Paying to avoid costs** Regulations
	Taxes
Sales of state-owned enterprises (privatization)	Prosecution (for illegal activities such as prostitution or gambling)
Access to government-controlled or regulated supplies of goods (raw materials, luxury goods, etc.), credit, foreign exchange, import and export licenses, other licenses or permits	Delays, red tape **Paying for official positions**

Consequences of corruption	
Inefficiencies Misallocation of government resources due to award of contracts to less efficient bidders	Incentives to create additional regulations or delays in order to collect bribes
Distortions in allocation of government expenditure	Lost national savings and lowered investment due to flight abroad of bribe "capital"
Distortions in allocation of privatized enterprises	**Inequities** Redistribution of assets from public sector to corrupt individuals
Inappropriate or poor quality infrastructure	Redistribution from relatively poorer to relatively wealthier individuals who are more likely to have access to government officials
Undersupply of public goods such as clean air or water	**Undermining of political legitimacy**

Sources: Rose-Ackerman (chapter 2), Johnston (chapter 3), and Mauro (chapter 4).

accountable that politicians and high-level officials are) the greater the opportunities will be to engage in corrupt behavior.

A cross-country study of administrative corruption in South Korea, Malaysia, Nepal, the Philippines, Singapore, Thailand, and Hong Kong analyzes the prevalent forms and incidence of corruption in three government functions: taxation, expenditure, and regulation (Alfiler 1986) (see also table 3 for a summary of opportunities for and consequences of corruption). The study found that bribery was the most common form of corruption (compared to nepotism and "internal" corruption, basically defined as the theft of government property). As might be expected, it found that reduction of taxes due was the primary corrupt objective in customs and other revenue collection agencies. With respect to government spending, the study found that overpricing, substandard quality, and the theft of government property for sale on the black market were the most common consequences of corruption. In the regulatory area, most of the cases look at police departments, where the most common outcome of corruption was protection of illegal vice, such as prostitution and gambling.

As Scott (1972, 66) has noted, "the pettiness of corruption refers only to the size of each transaction and not to its total impact on government income or policy." Indeed, widespread evasion of taxes including customs duties may seriously detract from the ability of the government to provide services. It is also likely to exacerbate the problem of low public-sector wages and further spread the corruption virus. Consistent with Shleifer and Vishny's analysis of corruption involving theft, the following example from Asia illustrates how competition among public officials in tax collection agencies can increase the volume of corruption:

> In Nepal, "chhoties"—customs offices situated in border areas—tried to compete with each other in attracting taxpayers. One way was to reduce their effective tax rates by charging duty only for a certain percentage of goods imported or exported. Businessmen naturally flocked to stations which charged the lowest rates. Some of these chhoties went to the extent of hiring bandits to harass traders using certain routes favorable to their competitors (Alfiler 1986, 48).

If the government is unable or unwilling to reduce expenditures, revenue shortfalls due to widespread corruption could also have severe macroeconomic consequences.

Other potential consequences of petty corruption include

- negative externalities from unenforced regulations (environmental degradation threats to worker or consumer health and safety),

- reduced government efficiency when hiring is based on favoritism rather than merit,

- shortages of subsidized necessities (due to theft and smuggling), and

- misallocation of talent from productive to nonproductive rent-seeking activities.[8]

Of course, similar illicit activities can occur at higher levels of bureaucracy. The more that higher level officials condone or engage in such behavior, the more pervasive corruption and its effects are likely to become.

---

8. For an analysis of the effects of rent-seeking opportunities on the allocation of talent, and the follow-on effects on growth, see Murphy, Shleifer, and Vishny (1993).

Certain decisions, such as those concerning government procurement and infrastructure, can only be made at higher levels of government. Even where particular projects respond to social needs, corruption may increase their costs, lower the quality, or lead to inappropriate choices of technology. (The more complex the project, the harder it is to prove that bribery rather than technical specifications determined the award of a contract.) Worse are "white elephant" projects that enrich officials and suppliers but serve little public purpose. A National Public Radio broadcast on corruption in Nigeria cited the construction of four incinerators in Lagos, none of which worked properly and which together represented considerable excess capacity (Morning Edition, 27 August 1996; see Rose-Ackerman, Ruzindana, and Tanzi for other examples).

Much of the corruption that comes to light involves white elephant projects or military procurement.[9] But data limitations and the plethora of factors determining government expenditures make it difficult to move beyond anecdotal evidence and demonstrate that in general more corrupt countries spend relatively more on these types of activities. Mauro, however, finds evidence that more corrupt countries spend relatively less on public education and perhaps less on health, though the evidence is weaker. This has two larger implications. First, some case studies have found an association between illiteracy and corruption (Alfiler 1986). Second and even more important is the contribution human capital makes to growth.

Corruption can also reduce the resources available to poor countries by facilitating capital flight or by driving away international donors. It is estimated that $60 billion left Russia between 1992 and 1996, with current capital flight continuing at $12 billion annually, almost all of it illegally (Financial Times, 14 February 1997, 3). Corruption may also contribute to capital flight because of the desire to hide illicit wealth from scrutiny or repossession, and the more uncertain the political situation, the more likely that the fruits of corruption will be stashed abroad.

The potential impact on aid flows was demonstrated in the Kenyan energy sector, which was suffering from inadequate capacity and regular power failures in 1995. "Donor allergy" had developed from what one source described as "a slap in the face of the donor community" during construction of the Turkwel Gorge dam several years earlier. The contract was awarded without competitive bidding. In the judgment of a report by the European Community, "the project ended up costing many times its original, already inflated price as a result of kickbacks paid to government officials" (Financial Times, 25 October 1995, 9). In late 1995, the Financial Times reported that international donors had not funded any power projects in Kenya for the previous five years.

---

9. Many of the deals that have been exposed as corrupt have involved military procurement.

Finally, decisions on government procurement may lead to less efficient resource allocation when bribery plays a role in the selection of the supplier. If all eligible firms are willing to bribe and have the same information, the most efficient supplier will be able to offer the highest bribe, so that corruption would have no impact on resource allocation. But some firms, including more efficient ones, may choose not to bribe or may be constrained from doing so (as US firms are by the FCPA). The secrecy surrounding corruption also makes information harder to obtain. Firms that may not be the most efficient but that spend the most time "making friends" may obtain inside information that allows them to learn how much to bid and whom and how much to bribe. Since favoritism is another common form of corruption, favored firms may also collude with officials to raise the price of winning bids while setting aside kickbacks for these cooperative officials.

Even though greater amounts of money will typically be required when individual transactions take place at the higher political and administrative levels, it is not clear that the aggregate effects of grand corruption are necessarily greater than those of petty corruption. The harassment element of petty corruption, in the form of extortion, for example, might be expected to have a broader negative effect on private economic behavior than would grand corruption, which is likely to be limited to fewer sectors. Rampant petty corruption may also be more politically corrosive over time because it affects more people on a regular basis.[10] The point is that although a little bit of high-level corruption may be more damaging to an economy than a little bit of low-level malfeasance, pervasive petty corruption may still be quite harmful. Of course, it is unlikely that petty corruption would become widespread in the absence of corruption at top levels of the government, but one should not underestimate the potential effects of low-level corruption simply because individual cases may involve small sums.

Competition, Credibility, and the Systemic Effects of Corruption

When corruption and its consequences cannot be controlled and contained, the credibility of government suffers, the security of property rights erodes, and the level of uncertainty and risk in the economy increases. If public officials cannot be relied upon to deliver on promises when bribed, or if necessary approvals for a project cannot be obtained at reasonable cost because officials at successive layers of bureaucracy demand a piece of the action, then corruption will prejudice economic activity more than if it were controlled and promises were credible.

---

10. I thank Michael Johnston for emphasizing this point. Also see Klitgaard (1988, 47-49).

Shleifer and Vishny (1993) analyze corruption markets that are monopolistic, competitive, or made up of independent monopolists. When the market structure is monopolistic, a king, dictator, or ruling party (for example the Communist Party in the old Soviet Union) is able to organize the market and ensure both predictability—it is known who must be bribed and by how much—and security of property rights over government goods or services once the bribes are paid. When the market among public officials is competitive, constituents shop around until they find an honest official and avoid paying a bribe. In the real world, however, a business owner or investor often needs several permits from more than one agency. If the public officials in this case act as independent monopolists, each setting a bribe price with no regard for what the others are doing, the total cost of the bribes will not be known in advance and may escalate to a level where the planned project becomes unprofitable. The problem will be particularly acute if there is free entry into the bribe market; that is, if bureaucrats can create new rules or regulations in order to get in on the action. In this case uncertainty is greater and property rights are not secure. Under these circumstances, economic activity that requires interaction with the government will either move into the informal sector, move abroad (or to another city or region), or in extreme cases, such as in Russia today, "mafias" may move in to provide the protection for property rights and contract enforcement that the government cannot.

This analysis provides the backdrop for the empirical evidence presented by Mauro (chapter 4, also 1995) on the impact of corruption on investment and growth. The cross-country data that are available do not clearly distinguish between corruption with and without "theft" or whether it is of the petty or grand variety. However the rankings that Mauro and others have used to study the effects of corruption typically attempt to measure the prevalence of corruption in a country. Thus, these assessments could be considered as indicative of the degree to which corruption is or is not controlled.

As might be expected from Shleifer and Vishny's model, Mauro finds that higher levels of corruption have a significant and negative correlation with lower levels of gross domestic investment. More recently, Wei (1997) also attributes a large negative impact on foreign direct investment (FDI) to corruption.[11] One problem in interpreting these results arises if corruption is endogenous to economic conditions; that is, the observed lower levels of investment are due to the effects of poverty

---

11. Wei, using the data on corruption from Mauro (1995) and data on FDI flows from 14 source countries into 45 host countries, finds that an increase in the level of corruption from that of Singapore to that of Mexico is equivalent to a 21 percentage point increase in the tax rate on multinationals. In his results, a one percentage point increase in the tax rate is associated with roughly a five percent reduction in FDI.

rather than corruption. In many cases, however, the causality is likely to run in both directions, with corruption and poverty reinforcing one another.[12]

While the negative relationship between corruption and investment may hold in general, some analysts argue that, in countries where the rule of law is weak, corruption may substitute for other forms of contract enforcement and *decrease* uncertainty for investors. Betancourt (1995) argues that China, as it undergoes the transition to a market economy, may benefit in the short run from corruption as a substitute for legal forms of contract enforcement. Wei observes that China in recent years has become the largest recipient of FDI among developing countries, and he argues that China may be a special case, because of the large proportion of its FDI from overseas Chinese. He notes that "overseas Chinese capital apparently is less sensitive to corruption, possibly because [these investors] are better able to use personal connections to substitute for the rule of law . . ." (Wei 1997, 14).

China aside, Wei concludes that "the dampening effect of corruption on FDI is greater for East Asian countries than for the world as a whole" (1997, 12).[13] Nevertheless, relatively high levels of corruption in many of the economies in that region appear not to have prevented relatively rapid growth. It is possible that these countries would have grown even faster had corruption levels been lower. Borner, Brunetti, and Weder (1995, 58-61), however, argue that it is the government's ability to keep promises and protect property rights that is the key to growth, not how corrupt it is. They cite the experience of a businessman who responded to a survey and had worked in both Brazil and Indonesia. Both countries received similarly poor ratings for the honesty and efficiency of the bureaucracy and judiciary but very different ratings for political credibility. The businessman commented "that while doing business in Brazil he was always afraid of large policy swings that could destroy his markets, whereas while working in Indonesia he was so convinced that this could not happen that he did not even read the newspapers."[14]

Borner, Brunetti, and Weder also note, however, that corruption typically has negative distributional consequences. In China, for example,

---

12. Mauro addresses the potential endogeneity problem by substituting an "instrumental variable" for corruption in some tests, as well as by controlling for per capita income.

13. Wei's results might also be skewed by the relatively small number of host countries in his sample and the absence of government policy indicators. For example, Japan and more recently South Korea have actively discouraged inward FDI in many sectors.

14. The issue of how some East Asian countries have been able to contain corruption and control its effects is obviously related to the larger issue of how the governments of these countries were able to intervene in their economies and use industrial policies relatively effectively when so many other countries have failed to do so.

where rapid economic growth is creating social strains among ethnic groups and economic classes and between rural and urban areas, corruption has become a rallying point for discontent. Recent economic troubles in Japan and South Korea also raise questions about the stability of corruption equilibriums. In particular, the corruption-linked collapse of Hanbo Steel, which may cost the South Korean government billions of dollars in payments to exposed banks and suppliers, underscores the risk of a failure in institutional controls and of corruption spinning out of control.

In sum, corruption that creates broadly felt negative externalities, such as unsafe infrastructure or environmental degradation, will be more damaging socially and politically than corruption that simply reallocates economic rents arising from government policy or imperfect competition. Most damaging of all, however, is corruption that is pervasive at all levels. Given the difficulties in controlling corruption, it is not likely to be compatible with sustainable long-term economic growth, just as it is not compatible with sustainable democracy.

Political Consequences of Corruption

A dog with a bone in his mouth cannot do two things: He cannot bark and he cannot bite. —Mexican Dictator Porfirio Díaz,
explaining how he ruled so long (1876-1911)

[Corruption is] the gangrene of democracy, the AIDS of democracy.
—Miguel Angel Burelli Rivas, Foreign Minister of Venezuela

Until recently, most of the literature on corruption was in the domain of political science or sociology. Whereas studies on corruption as a problem of economic development have focused on poor countries in the late twentieth century, the literature on the political causes and consequences of corruption covers early industrial England and the United States at least as extensively as it is does today's developing countries.[15] There is also a large and rapidly growing literature on the role of money in politics, influence peddling, and campaign finance reform.

Johnston (chapter 3) analyzes the political sources and consequences of corruption in terms of imbalances in domestic political and economic opportunities and in the relative accessibility and autonomy of elites. He identifies four syndromes. Two of them, interest-group bidding, typical of liberal democracies, and patronage machines, such as in Mexico, may involve corruption that is "significant but bounded in scope, serving more to limit the competitiveness of politics and the responsiveness of

---

15. See, for example, Heidenheimer (1970) and Heidenheimer, Johnston, and LeVine (1989).

government than to threaten their viability." In the other two syndromes—elite hegemony in China today, and fragmented patronage as in Italy or Russia—corruption may spiral out of control and threaten political stability.

That the political effects of corruption remain a concern for developed, as well as developing, countries is clear from the unseating of the Christian Democratic Party in Italy, the loosening of the Liberal Democratic Party's hold in Japan, several scandals in France and Belgium, and the growing demands for campaign finance reform in the wake of the most recent and expensive US presidential election in history. In the US case, there are few direct, tangible links between political contributions and policy outcomes, though unequal access certainly influences the policy-making environment. The primary political cost of influence-peddling "corruption" is increased cynicism among voters and the alienation of citizens from their government. Cynical use of corruption scandals by political opponents exacerbates the problem and may contribute to political gridlock. The need to raise large sums of money for political campaigns also dissuades some would-be office-seekers from becoming candidates.

Analyses of political corruption in less developed societies, especially those focusing on the operation of patronage machines, sometimes find beneficial effects. In this framework, corruption helps provide a separate, possibly more accessible communication network, soften the interaction between citizens and a government they may not understand, and may even prevent violence.[16] It is also argued that corruption sometimes provides access for groups otherwise excluded from political influence, for example, ethnic Chinese minorities in Thailand and Indonesia (see Scott 1972 and Schwarz 1995). Similarly, an expert on Asian politics argued recently that corruption in China had had some positive economic effects by providing access to marginalized groups, "which has led to the diversification and strengthening of the economy" (Hillstrom 1996, 4).

Professor Sun Yan concluded, however, that corruption had simultaneously "served to benefit the Mafia and entrenched elites," and that in general "its undemocratic and detrimental nature causes moral decay, social discontent, and political alienation" (Hillstrom 1996, 4). Johnston (1993, 193) also concludes that

> Sometimes corruption appears as an adaptive force, "humanizing" government and enabling citizens to influence policy. More often, corruption allows those with disproportionate money and access to protect and enhance their advantages. . . .

---

16. See Huntington (1968), Johnston (1993), McMullan (1970), and Scott (1972).

Equally important, as Johnston points out, in some cases "corruption props up institutions and regimes that might otherwise be ready for needed changes."

On the other hand, corruption may be destabilizing in situations where it is used as a club by the "outs" to attack the "ins" (see also McMullan 1970, 317-18). Opposition parties may exploit scandals, exaggerating or even inventing evidence of corruption in order to undermine support for reforms that affect their constituents or to gain power so they can get a piece of the action. The seemingly endless rotation of military coups and civilian governments in Nigeria is one example (Diamond 1993); Ghana during and after Nkrumah is another (Werlin 1979; LeVine 1989). Thus, in assessing the impact of corruption on political stability, it is important to distinguish between corruption and scandal (Johnston, chapter 3).

Corruption may be particularly dangerous and destabilizing during times of transition. During times of rapid change, the institutions that could control corruption may be weak or underdeveloped. Liberalization and deregulation of the economy, while helpful in the long run, may spur corruption in the short run if development of the institutional structure lags. And, if the gains of liberalization seemed to be skewed because of corruption, and corruption is associated with democratization and market capitalism, reforms become more difficult to implement and could even be short-circuited, as was feared might happen in Russia in its 1996 presidential election.

Distortion of International Trade and Investment

Most public statements about the evils of corruption include a reference to distortion of international competition and trade flows. Former US Trade Representative and Commerce Secretary Michael Kantor called corruption "a virus threatening the health of the international trading system" (Kantor 1996b). The United States has a particular interest in the impact of bribery on international transactions because of the perception that the US FCPA presents a significant competitive disadvantage for US firms competing with multinational firms from countries that do not penalize and may even implicitly encourage the use of bribes to win contracts abroad.

The net impact of corruption on trade is not clear, however. Bribes could lead to either an increase or a decrease in the volume of trade, depending on the circumstances. Although corruption may well affect the composition of trade, with regard to products and countries, it is not clear that focusing on corruption is a more effective policy response than focusing on the conditions that give rise to corruption or on the observable policy outcomes that may be influenced by corruption. The following sections examine these questions and analyze the potential impact of the FCPA on US trade and investment.

Corruption as an Impediment to International Trade

The general aims of the international trade rules under the WTO are to remove impediments to trade and, to a lesser degree, investment, and to eliminate discrimination among member countries. Depending on the circumstances, however, corruption may either increase or decrease impediments to trade and investment. Impediments will be increased if corruption is out of control, too costly, or primarily in the form of extortion. Impediments might be lower if corruption is a second-best response to existing barriers or other distortions. Also, many procurement markets, such as aircraft, are sectors with economies of scale and imperfect competition, so corruption may redistribute economic rents but have little effect on global welfare.[17] Moreover, while WTO rules are intended to constrain government trade policies, many instances of corruption subvert government policy. When illicit payments influence the outcome of government policy and lead to the creation of a new trade barrier or an illegal export subsidy, the existing rules will normally be sufficient to address the consequences.

Customs agencies are notorious for corruption in many countries. The net impact, however, is not obvious. Extortion of a shipper by customs officials, who, for example, threaten to allow a shipment of bananas to rot on the dock, could reduce the level of imports if the shipper is unable or unwilling to pay the bribe. But imagine an alternative scenario: suppose the exporter of the bananas offers a bribe if the customs official will lower the duty amount. In that case, rather than reducing trade, corruption might actually increase it (while lowering public revenues). And, since the anecdotal evidence suggests that tax evasion is perhaps the most common motive for bribery, it seems plausible that it might increase trade at the margin (Klitgaard 1988; Alfiler 1986). One would also expect that, the more restricted trade is, the more likely that an increase in trade will result from corruption.[18] Either scenario could cause problems for firms prevented from offering bribes—whether from moral sensitivity or by the law. In either case, exporters of homogeneous or highly perishable products would be most vulnerable, those selling specialized and technologically sophisticated products less so.

---

17. See the discussion of these issues in Rodrik and Rauch (chapter 5).

18. See Wei (1997) for a discussion of the black market and the smuggling of cigarettes and other products into China.

In developing an appropriate international policy response, the impact on the policy of the countries involved also matters. Does corruption influence the formulation of policy and lead to discrimination against imports or foreign investment? Or does it subvert the government's declared policy and international commitments? In the first case, the injured WTO member may be able to use existing rules to challenge the discriminatory policy directly. For example, several US steel companies recently asked the Clinton administration to file a complaint with the WTO claiming that South Korean government subsidies to Hanbo Steel, allegedly influenced by bribes to government officials, had distorted world steel markets (*Journal of Commerce*, 21 February 1997, 3A). In other cases where corruption subverts government policy, and particularly where it deprives the government of customs revenue, the government has an incentive to act, and the problem may reflect inadequate government capacity rather than intent to discriminate.

If corruption affects primarily the allocation of trade flows and not the volume and if any resulting discrimination among suppliers is due primarily to differences in treatment of transnational bribery among exporting countries (rather than the importing government's policy), it might be more appropriate to analyze the problem as a potential export subsidy. As with other export subsidies, which are generally prohibited by the WTO, no exporter gains relative to another if equivalent subsidies are available to all. The prevention of subsidy wars is in fact the major incentive for countries to negotiate agreements to constrain themselves. But in the case of transnational bribery, where a major competitor, the United States, is unilaterally constrained by the FCPA, the incentive for other countries to enact controls is weaker. This has been a major source of concern and frustration for US policymakers and firms.

The FCPA as a US Export Disincentive

Following the corruption scandals of the 1970s involving illicit payments by US multinational corporations to both US and foreign politicians, there was some international discussion of bribery in the context of codes of conduct for multinational investors. However, these discussions did not result in much concrete action (see Pieth and Heimann, chapters 6 and 8). Only in the United States did the Congress pass legislation, the FCPA, which was signed into law by President Jimmy Carter in 1977, making it illegal for US firms to pay bribes to foreign government officials.

From the beginning, some US firms complained that the unilateral nature of the FCPA placed them at a competitive disadvantage relative to international firms based in other countries. In the 1988 Omnibus Trade and Competitiveness Act, Congress amended the FCPA with the objective of reducing the burden of compliance. In that spirit, Congress also added a provision calling on the president to negotiate an agreement with other OECD members addressing transnational bribery. Little action was taken on the latter provision until President Bill Clinton took office in 1993 (see statement by Larson in appendix A). The attention given to the issue by the Clinton administration raises two questions: Why is international corruption suddenly so high on the US trade policy agenda? How significant a competitive disadvantage is the FCPA and how far should the United States go in addressing it unilaterally?

Why now? Not long after the Clinton administration entered office, Commerce Secretary Ron Brown launched a major export advocacy effort that eventually evolved into the "Big Emerging Markets" (BEM) strategy. As of 1996, the BEMs were considered to be Argentina, Brazil, Mexico, the Association of Southeast Asian Nations (Singapore, Indonesia, Thailand, Malaysia, the Philippines, Brunei, and Vietnam), the "Chinese Economic Area" (China, Hong Kong, and Taiwan), India, South Korea, Poland, Turkey, and South Africa (US Department of Commerce 1995). Comparing this list to table 2, one finds that the three largest BEMs, China, India, and Indonesia, along with the Philippines, are among the most corrupt of the 54 countries in the TI ranking. The TI rankings for Argentina, Brazil, Mexico, Thailand, and Turkey are also below the average score for the sample as a whole. The rankings for Taiwan and South Korea are at about average while Malaysia, Poland, and South Africa receive scores slightly above the average.

The administration also identified "big emerging sectors," including energy, health care, information, and transportation, which are among those most likely to have a large degree of state ownership or regulation in many countries. Firms in several of these sectors were also reported, during an investigation by the US Securities and Exchange Commission (SEC) of illicit payments in the 1970s, to have made questionable payments to foreign public officials (Jacoby, Nehemkis, and Eells 1977, 141). (Although the FCPA had not yet been passed and these payments were not illegal under US law, the SEC was investigating whether false reporting of the payments could have misled investors or deprived them of pertinent information.) Of the 63 health care, drug, or cosmetics firms responding to SEC investigators, 29 reported making "questionable payments." In addition, 31 percent of aerospace and 22.5 percent of air transport firms reported making such payments, while between 15 and 20 percent of the firms responding in office equipment, machinery, and electronics and electrical equipment admitted to making such payments. (Industry definitions can be found in Standard & Poor's "Classification of Industries" published at that time.) A cursory review of press articles over the past two years reveals that the big emerging sectors—and the military equipment sector—are also where corruption has been most often exposed.

But present levels of exports to these countries and in these sectors do not tell the whole story. These markets were selected not just because they were big but also because they were among the most rapidly growing. The size and rapid growth of the BEMs mean that their infrastructure needs are enormous. The US Commerce Department has estimated that new infrastructure projects in Asia alone may be worth over $1 trillion over the next decade, with perhaps another $500 billion in such projects being launched in Latin America (US Department of Commerce 1995, 22). With sluggish growth in much of the rest of the world, competition for exports to and investment in the BEMs is expected to be intense. This was why Secretary Brown in a 1995 report on the topic suggested that the US and its major allies and competitors should consider developing

> [a] framework for keeping competition in which governments themselves participate within bounds. That would mean taking a look together at all the tools which are being used, and trying to develop some rules of the game in terms of financing (including foreign aid), illicit payments and other kinds of arrangements which are being used to win deals (US Department of Commerce 1995, 45).

How important a competitive factor is the FCPA? For the FCPA to have an important overall effect on US sales abroad, at least the following three things would have to be true: all or most of the large markets in which US firms compete would have to be corrupt; evasion strategies would have to be difficult or nonexistent; and there would be no other offsetting factors.

Because of the nature of bribery, it is obviously difficult to estimate with much confidence the overall magnitude of the cost of corruption. The US Department of Commerce has estimated that bribes may have contributed to US firms losing some $11 billion in contracts over the period from early 1994 to late 1996 (Trade Promotion Coordinating Committee 1996, 12). The department regards this as a low estimate, because this figure includes only the contracts that have come to light and because it excludes potential follow-on sales (for example, of replacement parts). There has been some confusion over the magnitude of these estimates, however, and it is difficult to evaluate their validity because the analysis on which they are based remains classified (see box 1).

Moreover, in evaluating the effects on US exporters it is also important to keep in mind the *net* effects. As long as there are some situations where it is not necessary to bribe—because government officials are honest or other safeguards are in place—it is possible that bribes shift sources and destinations around without substantially changing global market shares. In a study of the Institute for International Economics on self-imposed export disincentives, Richardson (1993, 131) concluded that "Across-

Box 1　$45 billion or $11 billion—more or less?

According to congressional testimony by then-Secretary of Commerce Ron Brown in October 1995:

> Since the OECD approved recommendations to limit illicit payments in [April] 1994, the U.S. Government has learned of almost 100 cases of foreign firms using bribery to undercut U.S. firms' efforts to win international contracts worth about $45 billion (Department of Commerce press release, October 12, 1995).

This testimony and a later speech by then-US Trade Representative Michael Kantor that also cited the $45 billion figure received extensive press coverage (Kantor 1996a). The *Wall Street Journal*, for example, reported that "Mr. Kantor complained that U.S. companies . . . are losing some $45 billion annually to foreign companies that use bribes to win business deals" (7 March 1996, A2; on the same date, see also *Journal of Commerce*, 2A, and *Financial Times*, 5). Kantor repeated the figure in a July speech and then added, "Already this year we have learned of about $20 billion in additional lost contracts" (Kantor 1996b).[1]

Examination of the *National Export Strategy* report that contained the $45 billion estimate, however, shows that this is not the value of foreign contracts lost by US firms. Rather, it is the value of the "nearly ninety cases" in which foreign firms are alleged to have offered bribes while in competition with US firms for contracts (Trade Promotion Coordinating Committee 1995, 35). The report continues:

> Of these ninety cases, the U.S. firms have already lost more than twenty contracts—worth almost $7 billion—*at least in part* because of the bribes paid by their competitors [emphasis added].

With regard to the sixty or so other contracts, worth $38 billion, apparently the reason the contract was lost is unknown or contract negotiations have not concluded. The 1996 *National Export Strategy* report alleged there were 139 contracts worth $64 billion where bribes were offered, with estimated US losses in 36 cases worth $11 billion. The TPCC regards this estimate as low because "these figures represent only those cases which have come to our attention" (1996, 113).

Unfortunately, the *Foreign Competitive Practices Report* remains classified.[2] It is extremely difficult to judge the validity of any of these estimates without access to the underlying analysis or at least some idea of the methodology. Further complicating the issue, a preliminary (and apparently unpublished) Commerce Department summary of the review of bribery cases says that about half of them involved defense contracts. Given the political nature of most large sales of military equipment, it is even more difficult to determine the relative impact of bribes vis-à-vis other factors in these sales. It is also unlikely countries would ever agree to subject military sales to open, competitive bidding or that defense contracts will ever be decided on purely, or even primarily, economic grounds.

The raw figures must be put in context. Both the 1995 and 1996 reports conclude that firms offering bribes typically win 80 percent of contracts. But that figure is difficult to assess without knowledge of the percentage of contracts won by US or other firms when no bribes were offered. To provide some sort of baseline, the US share of total world exports in 1994 was about 12 percent; its shares of world exports of power-generating machinery and equipment (SITC 71) and aircraft and parts (SITC 792), two sectors thought to be plagued by corruption, were 21 percent and 40 percent, respectively (Statistics Canada 1996). The TPCC reports also emphasize US government actions to overcome these problems: the 1996 report claims that US government advocacy efforts over the previous two plus years had helped US firms win 230 contracts worth $40 billion (88).

---

1. Kantor succeeded Brown as Secretary of Commerce following Brown's death on 3 April 1996.
2. According to the *Wall Street Journal* (12 October 1995, A3) the report was compiled with the help of US intelligence agencies and contained "hundreds of examples of bribery and legitimate—often government-assisted—export promotion."

the-board regulatory burdens, such as procedures mandated for all businesses by the FCPA, seemed generally unimportant."[19]

Another widely cited study of the effects of the FCPA on US foreign direct investment and exports of aircraft did find a statistically significant negative impact on these variables following passage of that law in 1977 (Hines 1996). But the analysis is of the period immediately following passage of the original FCPA so it would not capture possible offsetting effects following the 1988 amendments or other possible adaptations by American firms (see below). Using a more recent and possibly more reliable data set, Wei (1997) finds that corruption on average has a depressing effect on foreign direct investment. But he finds no differential impact on US investors. Multinational firms in other countries apparently are just as cautious as are US investors when it comes to risking their capital in nations where corruption is widespread.

Even if past competitive effects have been limited, however, some of the fastest-growing markets and most lucrative project opportunities are in emerging markets, many of which have also been judged relatively corrupt. Thus, there will now be more demand for corruption-prone types of exports and contracts in more corrupt countries. A second source of growing concern for US exporters might be in the nature of the financing available for these projects. The World Bank and other official financial institutions, international and domestic, usually require international competitive bidding and the right to review contract awards before disbursing funds. A decade ago, the official development finance was 1.7 times greater than foreign private capital flows for developing countries ($36.7 billion versus $21.4 billion). In 1995, that relationship had roughly reversed, with private capital flows exceeding official flows by 60 percent ($78.7 billion private versus $48.6 percent official). With a greater number of large projects being financed by the private sector, it is possible that the bidding process could become less transparent and more vulnerable to corruption (World Bank 1996d, 35).[20]

---

19. This conclusion was based on an analysis of the impact of the regulatory costs of compliance with the FCPA, i.e., of the additional accounting and auditing costs of the disclosure requirements, and not the potential effects on competitiveness of being restrained from bribing in markets where competitors in fact do. Richardson's broader finding of little impact was based on the source-shifting behavior described above and on the fact that no firm interviewed by him mentioned the inability to bribe as a competitive disadvantage.

20. A second potential source of protection for US exporters when official finance is involved is the concern of the World Bank and other international financial institutions that the shares of officially funded procurements that supplier countries receive are not too out of line with their financial contributions to the organization. For example, the US share of World Bank payments to supplier countries for foreign procurements is roughly 19 percent (both for the 1996 fiscal year and cumulatively), slightly above its current quota of 17.4 percent (World Bank 1996a, 225, 239).

Just the same, the prohibition against bribing foreign officials may not be as great a handicap for US firms as has been claimed. Some firms have used the FCPA as a shield to protect themselves from extortion by corrupt foreign officials. George David, president and CEO of United Technologies Corporation, indicated at a meeting on ethics in 1993 that following a crackdown on illicit payments by a subsidiary in Mexico, not only were market share and profitability maintained, but the firm was "able to shorten [its] long, long overdue collection period on government receivables in one of the more notorious problem countries" (David 1994, 8). Just as a reputation for honesty may serve as a shield, a reputation for being willing to pay bribes may open one's firms to ceaseless demands for more. Some China observers note that whereas honest operations may be more challenging and time-consuming, they may avoid trouble in the long run (Ettore 1994, 21; see also Givant 1994). In another example, Colgate-Palmolive was reported to have used the FCPA as a shield to avoid paying bribes or being forced to engage in "nepotistic employment" practices while building a $20 million operation in Guangdong Province in 1992 (Pines 1994, 210-11).

Also, where bribes are an additional operating cost (as opposed to being offered to win a contract or other business), firms that can avoid internal corruption among employees and external corruption among suppliers, distributors, customers, and regulators should be relatively more cost-efficient and competitive. Furthermore, if corruption is as common as alleged, the losers must be paying bribes for nothing, further raising costs. Pines (1994, 211-12) notes that, because they lack access to reliable information, some firms may overpay or pay someone who fraudulently claims to have the "right connections." The perception that contracts can only be won through bribery could also result in reduced innovation and laziness on the part of some firms. Pitman and Sanford (1994, 18-19) argue that the FCPA could have offsetting benefits because it "mandates that [firms] find other, more effective methods to 'get the job done' when they previously may have thought bribery was their only option."

At the other end of the spectrum, some companies may decide to ignore the FCPA and risk getting caught. Lockheed Corporation (now Lockheed Martin Corp.), whose bribery of Japanese politicians in the 1970s brought down a government and contributed to the passage of the FCPA, pleaded guilty in 1995 to bribing an Egyptian official to win an aircraft supply contract (Wall Street Journal, 29 September 1995, 1). In early 1996, two other large US multinationals were under investigation for possible violations of the FCPA, but nearly a year later, charges had not been brought (National Journal, 20 April 1996, 871).[21]

---

21. As of early April 1997, the US Justice Department declined to confirm or deny whether the investigations were taking place. In March, however, following settlement of an FCPA

But there are also other, less risky methods of evasion. Among other changes, the amendments to the FCPA in the Omnibus Trade and Competitiveness Act of 1988 explicitly defined allowable facilitating payments for "routine governmental" services (licenses, permits, paper processing, provision of police protection, other government services) and created two affirmative defenses: that the payment is legal in the country where it occurs; or that the payment was for "reasonable and bona fide expenditure" such as travel or lodging for training or other trips abroad for government officials. According to a source at the US-China Business Council, "You'd think Disney World was a training site" (*Wall Street Journal*, 29 September 1995, 1; see also *New York Times*, 12 April 1996, A10). Wei (1997, 5n) also reports that conversations with Chinese businessmen and officials suggest more subtle, possibly legal forms of influence, such as study trips for officials to tour a foreign country, are more commonplace than outright bribes.

Finally, the aggressive advocacy and export promotion efforts of the Clinton administration can provide at least partial and, perhaps, temporary offsets for any hypothetical disadvantage posed by the FCPA.[22] For example, although the Middle East is widely thought to be one of the most corrupt regions in the world and aircraft one of the sectors most vulnerable to distortion by bribery, President Clinton's personal intervention in 1995 helped to clinch the sale to Saudi Arabia of $6 billion in commercial aircraft for Boeing and McDonnell Douglas. At the time, presidential spokesman Michael McCurry was quoted as saying that the President was not at all hesitant in using his influence to "go to bat for American companies" (*International Trade Reporter*, 1 November 1995, 1824; *Wall Street Journal*, 18 December 1995, 1). The 1996 national export strategy report claimed that US government advocacy efforts had helped US businesses to make deals worth over $40 billion, nearly four times more than the value of contracts allegedly lost to bribery (Trade Promotion Coordinating Committee 1996, 89).

Whatever the current or anticipated impact, the Clinton administration has stepped up efforts to get other countries, particularly OECD member states, to take action against transnational bribery. In 1996, the Department of Commerce revised its "advocacy guidelines" to buttress the FCPA and to ensure that US-based firms and especially subsidiaries

---

case with Triton Energy over questionable payments by its Indonesian subsidiary, the head of enforcement for the Securities and Exchange Commission, William McLucas, expressed concern that bribery of foreign officials might be becoming a significant problem for the first time since the FCPA was passed (*Bloomberg News*, 5 March 1997).

22. Some American businessmen and government officials argue that the United States lags behind other countries in these other forms of export promotion, so there is little or no counterweight to the disadvantage posed by the FCPA. See the Trade Promotion Coordinating Committee's report on *National Export Strategy* (1996).

of foreign-owned multinationals would not benefit from US export promotion programs if they or any part of their worldwide corporate family engaged in bribery. The new requirements state that for US-based subsidiaries or affiliates of foreign multinationals to qualify for US government support when bidding on an international contract, the parent corporation must actively enforce a policy prohibiting the bribery of foreign officials (Trade Policy Coordinating Committee [TPCC] 1996, 119-122).[23] The Export-Import Bank (Eximbank) and the Overseas Private Insurance Corporation (OPIC) also increased their reporting requirements for beneficiaries of their programs. US subsidiaries of foreign-owned companies are already covered by the FCPA. The major aim of the changes in the advocacy guidelines is to put pressure on their overseas parent corporations to adopt stronger policies against bribery.

Some American policymakers have advocated even stronger unilateral action. One proposal, going beyond the augmentation of reporting requirements, would have explicitly *conditioned* eligibility for assistance from the Eximbank or OPIC on the adoption and enforcement of an antibribery policy by the corporate parent. That position was rejected as overly intrusive in the affairs of recipient countries who would also be party to the contract. Potentially more controversial were the oft-voiced hints dropped by Michael Kantor when he was Secretary of Commerce, and earlier as US Trade Representative, that transnational bribery would be defined as an unfair foreign trade practice constituting grounds for retaliatory sanctions under section 301 of US trade law (see for example, Kantor 1996a).

In sum, there is little evidence that the FCPA has a major negative impact on overall US exports. The impact on particular sectors is more significant, and given the potential for more than $1.5 trillion in infrastructure projects in Asia and Latin America over the next decade, US firms in these sectors have reason to be concerned about possible distortions from bribery. With globalization and democratization making corruption less and less acceptable around the world, however, US firms that have been forced by the FCPA to become more innovative and aggressive should be well placed to reap the benefits. The FCPA could also be a competitive advantage in some newly democratizing countries where politicians or public officials concerned about negative publicity might prefer a US firm because they can more credibly claim that no corruption was involved. For these reasons, and also because meaningful international action against corruption will require cooperation from other governments, the United States should avoid aggressive unilateral actions in this area (see also Heimann, chapter 8, and Pieth, chapter 6).

---

23. According to the TPCC report, government support in this context "can take the form of letters, representations, or other interventions by US officials" (1996, 119).

Domestic and Institutional Reforms to Control Corruption

Just as the most important sources and consequences of corruption are internal to countries, the fundamental reforms that will most effectively reduce it over time must take place at the national level in the countries where it occurs. And since the specific sources, types, and consequences of corruption vary widely among countries, no simple prescription will fit all cases. Each country must individually identify the most important sources of corruption and the consequences that most cry out for attention. Nevertheless, any analysis of remedies to corruption must begin with its broad underlying sources: restricted economic and political competition, excessive bureaucratic or political discretion, and a lack of transparency and accountability. This section examines how broad-based economic and political reforms can reduce the opportunities for corruption, as well as how these reforms must be supplemented by institutional reforms to improve governance and state capacity to sustain reductions in rampant corruption.

Macro Reforms and Their Limits

Reforms that open up and liberalize the economy and increase competition, by, for example, lowering trade barriers, reduce the opportunities and the pool of rents available for bribery. Economic reforms that eliminate unnecessary regulations and simplify essential ones reduce the power and discretion of public officials, thereby removing opportunities for extortion. Political reforms that give more power to citizens as voters and as users of public services and endow the media with greater freedoms make corruption riskier and increase both the chances of detection and the potential penalty for politicians who get caught. In the long run, all of these reforms should limit the opportunities and incentives to engage in corrupt behavior.

In the short run, however, the balance between political and economic reforms, the sequencing of particular reforms, and the priority given to implementing corollary institutional reforms will determine whether corruption can in fact be reduced. The transfer of state-owned enterprises and other assets to the private sector illustrates many of the pitfalls awaiting would-be reformers. Privatization (or deregulation) in a situation where there is an underlying market failure or the market is not competitive may not result in net gains for social welfare. For example, corruption may be eliminated only to be replaced by private-sector collusion (Rose-Ackerman, chapter 2). When the privatization process itself is corrupt, state enterprises or other public resources may go not to the most competitive bidder but to favored insiders.

Whether ownership is public or private, the incentives persist to maintain rents in the form of direct subsidies, import protection, or other restrictions on competition. The technocratic policymakers in Indonesia were reported to have slowed down the pace of privatization of state-owned enterprises there because of concerns they would be bought up by cronies of Prime Minister Suharto who would then seek special favors such as continued import protection or subsidized access to credit (Schwarz 1995, 148). As Klitgaard (1988, 67) points out, whether a certain activity takes place in the public or private sector is not the issue; rather, whether it takes place in an environment of "*competition* and *accountability*" is what really counts (emphasis in original).

Perceptions that privatization and other reforms favor certain parties may feed public suspicions about market-oriented reforms and undermine their public support. Opposition parties and political dissidents may use corruption as an excuse to try to reverse reforms. In Russia and other parts of the former Soviet Union, the virulent and chaotic forms of corruption spawned by systemic collapse threaten to undermine the transition of those countries to more open political and economic systems. Rampant tax evasion has left the government unable to pay pensions or workers in the remaining state-owned enterprises, and the conspicuous consumption of those with new wealth also contributes to the nostalgia of some segments of the population for the days of stable Communist Party rule.

Thus, political and economic opening may expose old ways of doing business and open up possibilities for reform, but they may also introduce new opportunities for corruption and bring new players into the game. The *Wall Street Journal,* for example, reported that the movement toward freer markets and democracy in Latin America had also "democratized" corruption and that the inflows of capital following economic liberalization raised the incentives for corruption (1 July 1996, 1). Moreover, even successful economic reforms do not obviate the need for government entirely; the need to raise taxes, provide benefits, and regulate in many areas of public interest will persist. Micro reforms to strengthen government and social institutions must therefore accompany the macro reforms.

Reforming Institutions and Building State Capacity

Even under the best of circumstances, democratization and economic liberalization take time to consolidate. Naím (1995b, 8-11) in looking at the process of economic liberalization and Charlick (1992, 178) in focusing on democratization emphasize the importance of strengthening state capacity and improving governance to reduce corruption and consolidate reforms. Crucial areas for improved governance include civil service reform; greater tax collection capacity; and reforms to increase the capacity, independence, and honesty of the judiciary. Naím calls these "Stage II" reforms. Analysts who have focused closely on the need for institutional reforms emphasize the need to reduce inequities in access to information asymmetries and the need for changes in incentive structures. Improved information gathering allows agency leadership to acknowledge honest bureaucrats and investigate and punish dishonest ones.

Klitgaard (1988) analyzes several cases of efforts to reduce corruption and derives lessons for reformers. His most detailed case study concerns the efforts of Justice Efren Plana to reduce rampant corruption in the Philippines Bureau of Internal Revenue. In addition to improving information collection and creating an incentive structure to reward performance, Klitgaard recommends punishing "big fish" (i.e., prominent, high-level corrupt officials) to obtain a maximum demonstration effect. The big-fish tactic sends a signal of seriousness and lends credibility to anticorruption reforms. Box 2 summarizes other recommendations for improving information flows and changing incentives. Rose-Ackerman (chapter 2) offers similar recommendations for institutional reform, and as elsewhere (1978), she emphasizes the deterrent benefit of escalating penalties in proportion to the size of the bribe in the case of public employees and in proportion to the value of illicit gains in the case of the briber.

The benefits of incorporating transparency and accountability in the reform process are highlighted in Oldenburg (1987), who studied the example of a land consolidation program in India. The program, which sought to increase agricultural efficiency by consolidating scattered plots claimed by a single owner, seemed vulnerable to bribery that would influence outcomes. Yet it seems to have been largely free of corruption. Oldenburg attributes this in large part to the openness integrated into the program design. The proceedings were conducted largely in the villages with the participation of affected farmers. According to Oldenburg, "All proceedings [were] open and well publicized, and the records [were] open" (1987, 516). Moreover the farmers were given the right to appeal decisions, enhancing accountability by forcing officials to justify their decisions.

The importance of the right of appeal in making anticorruption reforms work underscores the need to create and maintain an honest and independent judiciary. If not addressed, judicial corruption could facilitate corruption elsewhere in the system by protecting restricted economic or political competition. It would almost certainly impede cleanup efforts if not dealt with because whistle-blowers would otherwise have no protection, reform-minded officials could be harassed, businesses suffering from discrimination would have no recourse, and corrupt officials and business people would not have to fear punishment. An honest judiciary could also provide recourse for third parties suffering the

Box 2 Using information and incentives to control corruption

Improving information gathering and analysis to detect and deter corruption

- Assess the organization's vulnerability to corruption and identify particular areas of concern.
- Look for evidence of corruption (red flags, including lifestyles more lavish than honesty would allow, random inspections, and statistical analysis).
- Increase access to information by opening channels to third parties (media and banks), clients, and the public.
- Strengthen internal "information agents" (auditors and investigators) and protect whistle blowers.
- Create specialized units or agencies (ombudsmen and anticorruption commissions).

Changing incentives to discourage corruption

Increase the rewards for honesty:

- Raise low-end salaries to reduce the need for illicit supplements.
- Introduce merit pay and incentive schemes that reward honest and efficient service, including nonmonetary rewards (for example, desirable transfers, training, travel, publicity, and praise).
- Use contingent contracts (for example, nonvested pensions for public employees and performance contracts for private contractors).

Increase the penalties for corrupt behavior:

- Raise the level of formal penalties. Where that is not possible (for political or other reasons), use nonformal penalties (for example, undesirable transfers, negative publicity, loss of professional standing, and blackballing).
- Increase authority to impose punishment.
- Link the penalty to the expected gain from corruption (the size of the bribe for the public employee; the size of the expected illicit profit for the briber).

Source: Adapted from Klitgaard (1988, 94-95) and Rose-Ackerman (1978).

---

consequences of corruption; for example, individuals injured when an unsafe building collapses. Thus, judicial reform should receive priority attention from anticorruption campaigners in countries where the judiciary is itself corrupt.

Changes in regulation, tax collection methods, and provision of benefits can reduce opportunities for corruption by reducing bureaucratic discretion (Rose-Ackerman, chapter 2). The adoption of more market-oriented methods of regulating private economic activity, for example auctioning pollution rights rather than setting limits by administrative fiat, often enhance efficiency and may also have antibribery benefits.[24]

---

24. This is an additional argument in favor of auctioning import and export quota licenses, though the authors of an Institute study on that topic did not recognize it at the time. See Bergsten, Elliott, Schott, and Takacs (1987).

Increased user fees for scarce government services could also address the excess demand problem that sometimes results in covert payments to affect the distribution of government benefits.

Just as corruption has costs, however, so does fighting it. As noted by Rose-Ackerman (chapter 2),

> Corruption can never be entirely eliminated. Under many realistic conditions, it will simply be too expensive to reduce corruption to zero. Furthermore, a single-minded focus on corruption prevention can have a negative impact on personal freedoms and human rights. Such a focus could produce a government that is rigid and unresponsive.

Reducing corruption takes real resources, for example to make civil service salaries and benefits competitive with the private sector or for monitoring and enforcement activities. Living beyond one's (apparent legal) means is frequently cited as potential evidence of illicit enrichment that should be grounds for investigation and prosecution of corrupt officials, but Moisés Naím has warned that witch hunts against public officials can precipitate the loss of some of the best talent in countries that can ill afford it. Overzealous anticorruption efforts may have other indirect costs, such as decreased morale among public employees or impaired government functioning because of too little discretion and overcentralization (see also Klitgaard 1988, 24-25). Thus, costs must also be considered in the development of anticorruption strategies and the selection of particular tactics.

Supporting Internal Reforms: The Role of the International Financial Institutions

The World Bank, International Monetary Fund (IMF), regional development banks, and bilateral aid agencies can lend valuable support for anticorruption efforts in a variety of ways. In the past, the World Bank and the IMF felt constrained in addressing corruption and other sensitive issues because of the requirement that they not interfere in members' internal political affairs. But both institutions, as well as other multilateral development banks (MDBs), have increasingly recognized the importance of governance issues in attaining development objectives. For the first time in public, Bank President James Wolfensohn and IMF Managing Director Michel Camdessus explicitly broached the issue of corruption in speeches at the joint annual meetings of their agencies in Washington in October 1996.

At the request of a member government, these agencies provide advice, technical assistance, and financial support for institutional and policy reforms that often help to reduce corruption either directly or indirectly. The contribution of the IMF comes primarily from the conditions it generally attaches to its loans, which encourage economic liberalization and, implicitly, reductions in the opportunities for corruption. The World Bank provides financial and technical assistance that can contribute more directly to both institutional reform and development in countries that need and desire such assistance. The argument has been put forth that lending be explicitly conditioned on efforts in borrower countries to reduce corruption, but this suggestion is more controversial.

The primary objective of IMF-sponsored programs is usually macroeconomic stabilization. In this context, the IMF urges national governments to reduce their interventions in the economy by reducing trade barriers, liberalizing financial markets, freeing up other prices, ending subsidies for food and other necessities, and privatizing state-owned enterprises (or at least cutting subsidies to them), among other measures. Whatever their other effects, these reforms also tend to reduce the opportunities for corruption.

But the central plank of most stabilization agreements is some measure of fiscal austerity, which may have unanticipated consequences if not handled carefully. One result of the combined inflation and policy-inspired squeeze on the public sector that occurred in many countries during the debt crisis of the 1980s was a large reduction in the real wages of public sector employees. These reductions, in turn, led to increased pressure to engage in bribery (Ul Haque and Sahay 1996; Klitgaard 1988, 197). When corruption is widespread in revenue collection agencies, as often occurs, a vicious cycle emerges in which austerity increases the incentives for corruption, which reduces government revenue, thereby leading to further austerity measures. Of course, governments can lower their total payroll costs by reducing the number of employees while maintaining the real wage level, but it is often more expedient not to act and simply allow inflation to erode wages. The IMF cannot and should not dictate exactly how a country achieves its fiscal targets, but it should work with borrowers to ensure that its recommendations do not make a bad situation worse.

The World Bank can more directly support anticorruption efforts because it provides lending for specific projects, in addition to providing resources for structural adjustment.[25] In a background paper circulated at the 1996 annual meetings, the World Bank identified key areas where it is contributing to anticorruption reforms:

■ support for and technical assistance in implementing *economic reforms* to reduce rent-seeking in the tax and regulatory areas, and to privatize state-owned enterprises or strengthen their regulation in uncompetitive markets and

---

25. The World Bank's rules intended to prevent corruption in government procurement in relation to the projects that it funds are discussed in more detail in the next section.

■ support for *institutional reforms* in the areas of government financial management (budgeting, accounting, and auditing systems); civil service reform; government procurement; and governance more broadly.

As one aspect of improved governance, the Bank is also supporting innovative programs, such as training workshops for journalists conducted in some countries by the Economic Development Institute (EDI) (World Bank 1996c). EDI has also worked with Transparency International (TI) to support establishment of "national integrity systems" in Tanzania and Uganda and to disseminate TI's "Source Book" for building such systems (United Republic of Tanzania 1995; Transparency International 1996). The Source Book discusses the role in combating corruption played by civil society, the press and the importance of judicial, legislative, and administrative reforms that would heighten monitoring, protect whistle-blowers, and promote open and transparent procurement systems and self-policing by the private sector.

The World Bank is also supporting the "Partnership for Capacity Building in Africa," which was instigated by the Bank's African Governors at the 1995 Annual Meetings with the goal of "strengthening or improvement of people, institutions and practices that enable countries to achieve their development goals" (World Bank Press Release, 28 September 1996). Even if not explicitly aimed at it, such capacity building should have anticorruption benefits. The World Bank also has increased its focus on human capital development and social spending (education and health), especially as private capital markets assume a larger role in financing large infrastructure projects. If Mauro's conclusion (chapter 4) that corruption is negatively correlated with government spending on education is borne out by further research, then increased international funding for education could help to offset the effects of corruption. Case studies indicate that illiteracy among government constituents facilitates petty corruption, so increased spending for education can help reduce such abuses.

Finally, some observers suggest that the World Bank and the regional development banks make reduction of corruption an explicit part of their conditionality. Certainly, the World Bank, the other MDBs, and the IMF should be less tolerant than they have been in the past toward corrupt governments. According to a detailed report in the *Financial Times*, the IMF, under pressure from the United States and other Western governments, lent Zaire more than $1 billion in the 1980s *after* receiving a report from a senior IMF official warning that Mobutu Sese Seko's government was completely corrupt (12 May 1996, 1-2). Total multilateral lending to Zaire between 1982 and 1994 totaled nearly $2 billion. With the obvious exception of procurement rules, however, it is not clear that it is either necessary or helpful to bring corruption explicitly into the general conditions attached to development assistance. How would corruption be defined and how would reductions be observed and measured? Where procurement rules and auditing procedures effectively insulate Bank projects from corruption, should lending be cut off because of corruption elsewhere in the government? If corruption does not obviously interfere with economic performance or the adoption of reforms is it a legitimate concern of these institutions? Given that pervasive corruption usually has an adverse impact on economic performance, is it necessary to introduce explicit conditionality in this area?

Even without explicit conditionality, the Bank has increasingly been emphasizing governance issues, including corruption, in its lending policies and in its policy dialogues with borrower countries. "Country Portfolio Performance Reviews" are conducted annually in most countries and focus on obstacles to the implementation of Bank projects (World Bank 1994, 38). "Country Assistance Strategy" (CAS) statements engage the Executive Board as part of the process of reviewing overall lending strategies in each country. The intent of these statements is to ensure that implementation problems "are taken into account in decisions on the volume and composition of lending." An analysis of a representative sample of 40 such statements in 1994, however, revealed that treatment of governance issues was generally restricted to the fairly narrow area of public sector management. Transparency, accountability, and issues concerning the rule of law were rarely raised in the statements reviewed (World Bank 1994, 38). For these reviews and assessments to be effective tools, however, the Bank must follow through by reducing or suspending assistance when corruption interferes with project implementation or broader development objectives. In these cases, however, the reason for interrupting lending programs is the impact on development goals, not the corruption per se.

The Role of Leadership

Finally, Ruzindana addresses the role of leadership (chapter 7). In his words, "corruption cannot exist without the connivance of the political leadership, even if passive." It is possible to have limited anticorruption reforms even when serious corruption involves top leadership, but political support is still required. Klitgaard's case study of the Philippines Bureau of Internal Revenue illustrates the potential for successfully tackling corruption despite otherwise rampant corruption at the top of the Marcos government (1988, chapters 2 and 3). Yet Marcos still appointed the anticorruption judge who cleaned up the agency and supported him when he punished high-level corrupt officials. Thus, even incremental steps require at least minimal political support.

With the political and economic reforms that are occurring around the world, however, such leadership should be more forthcoming. Moreover, leadership need not always be imposed from above; it can also come from below. In addition to top-level leadership, Ruzindana (chapter 7) emphasizes the role of civil society and the need to educate the public, to strengthen grassroots groups, and to protect and strengthen a free and independent media. These activities may be supported by the international community, but they must be homegrown to be effective.

International Initiatives to Combat Corruption

Corruption's effects on economic development and political legitimacy spill over a given country's borders, affecting global peace and prosperity. Thus, it is natural that corruption concerns the international community as a whole, just as distortions in international trade and investment flows are also concerns. The most important role of the international community is the one described above of providing financial and technical support to countries undertaking difficult anticorruption reforms.

Other international anticorruption initiatives focus on the role of multinational corporations in offering bribes and the impact on international transactions, particularly government procurement, where the public and private sectors do business directly. Potentially, the most important are the efforts in the OECD to deter and punish transnational bribery. Pieth (chapter 6) discusses the evolution of these efforts in detail, while recent breakthroughs are summarized below. Also discussed here are the Inter-American Convention against Corruption approved by the members of the Organization of American States (OAS), which includes measures to promote cooperation among member states in enforcing anticorruption laws and recent efforts by the World Bank and World Trade Organization to restrict the opportunities for corruption in government procurement contracts. Highlighting the need to address both supply and demand, the UN General Assembly approved a resolution in December 1996 calling on members to take "concrete action" against all forms of corruption. The nonbinding UN declaration incorporates elements of both the OAS Convention and the OECD recommendations discussed below. Some countries have proposed resuming negotiations on a universal anticorruption treaty under UN auspices, but little progress has been made to date and UN action on this issue remains primarily rhetorical.[26]

Corruption also raises global concerns because of how it facilitates

---

26. Some European countries that have been resisting strong action against transnational bribery in the OECD proposed universalizing the negotiations in the UN, reportedly in the hope that they would become bogged down as they did in the 1970s. For a brief history of the earlier UN negotiations, see Pieth (chapter 6).

international criminal activity, particularly drug trafficking and money laundering. Money laundering can have significant collateral economic effects and the liberalization of financial markets around the world has contributed to its spiraling growth. Nevertheless, the primary locus of concern is the criminal activity that spawns these activities and, while a reduction in corruption would clearly help, the primary policy responses must still focus on law enforcement, financial market regulation, and drug-addiction treatment.[27] Those issues are not addressed in this volume.

The Inter-American Convention Against Corruption

One of the striking things about the OAS anticorruption initiative is the leading role played by several South American countries in advancing the process. The first steps were taken in March 1994 when President Clinton invited heads of state in the Western Hemisphere to a summit to discuss strengthening and consolidating democracy and promoting economic growth in the region. Anticorruption action was an important American objective for the summit, but President Clinton initially spoke of the need for improved governance in the hemisphere without making explicit mention of corruption (Clinton 1994). Inclusion of an explicit anticorruption initiative on the summit agenda was then promoted by Ecuadorian Vice President Alberto Dahik, who was the chairman of the Advisory Council of Transparency International (TI) at the time, and Venezuelan President Rafael Caldera, who attributed the bank failures and financial crisis that struck his country shortly after he took office in 1993 to the corruption of his predecessors.[28]

At the Summit of the Americas held in Miami in December 1994, the leaders of 34 Western Hemisphere countries (all but Cuba) agreed on a "Declaration of Principles" and a "Plan of Action" for strengthening and expanding cooperation and economic integration in the region (Feinberg 1997). The portion of the plan of action that addresses measures to

---

27. The *Financial Times* recently reported that global earnings from organized crime, mostly from drug trafficking, reached an estimated $1 trillion in 1996 (14 February 1997, 1). See Pieth (chapter 6) for a brief discussion of the Financial Action Task Force, which was established in 1990 to address money laundering of criminal proceeds. For analysis of the sources, scope, and potential threat to macroeconomic and financial market stability from money laundering, see Quirk (1996) and Tanzi (1996). For discussions of international organized crime and US policies on international drug trafficking, see Raine and Cilluffo (1994) and the Council on Foreign Relations (1997), respectively.

28. See Transparency International (1995) and Andres Oppenheimer in the *Miami Herald*, 4 December 1994. Ironically, Vice President Dahik is now in exile in Costa Rica, having fled Ecuador to avoid prosecution on charges of corruption. Dahik claims that the corruption charges are simply part of a political vendetta against him.

strengthen democracy included an initiative against corruption.[29] Although this initiative listed several steps that countries should consider taking to combat corruption and improve governance, including potentially far-reaching institutional reforms, the initial focus was on the provision calling for development within the OAS of "a hemispheric approach to acts of corruption in both the public and private sectors that would include extradition and prosecution of individuals so charged." The leaders also called on "the governments of the world to adopt and enforce measures against bribery in all financial or commercial transactions with the Hemisphere." At the urging of the United States, the leaders also included a suggestion that the OAS establish a liaison with the OECD Working Group on Bribery in International Transactions.

The resulting Inter-American Convention against Corruption was adopted 29 March 1996 in Caracas, a little more than a year after it had been proposed. It was signed there by representatives of 21 countries in a special session. The United States signed before the OAS General Assembly in Panama the following June, after the treaty had been thoroughly examined by the US Justice Department. The principal provisions of the convention require adherents to criminally sanction bribery, transnational bribery, and "illicit enrichment," and to cooperate with one another in the investigation and prosecution of acts defined as corrupt in the convention, through extradition and assistance in recovering illicitly acquired property or wealth. The convention also discourages the use of bank secrecy laws as the basis for withholding cooperation from investigations of corruption.

The key provision from the US perspective is Article VIII, which effectively internationalizes the FCPA by requiring parties to the convention to make it a crime to bribe foreign public officials. Article IX requires each member state to "establish under its laws as an offense a significant increase in the assets of a government official that he cannot reasonably explain in relation to his lawful earnings during the performance of his functions." This provision has been depicted as an essential tool in combating a phenomenon cloaked in secrecy and deception. But it was also the most troublesome for US negotiators and prevented the United States from immediately signing the convention in Caracas. Although implementation is subject to the Constitution and fundamental legal principles of each member state, the US Justice Department wanted to ensure that the language did not conflict with the US Constitution and legal tradition that the accused is innocent until proven guilty.

Thus, the focus in the convention is on criminal sanctions and enforcement. Though the scope for an international role is limited, corollary domestic and institutional reforms are still rather weakly dealt with

---

29. For more detail on the convention and its negotiation, see Elliott (1996).

in the convention. Article III refers to "preventive measures" that members "agree to consider . . . within their own institutional systems." These measures include standards of conduct for public officials, "mechanisms to enforce these standards," and strengthening government procedures in the areas of hiring, government procurement, and tax collection. Signatories also agree to consider "whistle-blower" protection and "oversight bodies with a view to implementing modern mechanisms for preventing, detecting, punishing, and eradicating corrupt acts." Article III notes the need for "mechanisms to encourage participation by civil society" and NGOs and the "study of further preventive measures that take into account the relationship between equitable compensation and probity in public service." These domestic reforms are crucial if the convention is to be an effective anticorruption instrument. Unfortunately, there are no follow-up measures specified in the convention to support or monitor the implementation of these reforms.

As of the end of 1996, only a handful of countries had ratified the OAS convention, and the Clinton administration had not yet submitted it to the US Senate. OAS Secretary General César Gaviria has suggested that the OAS could assist in the drafting of "model laws" aimed at detecting and punishing corruption and at modernizing the state in ways that reduce the opportunities for corruption. To this end, Gaviria has also suggested that the OAS encourage "horizontal cooperation and exchange of experience in the area of combating corruption and set up a data base of success stories in this field" (Gaviria 1995). The Inter-American Development Bank has also identified ways in which it can support anticorruption efforts, in particular its support of judicial and civil service reforms in the region.

The Inter-American Convention against Corruption is the first document of its kind, codifying anticorruption measures in a treaty reached by both developed and developing countries. If the potential is to be realized, however, a number of steps must be taken. First, the United States should set an example by quickly ratifying the convention. In a recent speech, US Ambassador to the OAS Harriet Babbit said that she hoped to see ratification before the end of the year, that is, about 18 months after it was signed. At the time of her remarks, only Paraguay and Bolivia had submitted instruments of ratification to the OAS. The United States should move as rapidly as possible toward ratification and, along with Secretary General Gaviria, should encourage all OAS members to ratify the convention prior to next year's summit in Santiago, Chile.

Second, greater attention to other implementation issues is needed. Secretary General Gaviria's commitment to having the OAS monitor and review implementation, which was not explicitly mandated in the convention, is a useful demonstration of his overall support. His first report on the implementation of the convention is due to be presented to the

General Assembly in 1997. It will be the first indication of how effective the OAS can be in this area. The technical assistance and financial support of the Inter-American Development Band will also be helpful in meeting the challenge of far-reaching domestic reforms that will be necessary in some countries.

Controlling the Supply of Bribes: The Organization of Economic Cooperation and Development and the International Chamber of Commerce

The initiatives of the ICC and OECD focus on deterring the use of bribery by multinational enterprises in the course of business operations in foreign countries, allegedly a major source of illicit payments. Like the United Nations, the ICC and OECD initially considered the problem of transnational bribery in the 1970s, following a series of scandals and the passage in the United States of the FCPA. These initial efforts failed to make an impact, but interest has been renewed in the 1990s.

The OECD revived its interest in the corruption issue in 1993 under the prompting of the Clinton administration. In early 1994, the Committee on International Investment and Multinational Enterprises approved a recommendation for submission to the Council that urged members to "take concrete and meaningful steps" against the bribery of foreign officials. The recommendation, which also created a Working Group on Bribery in International Business Transactions, was formally adopted by the OECD Council of Ministers later that spring (see Pieth, chapter 6). This was followed two years later by a second recommendation approved by the Council that called on members to end the tax deductibility of transnational bribes and to consider means of imposing criminal sanctions on such behavior.[30] Neither recommendation is legally binding on members, but both contain provisions for the monitoring and review of actions taken to implement the recommendations. The working group has also been developing "best practice" principles for accounting and auditing procedures to facilitate effective enforcement. Secrecy is an essential component in the bribery transaction, so transparency and thorough record keeping are important tools to control corruption.

The results with respect to national implementation of the recommendations are thus far mixed, however. Recently, the United Kingdom concluded that a 1906 antibribery law could be interpreted as covering bribery of foreign officials, though it had not previously been used for that purpose. Japan also not long ago announced that it would take

---

30. At the time the recommendation was approved, Austria, Belgium, Luxembourg, Netherlands, Germany, and Greece allowed "commissions" to be deducted as a business expense with few restrictions. Australia, Canada, Denmark, France, Ireland, Norway, New Zealand, Spain, and Switzerland allowed tax deductibility if the recipient was identified.

steps to criminally sanction transnational bribery, probably by amending its Law for the Prevention of Unfair Competition, which carries criminal sanctions. The Japanese government expects the measure to be passed and to take effect in April 1998, but concerns have been raised as to whether Japan's Fair Trade Commission will be more effective on this issue than it has been on other fair competition issues in the past.

Regarding the tax deductibility of bribes, only Norway has completely implemented the recommendation; a handful of countries have legislation pending, but most OECD members have not moved to implement the recommendation on tax deductibility. France and Germany have said they cannot eliminate tax deductibility until the criminalization issue is resolved *(Transparency International USA Newsletter*, March/April 1997, 2). One OECD member state has taken steps to end tax deductibility for bribes, but only following a criminal conviction for bribery, presumably in the country where it occurs.

The breakthrough in the OECD came in May 1997 when the members agreed to quickly negotiate and promptly implement an international convention to criminalize transnational bribery. Although the United States, supported by most other OECD members, had opposed the convention approach because of the legal complexity and delay involved, France and Germany, supported by Japan and Spain, insisted that criminal sanctions be codified in a formal convention (*Washington Post*, 9 May 1997, A22). The compromise involved setting tight deadlines for final implementation of treaty provisions. The final convention would be based on the draft principles for criminalization developed by the OECD working group. That text defines the perpetrators and collaborators in acts of bribery, acts that would constitute a criminal violation, how to establish jurisdiction, and how to ensure effective enforcement in light of the different legal and judicial systems among OECD countries (OECD 1996). Continued progress depends primarily on peer pressure among governments, as well as the pressure of public opinion in countries suffering domestic corruption of their own (see also Glynn, Kobrin, and Naím in chapter 1).

As the OECD has progressed in its efforts to prevent international corruption, interest in codes of conduct and compliance programs for multinational cooperation has increased. The ICC appointed a committee in 1994 to review its earlier report on transnational bribery, issued in 1977, and to update the recommendations as appropriate (see Heimann, chapter 8 for further detail). Major contributions of the new report include the strengthened "rules of conduct" for preventing illicit payments and a recommendation to establish a standing committee "to promote widespread use of the rules and to stimulate cooperation between governments and world business." The report, approved by the ICC executive board in March 1996, also calls on governments to make procurement procedures more transparent, to condition government contracts with corporations on their abstaining from bribery, and to implement promptly the steps recommended by the OECD on this issue. The proposed standing committee has been appointed with one group focusing on developing a detailed compliance program to flesh out the general principles in the code. A second group is working with ICC national committees to get member companies to adopt the proposed code.

Targeting Grand Corruption in Government Procurement: the World Bank and the World Trade Organization

The World Bank and most other international and national aid agencies require international competitive bidding when official funds are used in whole or in part to fund government procurement of goods, services, or projects. The World Trade Organization (WTO) also oversees rules on government procurement, but they are incorporated in a multilateral agreement currently subscribed to by only 22 countries (the United States, the 15 countries of the European Community, Canada, Israel, Japan, Norway, South Korea, and Switzerland). The issue currently before the WTO is how to expand the country coverage of rules on transparency and due process in government procurement.

For those procurements where international competitive bidding is appropriate, World Bank guidelines emphasize transparency at all stages of the bidding process, from the public call for bids through the award of contracts. They also provide for the World Bank to review and evaluate bids and award contracts. The Bank may declare a "misprocurement" if procedures are not followed or if it later finds it had received "incomplete, inaccurate, or misleading information" or if corruption influenced the award. In July 1996, the World Bank further tightened its guidelines by removing the constraint that misprocurement due to corrupt practices can only be declared following a decision by a court of law, by revising the standard bidding documents that must be used in Bank-funded procurements to require disclosure of commissions paid to agents or other third-party intermediaries in the bidding process, and by introducing sanctions against borrowing countries and international firms that engage in corrupt practices. The potential sanctions include rejection of contract awards or cancellation of the portion of a loan linked to fraudulent or corrupt practices, and the blacklisting of firms that engage in such practices, either indefinitely or for a specified period of time (World Bank 1996b).

TI has further suggested that the World Bank should encourage the use of corporate codes of conduct by making them a condition for bidding on Bank-funded projects (see Heimann, chapter 8). Some in the World Bank have resisted this proposal, however, because it could reduce competition (because so few firms outside the United States currently have codes), and it would increase the paperwork and red tape, which are already substantial. Those in the bank opposed to the proposal also argue that the offsetting benefits may be few because of the difficulties in ensuring that newly created codes are no more than fig leaves.

Finally, recent changes in how the Bank evaluates its own performance, though adopted for other reasons, could have anticorruption benefits. Both personal and institutional success previously were measured by the volume of loan approvals. Complaints from NGOs and other groups about the consequences of this approach in relation to the environment, human rights, and other areas contributed to a reassessment of project review and loan approval. More careful analysis of the development impact of proposed projects should reduce the likelihood that "white elephant" projects receive funding approval. The most important way in which the Bank (and other international financial institutions) can contribute to the fight against corruption, however, is through capacity building and promotion of institutional reforms, as discussed above.

Although bribery and nepotism are recognized as anathema for efficient government procurement, most governments *openly* intervene in favor of domestic suppliers for a variety of procurement projects, arguing national security or industrialization goals. The current WTO Government Procurement Agreement (GPA) is primarily intended to reduce the level of explicit discrimination in favor of domestic suppliers and to introduce greater competition into these markets. In addition to listing the government entities and activities subject to its rules, the GPA specifies extensive and detailed bidding procedures regarded by representatives of some countries as excessively complex and burdensome. Although Taiwan and Singapore are currently involved in negotiations on access to the agreement, few additional countries are expected to join any time soon.

Because the membership of the GPA is limited, the United States is seeking an agreement on transparency, openness, and due process in government procurement that would be mandatory for all WTO members.[31] Under such an agreement, which US negotiators hope would be an interim step to full acceptance of GPA disciplines, WTO members would not have to reduce home-country preferences or otherwise liberalize their government procurement regimes, but they would have to abide by agreed on procedural rules. A major objective of the proposed rules would be to ensure that when international bids are entertained, the process is not distorted by bribery. At the WTO ministerial meeting in Singapore in December 1996, however, few other countries embraced the US proposal to conclude within a year an agreement on transpar-

---

31. It should be noted that 75 percent of US exports in 1995 went to countries that are already members of the GPA or are in the process of joining it, or to Mexico, which is covered by the government procurement rules of NAFTA.

ency in government procurement. US negotiators were only able to obtain a rather weak call to "establish a working group to conduct a study on transparency in government procurement practices . . . and, based on this study, to develop elements for inclusion in an appropriate agreement . . ." (World Trade Organization 1996).

Another recent proposal for reducing corruption in government procurement comes from David Finch, a former IMF official (Finch 1996). He recommends that the Berne Union, an international association of export credit agencies primarily from OECD-member countries, require supervised international competitive bidding for appropriate sales guaranteed by them (he excludes military contracts, for example).[32] Finch suggests having the World Bank supervise the bidding procedures in these sales, because it already has experience in monitoring its own procurement guidelines. But the World Bank may reject additional responsibilities, and it is not clear that such an agreement would have more than symbolic impact, because OECD figures show that only 3.2 percent of OECD manufactured exports were covered by official export credits in 1992 (cited in Ray 1995, 7).

Finally, World Bank President Robert McNamara has proposed the use of "antibribery" pacts to increase transparency and stem the opportunities for corruption in government procurement. As described in Heimann (chapter 8), antibribery pacts could be developed to fit the needs of countries or even particular agencies adopting them. The key elements would include commitments by the procuring agency or government to use transparent bidding procedures, guard against extortion by their officials, and establish procedures for monitoring compliance and sanctioning violations; only firms willing to sign the antibribery pact would be allowed to bid and they would also have to commit publicly to refrain from paying bribes and to establish a corporate code of conduct and a program to enforce compliance.

The motivation behind the antibribery pact is, first, to allow reformers to prominently signal that the rules for doing business in their country have changed and, second, to help firms avoid the collective action problem in refraining from offering bribes. Many firms claim that they prefer not to bribe but fear being edged out by a competitor if they unilaterally refrain. The pact is aimed at leveling the playing field.

Priorities for an International Anticorruption Strategy

There are no quick fixes or simple solutions for corruption. The sources and consequences of corruption differ from place to place, and each

---

32. The OECD, which has rules governing tied aid and subsidized export financing, is also studying this issue.

country must set its priorities and fashion its own responses based on its particular needs. In general, however, reforms that increase political accountability and economic competition are the keys to reducing opportunities for corruption. Contested elections, greater transparency in the policymaking process, and a free media increase the potential costs of corruption, while a more open economy reduces the potential gains.

While many countries today are pursuing democratization and opening up their economies to competition, the institutional reforms needed to consolidate and build upon these efforts often lag. Without "institutional adjustment" or "therapy" (see Klitgaard 1995 and Naím 1995b, respectively) these initial macro reforms may not be sustainable. Among the micro reforms that will support broader systemic reforms and address corruption are

- judicial reforms to ensure honesty and independence and build capacity;

- civil service and other institutional reforms to improve information flows and increase the incentives for honesty and performance while discouraging dishonesty;

- simplification of tax and regulatory systems;

- use of auctions, competitive bidding schemes, and market-based regulatory mechanisms whenever possible to reduce bureaucratic discretion;

- strengthening campaign finance laws and rules on conflict of interest; and

- strengthening the institutions of civil society, including the media, NGOs, and other grassroots groups.

Difficult and far-reaching internal reforms such as these are the building blocks for an anticorruption strategy, but the international community also has a role to play. First, it can encourage and support the internal reforms and, second, it must tackle the international sources and consequences of corruption. The recent OECD commitment to implement an international convention criminalizing bribery of foreign public officials is potentially a major step in this direction.

International Support for Internal Reforms

The international financial institutions already support internal anticorruption strategies in developing countries in a variety of ways, but they could do more. The World Bank and IMF support anticorruption reforms most importantly through loan conditionality focusing on procompetitive, market-oriented economic reforms. The Bank also directly addresses corruption in its guidelines governing procurement that uses Bank funds. It beefed up those regulations in the summer of 1996 and stated more clearly than ever before that it will cancel procurements and punish responsible parties if it finds corruption. To maximize the impact, the World Bank and other MDBs should act quickly on the recent recommendation of the G-7 finance ministers to cooperate in standardizing their procurement guidelines based on the World Bank model.

The international financial institutions also provide technical and financial assistance for institutional reform and capacity building, but they need to focus more attention on governance issues. World Bank staff have begun to use their "country portfolio performance reviews" and "country assistance strategy" statements to explicitly link governance issues and economic development. Early assessments, however, suggest they focus too narrowly on "public sector management issues" and need to include governance issues more systematically in their discussions with borrower countries.

Where corruption is widespread but safeguards against malfeasance in particular projects are possible, the Bank should redirect loans to activities neglected or undermined as a result of corruption, such as education and health. If it is not possible to ensure that official funds will be effectively used or that they are not being stolen or diverted, lending should obviously be suspended and funds withheld in these cases. In such situations, standard conditionality regarding project implementation and economic performance is likely to provide ample ammunition for reduced lending. In some situations, however, it may send a useful signal if the World Bank highlights the role of corruption in blocking a country's development.

Corruption in International Business

Most countries have laws against bribing their own public officials, but many lack the legal and institutional capacity to effectively deter and punish such behavior. By criminalizing bribery of foreign officials by their nationals and corporations, OECD countries will help to fill this gap. In addition, the World Bank, WTO, and others are studying how to expand the use of open, competitive bidding so that government procurement contracts will not be distorted by corruption. Though bribery in international transactions is only part of the problem, such agreements are an important component of an overall anticorruption strategy.

At the May 1997 ministerial meeting, OECD members committed to implementing by the end of 1998 a multilateral convention to deter and punish transnational bribery. A potential obstacle, however, is the difficulty in observing and documenting illicit payments, which raises concerns about free riders—countries who may commit themselves to sanction such behavior but then fail to enforce with vigor. Thus, the key to finalizing the agreement and making it effective will be establishing a monitoring process to ensure expeditious and vigorous enforcement.

The model for rigorous monitoring and peer review adopted by the OECD is that of the Financial Action Task Force (FATF) for monitoring implementation of its recommendations to combat money laundering. The first step involves self-reporting by OECD governments on the steps they take to implement anticorruption recommendations. The second step involves review by the Working Group on Transnational Bribery to independently evaluate the speed and scope of actions taken by member countries and to assess whether these actions are likely in practice to be effective.[33] The OECD recommendation calls vaguely for the "provision of regular information to the public." Both the national reports and the Working Group assessments should be publicly available for outside review by citizen groups and NGOs such as Transparency International, which could then add their own assessments as well as additional public pressure if necessary.

The major weakness of the OECD agreement is that the Agreed Commons Elements for criminalization define only bribery related to obtaining or retaining business as an offense. This addresses only bribery in contracting and would still permit firms to pay bribes in order to evade customs duties or other taxes or to avoid regulations protecting the environment or health and safety. Corruption in these areas are potentially more socially damaging than allocative inefficiencies related to government procurement, and this lacuna should be addressed in the treaty negotiations.

Other mechanisms intended to increase transparency and guard against corruption in international business include the proposal by former World Bank President Robert McNamara for "antibribery pacts," similar to the TI proposal for "islands of integrity" and the proposal that the World Bank require corporate codes of conduct and effective compliance programs as a condition for bidding on its projects. Under the pact, both government officials and bidding firms would publicly pledge not to offer or accept bribes and would take additional steps to guard against corruption in particular countries, agencies, or single projects.

Because the World Bank already requires international competitive bidding for major procurements, antibribery pacts would be most helpful in procurements not already subject to external supervision. The pacts should be used by countries wanting to lend credibility to their anticorruption efforts, to send a signal to their own officials that the rules have changed and as a signal to multinational corporations that they can no longer do business as usual. Widespread adoption of the antibribery

---

33. For example, Japan has proposed to sanction transnational bribery under its unfair competition law but some observers fear this will have little impact in practice, because Japan's competition watchdog, the Japan Fair Trade Commission, has been widely criticized as ineffective.

pacts would also put pressure on international corporations to adopt and enforce corporate codes of conduct and would reinforce OECD efforts to control transnational bribery.

The World Bank can reinforce these efforts and those of the OECD by requiring multinational corporations bidding on Bank-funded projects to have a code of conduct in place. The Bank's concerns about reducing competition by limiting the pool of eligible bidders could be mitigated by announcing with sufficient notice (a few months to a year) that the codes would be required. That would give firms time to develop codes and compliance programs. To minimize the additional paperwork required, the Bank could enforce the requirement by adding a one- or two-sentence addendum to existing bidding documents. To raise the profile of the issue and further deter violations, the addendum should be signed by a high-level officer affirming that the parent corporation and all applicable subsidiaries have and enforce codes of conduct and that they will abide by the borrowing country's laws and regulations relating to corruption in government procurement. It is likely, as the Bank fears, that many firms will nominally adopt a code but not enforce it. Nevertheless, when corruption is alleged in a particular case, evidence as to the steps a firm has taken to enforce compliance, for example, getting a signed statement from local representatives and agents that they have received and read a copy of the code, could be helpful in identifying possible violations.

If, as recommended, other multilateral development banks standardized their regulations on the World Bank model, procurement rules emphasizing transparency and competitive bidding would cover as much as 15 to 18 percent of total nondefense government expenditure on goods and services in 88 low- and middle-income countries (Hoekman 1996, 39). In May 1996, Development Assistance Committee (DAC) members adopted a statement of principle that anticorruption provisions should be included in bilaterally funded procurement contracts. Since October 1996, the US Agency for International Development has included a statement explicitly prohibiting bribery in all contracts and providing for cancellation and legal action in the case of violations (TPCC 1996, 121). If other countries enforce similar rules, the ratio of covered government purchases would rise to somewhere between one-third and one-half of nondefense expenditures in recipient countries (Hoekman, 1996, 39). This could significantly boost anticorruption efforts in many countries, though tied aid, by reducing the level of competition, will reduce the potential benefits.

To expand the coverage of anticorruption safeguards even further, the World Trade Organization should act on the proposal made by the United States in Singapore last December to negotiate an agreement on transparency and due process in government procurement. The procedural safeguards in the Government Procurement Agreement (GPA) could serve as the basis for a separate agreement that would be binding on all

WTO members. Countries that are not signatories to the GPA, however, would not be required to take on its broader nondiscrimination commitments and would be under no obligation to open their government procurement to international competition. They would simply have to be open in the process of awarding contracts, which would tend to reduce the opportunities for corruption. Indeed, an analysis of the costs and benefits of the GPA for less developed countries concluded that "transparency arising from the procedural requirements of the GPA may well be the primary benefit of membership for developing countries—even if strict nondiscrimination is not pursued" (Hoekman 1996, 10).

A phenomenon that has been with us since before biblical times will not be eradicated overnight. But the day when bribes were considered mere gifts, and corruption was a way of doing business, are in the past. While tolerance of corruption may continue to prevail in some quarters, it is no longer publicly expressed. This change in attitude is a big step, but, to reiterate, the international community must take additional steps if the current momentum is to be maintained:

- The World Bank, International Monetary Fund, and other multilateral and bilateral development agencies should emphasize the role of effective governance in economic development and should devote more resources and technical assistance to institutional reforms and capacity building in countries where corruption is rampant. Where corruption blocks reform, the IFIs should cut off countries far more quickly than they did in Mobutu's Zaire.

- Other MDBs should conform their procurement guidelines to the World Bank's high standards.

- All DAC members should adopt anticorruption guidelines for their aid programs, and both MDBs and bilateral aid agencies should be even more vigilant in supervising bidding procedures and auditing project implementation to ensure that scarce public resources are not siphoned off for personal use.

- OECD countries should meet or even beat the deadlines they have set for themselves to criminalize transnational bribery and end tax deductibility of bribes. They should also expand the definition of the crime to encompass bribes paid in the course of doing business.

- The members of the World Trade Organization should conclude an agreement providing for transparency and due process in government procurement markets.

Of course, the ultimate responsibility for ending corruption still lies with the leaders of each nation and the citizens who must hold them accountable.

References

Ades, Alberto, and Rafael Di Tella. 1994. Competition and Corruption. Oxford Applied Economics Discussion Paper Series, no. 169 (April).

Ades, Alberto, and Rafael Di Tella. 1995. National Champions and Corruption: Some Unpleasant Competitiveness Arithmetic. Unpublished (August).

Alam, M. Sahid. 1990. Some Economic Costs of Corruption in LDCs. *Journal of Development Studies* 27, no. 1 (October): 89-97.

Alam, M. Sahid. 1995. A Theory of Limits on Corruption and Some Applications. *Kyklos* 48, no. 3: 419-35.

Alfiler, Ma. Concepcion P. 1986. The Process of Bureaucratic Corruption in Asia: Emerging Patterns. In Ledivina V. Cariño, *Bureaucratic Corruption in Asia: Causes, Consequences, and Control*. Quezon City: JMC Press, Inc. for College of Public Administration, University of the Philippines.

Banfield, Edward. 1975. Corruption as a Feature of Governmental Organization. *Journal of Law and Economics* 18, no. 3 (December): 587-605.

Bayley, David H. 1970. The Effects of Corruption in a Developing Nation. In Arnold J. Heidenheimer, *Political Corruption: Readings in Comparative Analysis*. New York: Holt, Rinehart, and Winston.

Bergsten, C. Fred, Kimberly Ann Elliott, Jeffrey J. Schott, and Wendy Takacs. 1987. *Auction Quotas in United States Trade Policy*. POLICY ANALYSES IN INTERNATIONAL ECONOMICS 19. Washington: Institute for International Economics.

Betancourt, Roger R. 1995. *Markets, the State and Corruption in a PCPC Reform Process: Why China and Vietnam Grow while Cuba Stagnates*. IRIS Working Paper no. 180. Maryland: University of Maryland, Center for Institutional Reform and the Informal Sector.

Bhagwati, Jagdish. 1982. Directly Unproductive, Profit Seeking (DUP) Activities. *Journal of Political Economy* 90, no. 5 (March): 142-47

Borner, Silvio, Aymo Brunetti, and Beatrice Weder. 1995. *Political Credibility and Economic Development*. New York: St. Martin's Press.

Charlick, Robert. 1992. Corruption in Political Transition: A Governance Perspective. *Corruption and Reform* 7: 177-87.

Clinton, William J. 1994. Remarks by the President at the Announcement of the Summit of the Americas. White House Press Release, 11 March.

Congressional Budget Office (CBO). 1992. *The Economic Effects of the Savings & Loan Crisis*. Washington: Congress of the United States.

Congressional Budget Office (CBO). 1993. *Resolving the Thrift Crisis*. Washington: Congress of the United States.

Council on Foreign Relations (CFR). 1997. *Rethinking International Drug Control: New Directions for U.S. Policy*. Task Force Report (Mathea Falco, Chair). New York: Council on Foreign Relations.

David, George. 1994. Notable and Quotable. *Corporate Crime Reporter* 8, no. 45 (21 November): 8-9.

Diamond, Larry. 1993. Nigeria's Perennial Struggle. In Larry Diamond and Marc F. Plattner, *The Global Resurgence of Democracy*. Baltimore and London: The Johns Hopkins University Press.

Elliott, Kimberly Ann. 1996. *Implementing the Summit of the Americas: Combatting Corruption*. A North-South Center Working Paper. Coral Gables, FL: University of Miami.

Ettore, Barbara. 1994. Why Overseas Bribery Won't Last. *Management Review* 83, no. 6 (June): 20-25.

Feinberg, Richard E. 1997. *Summitry in the Americas: A Progress Report*. Washington: Institute for International Economics.

Finch, C. David. 1996. G7 Corruption Project. *International Economy* X, no. 6 (November/December): 22-26.

Gaviria, César. 1995. *A New Vision of the OAS*. Working Document, General Secretariat of the Permanent Council, Organization of American States. Washington (6 April).

Givant, Norman. 1994. The Sword that Shields. *The China Business Review* 21, no. 3 (May-June): 29-31.

Gould, David J., and Jose A. Amaro-Reyes. 1983. *The Effects of Corruption on Administrative Performance: Illustrations from Developing Countries*. World Bank Staff Working Paper no. 580, Management and Development Series no. 7. Washington: World Bank.

Heidenheimer, Arnold J. 1970. *Political Corruption: Readings in Comparative Analysis*. New York: Holt, Rinehart, and Winston.

Heidenheimer, Arnold J., Michael Johnston, and Victor T. LeVine, eds. 1989. *Political Corruption: A Handbook*. Brunswick, NJ: Transaction Books.

Hillstrom, Britta. 1996. Effects of Corruption on Democracies in Asia, Latin America, and Russia. *The Woodrow Wilson Center Report* 8, no. 3 (December): 3-40.

Hines, James. 1996. *Forbidden Payment: Foreign Bribery and American Business after 1977*. NBER Working Paper, no. 5266. Cambridge, MA: National Bureau of Economic Research.

Hoekman, Bernard. 1996. *Multilateral Disciplines on Government Procurement: What's in It for Developing Countries?* Centre for Economic Policy Research Discussion Paper, no. 1502. London: Centre for Economic Policy Research.

Huntington, Samuel. 1968. *Political Order in Changing Societies*. New Haven, CT: Yale University Press.

Jacoby, Neil, Peter Nehemkis, and Richard Eells. 1977. *Bribery and Extortion in World Business*. New York: Macmillan.

Johnston, Michael. 1993. "Micro" and "Macro" Possibilities for Reform. *Corruption and Reform* 7: 189-204.

Kantor, Michael. 1996a. Remarks. Prepared for delivery before the Emergency Committee for American Trade. Office of the US Trade Representative, Washington, 6 March.

Kantor, Michael. 1996b. Remarks. Prepared for delivery before the Detroit Economic Club. US Department of Commerce, 25 July.

Kjellberg, Francesco. 1995. Conflict of Interest, Corruption or (Simply) Scandals? *Crime, Law & Social Change* 22, no. 4: 339-60.

Klitgaard, Robert. 1988. *Controlling Corruption*. Berkeley: University of California Press.

Klitgaard, Robert. 1991. Gifts and Bribes. In Richard J. Zeckhauser, *Strategy and Choice*. Cambridge, MA: The MIT Press.

Klitgaard, Robert. 1993. Strategies for Reform. In Larry Diamond and Marc F. Plattner, *The Global Resurgence of Democracy*. Baltimore and London: The Johns Hopkins University Press.

Klitgaard, Robert. 1995. *Institutional Adjustment and Adjusting to Institutions*. World Bank Discussion Papers, no. 303. Washington: World Bank.

Krueger, Anne O. 1974. The Political Economy of the Rent-Seeking Society. *American Economic Review* 64, no. 3 (June): 291-303.

LaPalombara, Joseph. 1994. Structural and Institutional Aspects of Corruption. *Social Research* 61, no. 2 (Summer): 325-50.

Lee, Rance P. L. 1986. Bureaucratic Corruption in Asia: The Problem of Incongruence between Legal Norms and Folk Norms. In Ledivina V. Cariño, *Bureaucratic Corruption in Asia: Causes, Consequences, and Control*. Quezon City: JMC Press, Inc. for College of Public Administration, University of the Philippines.

Leff, Nathaniel H. 1970. Economic Development through Bureaucratic Corruption. In Arnold J. Heidenheimer, *Political Corruption: Readings in Comparative Analysis*. New York: Holt, Rinehart, and Winston.

LeVine, Victor T. 1989. Supportive Values of the Culture of Corruption in Ghana. In Arnold J. Heidenheimer, Michael Johnston, and Victor T. LeVine, *Political Corruption: A Handbook*. Brunswick, NJ: Transaction Books.

Leys, Colin. 1965. What is the Problem about Corruption? *The Journal of Modern African Studies* 3, no. 2 (June).

Mauro, Paolo. 1995. Corruption and Growth. *Quarterly Journal of Economics* CX, no. 2, no. 441 (August): 681-712.

McMullan, M. 1970. Corruption in the Public Services of British Colonies and Ex-Colonies in West Africa. In Arnold J. Heidenheimer, *Political Corruption: Readings in Comparative Analysis*. New York: Holt, Rinehart, and Winston.

Meny, Yves. 1996. "Fin de Siècle" Corruption: Change, Crisis and Shifting Values. *International Social Science Journal* 28, no. 3 (September): 309-20.

Murphy, Kevin M., Andrei Shleifer, and Robert W. Vishny. 1993. Why is Rent-Seeking So Costly to Growth? *American Economic Review* 83, no. 2: 409-14.

Myrdal, Gunnar. 1970. Corruption: Its Causes and Effects. In Arnold J. Heidenheimer, *Political Corruption: Readings in Comparative Analysis*. New York: Holt, Rinehart, and Winston.

Naím, Moisés. 1995a. The Corruption Eruption. *Brown Journal of World Affairs* 2, no. 2 (Summer): 245-61.

Naím, Moisés. 1995b. *Latin America's Journey to the Market: From Macroeconomic Shocks to Institutional Therapy*. International Center for Economic Growth Occasional Paper, no. 62. San Francisco: ICS Press.

Noonan, John T. 1984. *Bribes*. New York: Macmillan.

Nye, Joseph S. 1970. Corruption and Political Development: A Cost-Benefit Analysis. In Arnold J. Heidenheimer, *Political Corruption: Readings in Comparative Analysis*. New York: Holt, Rinehart, and Winston.

Oldenburg, Philip. 1987. Middlemen in Third-World Corruption: Implications of an Indian Case. *World Politics* 34, no. 4 (July): 508-35.

Organization for Economic Cooperation and Development (OECD). 1996. Implementation of the Recommendation on Bribery in International Business Transactions. Report of the OECD Committee on International Investment and Multinational Enterprises (CIME) to the 1996 meeting of the OECD Council of Ministers. Paris. http://www.oecd.org.

Ouma, Stephen. 1991. Corruption in Public Policy and Its Impact on Development: The Case of Uganda since 1979. *Public Administration and Development* 11, no. 5 (September/October): 473-90.

Pines, Daniel. 1994. Amending the Foreign Corrupt Practices Act to Include a Private Right of Action. *California Law Review* 82, no. 1 (January): 185-229.

Pitman, Glenn A., and James P. Sanford. 1994. The Foreign Corrupt Practices Act Revisited: Attempting to Regulate "Ethical Bribes" in Global Business. *International Journal of Purchasing and Materials Management* 30, no. 3 (Summer): 15-20.

Quirk, Peter J. 1996. *Macroeconomic Implications of Money Laundering*. IMF Working Paper, no. 96/66. Washington: International Monetary Fund.

Raine, Linnea P., and Frank J. Cilluffo. 1994. *Global Organized Crime: The New Empire of Evil*. Washington: Center for Strategic and International Studies.

Ray, John E. 1995. *Managing Official Export Credits*. Washington: Institute for International Economics.

Richardson, J. David. 1993. *Sizing Up U.S. Export Disincentives*. Washington: Institute for International Economics.

Rose-Ackerman, Susan. 1978. *Corruption: A Study in Political Economy*. New York: Academic Press.

Schwarz, Adam. 1995. *A Nation in Waiting: Indonesia in the 1990s*. Boulder, CO: Westview Press.

Scott, James C. 1972. *Comparative Political Corruption*. Englewood Cliffs, NJ: Prentice-Hall.

Shleifer, Andrei, and Robert W. Vishny. 1993. Corruption. *Quarterly Journal of Economics* CVIII, no. 3, no. 434 (August): 599-618.

Statistics Canada. 1996. *World Trade Database on CD-ROM*. Ottawa: Government of Canada, International Trade Division.

Tanzi, Vito. 1996. *Money Laundering and the International Financial System*. IMF Working Paper No. 96/55. Washington: International Monetary Fund.

Tilman, Robert O. 1970. Black-Market Bureaucracy. In Arnold J. Heidenheimer, *Political Corruption: Readings in Comparative Analysis*. New York: Holt, Rinehart, and Winston.

Trade Promotion Coordinating Committee (TPCC). 1995. *Meeting Foreign Competition*. Third Annual Report to the United States Congress on National Export Strategy. Washington (October).

Trade Promotion Coordinating Committee (TPCC). 1996. *Toward the Next American Century: A U.S. Strategic Response to Foreign Competitive Practices*. Fourth Annual Report to the United States Congress on National Export Strategy. Washington (October).

Transparency International (TI). 1995. *Building a Global Coalition against Corruption*. Annual Report. Berlin: Transparency International.

Transparency International (TI). 1996. *National Integrity Systems: The TI Source Book*. Berlin: Transparency International.

Ul Haque, Nadeem, and Ratna Sahay. 1996. Do Government Wage Cuts Close Budget Deficits? The Costs of Corruption. *IMF Staff Papers* 43, no. 4 (December): 754-78.

United Republic of Tanzania. 1995. *The National Integrity System in Tanzania*. Proceedings of a Workshop convened by the Prevention of Corruption Bureau, Government of Tanzania, Arusha, 10-12 August, facilitated by Transparency International and the Economic Development Institute of the World Bank.

US Department of Commerce. 1995. *The Big Emerging Markets: 1996 Outlook and Sourcebook*. Lanham, MD: Bernan Press.

Wei, Shang-Jin. 1997. How Taxing is Corruption on International Investors? Processed. Harvard University, Kennedy School of Government, 25 February.

Werlin, Herbert H. 1979. The Consequences of Corruption: The Ghanaian Experience. In Monday Ekpo, *Bureaucratic Corruption in Sub-Saharan Africa: Toward a Search of Causes and Consequences*. Washington: University Press of America.

World Bank. 1994. *Governance: The World Bank's Experience*. Washington: World Bank.

World Bank. 1996a. *Annual Report 1996*. Washington: World Bank.

World Bank. 1996b. *Procurement Guidelines*. Washington: World Bank.

World Bank. 1996c. The Corruption Issue. Annual Meetings Backgrounder, External Affairs. Washington, 24 September.

World Bank. 1996d. *Financial Flows and the Developing Countries*. Washington: World Bank (May): 35.

World Trade Organization (WTO). 1996. Text of Ministerial Declaration. Released in Singapore, 13 December.

APPENDICES

A

US Policy on Corruption

ALAN LARSON

In the United States, government involvement in curtailing transnational bribery began in 1977 with the enactment of the Foreign Corrupt Practices Act (FCPA). I will outline the evolution of US involvement in this effort, highlight the work we have already done, and describe future initiatives against corruption.

As international corruption scandals flourished throughout the 1980s and 1990s, a growing number of business leaders and policymakers began to see that bribery threatened interests of vital importance.

■ First, bribery distorts global markets and hinders economic development by substituting graft for quality, performance, and suitability.

■ Second, bribes undermine democratic accountability. Corruption further weakens unstable governments and threatens emergent democracies.

■ Third, bribery creates a type of nontariff barrier to trade against companies that refuse to engage in the practice—or are legally barred from doing so, as US firms are by the FCPA. Thus companies with legitimate business practices are penalized.

Let me emphasize that US action against corruption is motivated by all three of these interests. While we naturally regard the competitive

Alan Larson is Assistant Secretary of State for Economic and Business Affairs.

disadvantage to US companies as significant and unacceptable, bribery's effects on economic development and democratic accountability also impel us. To put it in colloquial terms, our goal is not only to level the playing field for US firms, but also to strengthen the rules of the game so that international economic competition will serve to foster economic development and support democratic institutions.

The United States made episodic efforts to address these vital interests as early as 1978. At the time, there was little support for initiatives against corruption in the Organization for Economic Cooperation and Development (OECD) and the United Nations (UN), and it languished. The amendments to the FCPA in the 1988 trade act included a suggestion that the president negotiate an international agreement on the prohibition of overseas bribery. In 1989, I directed the US delegation to propose such a negotiation in the OECD. Although an Ad Hoc Group on Illicit Payments was launched to study the issue, the negotiations made slow progress. To keep the negotiations alive, I organized two breakfast meetings with US negotiators and other key delegations during my tenure as ambassador to the OECD.

However, the fight against corruption made real progress early in Clinton administration. Secretary of State Warren Christopher reviewed the information on illicit payments and decided it was time to put more political muscle behind the US effort in the OECD; my former boss, Dan Tarullo, raised the issue at policy levels. Less than a year later, the United States had successfully convinced OECD members to approve the Recommendation on Bribery in International Business Transactions, a remarkable breakthrough in the battle against corruption. The recommendation calls on member states to take "concrete and meaningful steps" to combat bribery and I would like to briefly discuss the OECD initiative (for details on the OECD, see Pieth, chapter 6).

Successful negotiation of the 1994 recommendation set into motion various initiatives in the OECD and other forums. In April 1996, OECD members agreed that bribes paid to foreign officials should no longer be tax deductible. In addition to their substantive value, these two important OECD recommendations have broader implications. First, they counter the perception that in multilateral forums the group instinct is to talk, not act. The recommendations also prove that if there is political will and strong leadership much can be accomplished. Finally, the OECD initiatives created tremendous momentum that has spurred additional, and sometimes successful work against illicit payments.

US involvement in the OECD initiatives is an obvious indication of our commitment to the multilateral process and our successes encourage us to redouble our multilateral efforts. At the same time, the OECD recommendation calls on members to consider national action, including reviewing "laws and regulations relating to public subsidies . . . or other public advantages so that advantages could be denied as a sanction for bribery." The United States negotiated with the US Overseas Private Insurance Corporation (OPIC) to require a project company seeking OPIC financing to certify that bribery was not used to obtain the contract. Similarly, we are considering ways of amending export advocacy guidelines to ensure that the United States is not advocating for companies that have paid bribes.

National measures like the ones described are useful resources that we will not hesitate to deploy in the war against corruption. Indeed, national action is often necessary to give effect to multilateral agreements and we intend to pursue a variety of these national measures to foster and support multilateral efforts to combat corruption.

In addition to the OECD recommendations, the United States has successfully shepherded other multilateral initiatives. On 29 March 1996, the Organization of American States concluded the Inter-American Convention against Corruption. The convention serves as a powerful political statement by leaders of the Western Hemisphere that they will no longer tolerate the corrosive effects of corruption on free markets and the democratic system. From the US perspective, the crown jewel of this convention is the obligation it creates for signatories to criminalize transnational bribery of public officials. The convention also makes transnational bribery an extraditable offense, provides mutual legal assistance in investigations of corruption, and calls for the seizure and forfeiture of illicit gains.

Another hemispheric success involves the creation of the North American Development Bank (NADB) by the North American Free Trade Agreement (NAFTA). As a result of a joint initiative by the US Departments of State and Treasury, the NADB charter requires companies to certify that they have not engaged in bribery of foreign or domestic officials in furtherance of a Bank project. Companies must also have active corporate policies that prohibit bribery in pursuit of corporate activity, and they must assert that there has been no conviction of bribery within five years of certification. If the Bank discovers that a company has been convicted of bribery, it may debar that company from any future participation in a Bank-funded or guaranteed project.

The New Transatlantic Agenda, the product of last year's US-EU summit, urges EU members to combat illicit payments by implementing the 1994 OECD Recommendation on Bribery in International Business Transactions. The private sector counterpart to the Transatlantic Agenda, the Transatlantic Business Dialogue, went a step further and called on EU nations to criminalize bribery.

One area that is ripe for change and where the United States will channel much energy in the future is government procurement. Procurement markets account for trillions of dollars in commercial transactions. In such a lucrative environment, anticompetitive and illicit behavior flourishes. Countries have responded enthusiastically to US proposals to increase transparency in procurement procedures. The United States has made such a suggestion in APEC.

Similarly, the United States has set its sight on ensuring that the international procurement process is open and transparent in the World Trade Organization (WTO). The WTO Government Procurement Agreement (GPA) satisfies this standard, but it is of limited use, with only 26 signatories thus far, mainly because few countries can meet its rigorous procedural requirements. The United States will continue to press for universal accession to the GPA, but in the interim, we have developed an alternative strategy. We will seek a mandate at the WTO ministerial meeting in Singapore in December 1996 to negotiate an interim, stand alone procurement arrangement on transparency, due process, and openness in government procurement.[1]

In conclusion, let me simply say that success has many parents while failure is an orphan. The best evidence that combating overseas bribery has come of age as a policy issue is the fact that senior policymakers are clamoring to get involved in it. For leaders like Mark Pieth, who were involved with this issue when no one else seemed to care, this must be an immensely satisfying development.

---

1. At the ministerial, WTO members agreed only to establish a working group to study the issue. See Elliott, chapter 10.

B

Data Sources for Cross-Country Analysis of Corruption

KIMBERLY ANN ELLIOTT

There has recently been a flurry of cross-country empirical studies of the sources and effects of corruption. The chapter by Mauro (chapter 4) on the effects of corruption on investment, growth, and government expenditure is an extension of his article in the August 1995 *Quarterly Journal of Economics*, which in turn is based on his doctoral thesis. Alberto Ades and Rafael Di Tella have co-authored two papers on how competition and industrial policies inhibit or foster corruption. James Hines has studied the effects of the US Foreign Corrupt Practices Act on US exports to and investment in more and less corrupt countries. Along similar lines and using similar data sources, a number of studies have looked at the effects of institutions and political stability on economic growth. These studies include Keefer and Knack (1994), Fedderke and Klitgaard (1996), and Barro (1991).

The data on corruption used in these studies are of two basic types: expert assessments and surveys of international businessmen or other observers within countries. Firms that provide political risk information and analysis for multinational firms are usually the sources for this data. One corruption index used in this chapter is based on a data set compiled by the Center for Institutional Reform and the Informal Sector (IRIS) at the University of Maryland from data originally collected by Political Risk Services and published in the *International Country Risk Guide* (ICRG). The IRIS data set is described in Keefer and Knack (1994). This data set includes a number of political risk variables including an assessment of the degree to which payments are required at high political levels for large transactions and at lower levels for routine government functions, such as licensing, customs clearance, etc. The index covers 148 countries. The scale ranges from 0, indicating payments are "generally expected," to 6, indicating little corruption. To be consistent with the second data source (described below), the index was converted to a 10-point scale.

Transparency International (TI) is the second data source for this chapter. In 1995 and 1996 TI released rankings of perceived corruption in various countries. The TI ranking is based on a survey of surveys, incorporating information from six different sources, including the ICRG/IRIS index described above; the World Competitiveness Report of the Institute for Management and Development (IMD), which covers 37 to 48 countries (depending on the year), the Asian consulting firm Political and Economic Research Consulting (PERC), which covers only 10-12 Asian countries (again depending on the year); and a staff assessment for 105 countries compiled by DRI/McGraw-Hill Global Risk Service. For the early 1980s, there are data from Business International (BI, since taken over by the Economist Intelligence Unit), which cover 68 countries. Finally, there is a survey of embassies and chambers of commerce in 103 countries compiled by Peter Neumann and published in a German monthly, and a ranking of 58 countries compiled at Goettingen University based on responses to an internet solicitation of anonymous contributions and interviews of employees of multinational firms and international institutions.

For the 1996 index, TI used three surveys each from PERC and IMD (for 1993-95) and the most recent survey from the other sources, except BI. A country had to be included in at least four of the indices in order to be included in the TI ranking, which resulted in a list of 54 countries. More information on how the TI ranking was compiled and the underlying sources can be obtained from the Internet website maintained by the ranking's creator, Dr. Johann Graf Lambsdorff of Goettingen University (http://www.gwdg.de/~uwvw/icr.htm).

The index used in this chapter differs slightly from that used by Mauro in chapter 4. The index he uses is the simple average of the ICRG index (averaged over 1982-95) and the BI corruption index (averaged over 1980-83), where both are available, and the ICRG index otherwise. The index used here combines the 1996 TI and ICRG indices (averaged as Mauro does over 1982-95 or a minimum of 10 years). The TI index is used where it is available in the expectation that, because it incorporates data from a variety of sources, it should contain fewer anomalies than a single source. But because the TI ranking covers only 54 countries, the ICRG index was used to expand the sample. After excluding countries in the ICRG sample not covered a full 10 years, 111 countries remained, doubling the TI sample size.

The correlation matrices provided by TI indicate that the various measures of corruption are fairly highly correlated with one another. The TI

1996 ranking is also highly correlated with the ICRG index alone (0.89 when averaged over 1982-95 and 0.88 when averaged over 1992-95), the "bureaucratic efficiency" index compiled by Mauro (1995) from the BI data for 1980-83 (0.91), and the hybrid ICRG/BI index used by Mauro in this volume (0.91). The TI ranking is consistently more closely correlated with other data expected to either cause or be a consequence of corruption. Unfortunately it is impossible to know whether this is because the TI data better reflect "reality" (at least as seen through the eyes of international businessmen) or whether it is simply the case that the larger the number of countries, the weaker the conclusions that generally apply.

Other Data Used

The data on per capita income and trade as a share of GDP are from Summers and Heston (1991). The data on government expenditure as a share of GDP are from the World Bank World Tables (on CD-ROM); the data on the role of state-owned enterprises are also from the World Bank (1995, 272-75). The measure of "political openness" is based on the Freedom House (1996a) ranking of countries, from "free" (a score of 1) to "not free" (a score of 7) and is available for all 111 countries in the sample using the combined IRIS/TI corruption index. To be consistent with the economic freedom index (described below), the political freedom index was inverted, with 1 indicating the unfree and 7 indicating the free. The measure of "economic openness" is based on a new Freedom House (1996b) assessment of the degree of economic freedom in 66 countries, ranging from free (a score of 16) to not free (a score of 0). The economic freedom index is the sum of 6 separate variables, including the freedom to own property (scored from 0-3), freedom to earn a living (0-3), freedom to own and conduct business (0-3), freedom to invest one's earnings (0-3), freedom to trade (0-2), and freedom to participate in a market economy (0-2). The last variable includes an assessment of the degree of corruption in the economy. It was subtracted from each country's score, thus reducing the possible score to a range of 0 to 14.

References

Barro, Robert J. 1991. Economic Growth in a Cross-Section of Countries. *Quarterly Journal of Economics* 106, no. 2, no. 425 (May): 407-43.

Fedderke, Johannes, and Robert Klitgaard. 1996. Economic Growth and Social Indicators: An Exploratory Analysis. Unpublished (March).

Freedom House. 1996a. *Freedom in the World: The Annual Survey of Political Rights and Civil Liberties, 1995-96*. New York: Freedom House.

Freedom House. 1996b. *World Survey of Economic Freedom 1995-96*. New York: Freedom House.

Keefer, Philip, and Stephen Knack. 1994. *Institutions and Economic Performance: Cross-Country Tests Using Alternative Institutional Measures.* IRIS Working Paper No. 109. Maryland: University of Maryland, Center for Institutional Reform and the Informal Sector.

Summers, Robert, and Alan Heston. 1991. *Penn World Tables.* On diskette, available from National Bureau of Economic Research, Cambridge, MA.

World Bank. 1995. *Bureaucrats in Business: The Economics and Politics of Government Ownership.* London: Oxford University Press for the World Bank.

Other Publications from the
Institute for International Economics

WORKS IN PROGRESS

Reconcilable Differences, Second Edition
C. Fred Bergsten, Marcus Noland, and Takatoshi Ito

Whither APEC?
C. Fred Bergsten, editor

Trade, Jobs, and Income Distribution
William R. Cline

China's Entry to the World Economy
Richard N. Cooper

Economic Policy/ Foreign Policy
Bowman Cutter

Liberalizing Financial Services
Wendy Dobson and Pierre Jacquet

Economic Sanctions After the Cold War
Kimberly Ann Elliott, Gary C. Hufbauer and Jeffrey J. Schott

Trade and Labor Standards
Kimberly Ann Elliott and Richard Freeman

Regional Trading Blocs in the World Economic System
Jeffrey A. Frankel

Forecasting Financial Crises: Early Warning Signs for Emerging Markets
Morris Goldstein and Carmen Reinhart

Overseeing Global Capital Markets
Morris Goldstein and Peter Garber

Global Competition Policy
Edward M. Graham and J. David Richardson

Prospects for Western Hemisphere Free Trade
Gary Clyde Hufbauer and Jeffrey J. Schott

Trade Policy Review
Donald Keesing

The Future of U.S. Foreign Aid
Carol Lancaster

The Economics of Korean Unification
Marcus Noland

Foreign Direct Investment
Theodore Moran

The Case for Trade: A Modern Reconsideration
J. David Richardson

Measuring the Cost of Protection in China
Zhang Shuguang, Zhang Yansheng, and Wan Zhongxin

Who's Bashing Whom? Trade Conflict in High-Technology Industries, Second Edition
Laura D'Andrea Tyson

Canadian customers	RENOUF BOOKSTORE
can order from	5369 Canotek Road, Unit 1, Ottawa, Ontario K1J 9J3, Canada
the Institute or from:	Telephone: (613) 745-2665 Fax: (613) 745-7660

Visit our website at: http:/ / www.iie.com   **E-mail address: orders@iie.com**